SIMPLIFIED SENTENCE SKILLS

SIMPLIFIED SENTENCE SKILLS

BARBARA HANSEN
REBECCA MCDANIEL

UNIVERSITY OF CINCINNATI ◆ RAYMOND WALTERS COLLEGE

NTC Publishing Group
a division of NTC/CONTEMPORARY PUBLISHING COMPANY
Lincolnwood, Illinois USA

To Maurice McDaniel and Joseph Hansen, the most important men in our lives.

Executive Editor: Marisa L. L'Heureux
Design Manager: Ophelia M. Chambliss
Production Manager: Margo Goia

CONTENTS

PREFACE

If you think this course is going to be easy, you're wrong. Learning a new skill is never easy. Anything worth achieving has a price, and the price of knowledge is self-discipline and hard work. Are you willing to pay the price? If you are, this book can be a great help to you. The book is not intended to teach you "everything you always wanted to know about English but were afraid to ask." Rather, it will teach you everything you need to know about English but haven't learned.

Learning to write is in some ways like learning to walk. We have to begin by taking slow, simple steps before we can walk easily, let alone do creative variations like skipping, jumping, or dancing. Because writing is much too complex to master in one course, this book will give only a few of the beginning steps, steps you possibly were already taught somewhere in your education but never really understood. If you learn these beginning steps thoroughly, you will have a solid foundation for all the additional steps, all the creative variations, you will make later in your life.

After you're introduced to these basic rules of writing, you will be given many opportunities to practice each of them. That's what learning any skill is all about: practice. People do not become skilled swimmers by reading a book or listening to a teacher; they become skilled by getting into the water and swimming. It's true that learners use the information received from swimming instructors, but only by repeated practice will they master the skill of swimming. That's exactly how you will master the skill of writing.

This repetition of basic rules will help you with the simplest steps of writing. *Rules* and *repetition* are not the bad words some educators have made them; they only become "bad" when misunderstood. Some texts and instructors avoid using the word *rule* as carefully as they avoid using all nonacceptable four-letter words. To them, rules imply a rigid standard forced on the student, a strait-jacket allowing no freedom. Rather than limiting your freedom, however, we believe that rules allow the greater freedom that comes from discipline. Without rules, you flounder in uncertainty; with rules, you flourish in security.

This security comes from knowing what is acceptable for most readers, most of the time; and that's all rules really are. These rules of writing were not handed down by some all-knowing English instructor; they simply reflect how the language works—most of the time. If the majority of educated people in a given geographic area use the language in a certain way, that usage becomes a rule. Because educated people's usage differs, rules are flexible and have exceptions. This flexibility, however, does not mean that rules are bad. It does mean a rule won't work 100 percent of the time; our language is just too varied for that. If a rule works 95 percent of the time, however, it's worth knowing. This book will help you learn what is acceptable to most people, most of the time.

FEATURES OF SIMPLIFIED SENTENCE SKILLS

Simplified Sentence Skills is an effective text for individualized, laboratory, or traditional instruction. The book has unique strengths that simplify both the learning and the teaching of basic skills.

Nuances of language that beginning writers do not need are carefully avoided. For example, the unit on verbs omits voice and mood. Likewise, verbals are included only to show that they are not main verbs, without naming all the types possible. Pronoun case is taught without including the confusing *who/whom* rules. Terminology is presented only when needed.

Only basic rules are included; the book alludes to rules that are omitted but does not teach them. If a rule works 95 percent of the time, we see no reason to confuse you by teaching the 5 percent of exceptions.

The book's clear structure helps show the relationship of the rules to each other. For example, skill with linking verbs is shown to be necessary for distinguishing predicate adjectives from direct objects; skill with direct objects makes the *lie/lay, sit/set, rise/raise* distinctions easier; skill with independent clauses forms the basis for over half of the punctuation rules. The interdependence of rules is constantly brought to your attention.

There are over two thousand excellent practice items in this book. These items are used in four different types of exercises: Try-It Exercises, Practice Exercises, Review Exercises, and Chapter Quizzes. Each type of exercise serves a separate function:

- The Try-It Exercises, which are placed within each chapter, give you immediate, in-depth feedback, for the answers are in the paragraphs that follow the exercise.

© NTC/CONTEMPORARY PUBLISHING COMPANY

- The Practice Exercises, which are placed within each chapter, come in sets of two: one side of the page has objective exercises, and the other side has generative exercises in which you write sentences using the rule you have just practiced on the other side of the page. The answers to the objective exercises are in the back of the book. These exercises will be perforated, so your instructor can collect and evaluate the generative (or objective) exercises if he or she wishes.

- The Review Exercises, which are at the end of each chapter, move from simple concepts to more difficult ones. You can get an immediate sense of how well you have mastered the skills for each chapter by consulting the answer key in the back of the book.

- The Chapter Quizzes are exercises that review all areas taught.

ACKNOWLEDGMENTS

We are indebted to NTC/Contemporary Publishing Company for publishing this text, especially to Marisa L. L'Heureux, Executive Editor of English and Communication Arts, whose keen mind and editorial suggestions improved each draft of this book. We also appreciate the detailed work of the copy editor, Elizabeth Fresen, whose copy editing skills were brilliant.

Acknowledgment is made to Linda Wheeler Donahue, Naugatuck Valley College; C. Jeriel Howard, Northeastern Illinois University; Janet Marting, The University of Akron; John N. Miller, Normandale Community College; and Katherine Ploeger, Modesto Junior College. Their suggestions helped strengthen the text.

We are especially grateful to our students for showing us what needs to be taught and how best to teach it.

SENTENCE STRUCTURE

1

VERBS, SUBJECTS, COMPLEMENTS, AND COMPOUNDS

You know that learning to count to one hundred does not provide you with the ability to add and subtract. Yet without an understanding of individual numbers, you would not be able to learn the basic mathematical functions of addition and subtraction. And without a foundation in basic math, comprehension of geometry, algebra, or trigonometry certainly would be impossible. The same need to understand basics applies to written English as well. If you have been struggling at writing for several years now, it is very likely that your problem is due to insufficient knowledge of the beginning skills. And in turn, that weakness has made your attempts at more advanced writing unsuccessful, or at least less successful than you would like.

To help you gain the knowledge you will need to write well, we are going to start at the simplest level and progress to more difficult sentence skills. We are not going to assume that you have an advanced knowledge of the language. Mastering the simple basics will make you more comfortable with your language and more able to use it effectively to communicate in writing. In short, by learning these simple basics, you will be free to focus on creating strong sentences.

Just as you learned to count consecutively before you learned to add and subtract, you must learn certain terms in order to understand English. Do not be concerned, however, that you will have to learn an overwhelming number of confusing definitions. In this book we will introduce only those terms you need to know in order to strengthen your skills. In time, you will discover that knowing these terms will help you become a more competent writer.

VERBS

In order to write a correct sentence consistently, you first must understand its components. A **sentence** is a group of words that has a main verb and a subject, expresses a completed thought, and can stand alone. Although a sentence *must* have a main verb and a subject, it *may* also have a complement. In addition, there can be any number of phrases or clauses attached to it. All of these elements of a sentence—complements, phrases, and clauses—will be explained later in this book.

The first element of a sentence that we will learn is the verb. Another word for verb that means the same thing is simple predicate. The term **main verb** refers to the word that expresses action or helps to make a statement complete. The main verb can be either an action or a linking verb. Although the main verb consists of only one word, it may have helping verbs in front of it. In this chapter, you will learn to identify main verbs as action or linking, as well as to identify helping verbs and fake verbs.

Look at the italicized words in the following sentences:

Michelle *studied* her lesson.

Michelle *has studied* her lesson.

Michelle *is* a good student.

Michelle *might be* a good student.

Studying her lesson, Michelle *gained* knowledge.

To study her lesson, Michelle *went* to the library.

In the first sentence, *studied* is the main verb. In the second sentence *has* is a helping verb and *studied* is the main verb. In the third sentence, *is* is the main verb. In the fourth sentence, *might* is the helping verb and *be* is the main verb. In the fifth sentence, *gained* is the main verb and *studying* is a fake verb. In the sixth sentence *went* is the main verb and *to study* is a fake verb.

The reason you will learn about verbs first is that *the main verb is the very first thing you must find* in order to determine whether you have a sentence. After you finish this section, you will feel comfortable using the term *verb* and finding the verbs in sentences.

We will begin by explaining the categories of verbs.

Action Verbs

An **action verb** expresses either physical or mental action. Of all the verbs, action verbs are the most common and the easiest to recognize. If you remember that action can be either physical (run, jog, hit, jump, play, etc.) or mental (think, perceive, understand, contemplate, etc.), action verbs will not cause you difficulty. Consider the action verbs in the following sentences:

© NTC/CONTEMPORARY PUBLISHING COMPANY

Meghan *ran* the fastest race.

Meghan *jogged* two miles with her mother.

Meghan *understands* the value of exercise.

Meghan *thinks* positive thoughts before each race.

As Meghan *hugged* her Dad, she *comprehended* the power of self-confidence.

Each verb is an action verb. The verbs *ran* and *jogged* in the first and second sentences show physical action, while the verbs *understands* and *thinks* in the third and fourth sentences show mental action. In the fifth sentence, the verb *hugged* shows physical action and the verb *comprehended* shows mental action.

TRY-IT
EXERCISE

As you read the following sentences, underline any word that shows action.

1. The students walked into the classroom.
2. They sat at their desks.
3. They soon realized a whole new world of words.
4. The students listened and took notes.
5. As they discussed the lesson, the students learned new skills.
6. These students gained control of the written word.

In the first sentence, the action word (verb) is *walked;* in the second, the verb is *sat;* in the third, the verb is *realized;* in the fourth, the verbs are *listened* and *took;* in the fifth, the verbs are *discussed* and *learned;* and in the sixth sentence, the verb is *gained.*

PRACTICE
EXERCISE 1-1

IDENTIFYING ACTION VERBS

Underline the action verb in each of the following sentences.

EXAMPLE: My brothers <u>run</u> two miles each morning.

1. I ride a stationary bicycle for exercise.
2. My dad plays golf for his exercise.
3. He often lectures us about our health.
4. Mom thinks positive thoughts for her exercise!
5. Nevertheless, she agrees with Dad about the importance of health.
6. They define *health* differently.
7. My brother and I gain fitness from sports.
8. I praise his self-discipline and stamina.
9. He blushes at my comments.
10. However, he enjoys the praise.

NAME _____ DATE _____

INSTRUCTOR _____ CLASS TIME _____

PRACTICE	# USING ACTION VERBS
EXERCISE 1-2	

For each of the following, create a sentence using the action verb listed.

EXAMPLE: want _I want a mountain bike for my birthday._

1. jog _every morning I want to jog_
2. memorize _my brother the memories the_
3. drive _driven the car of my friend_
4. watch _____
5. talk _____
6. decide _____
7. work _____
8. like _____
9. type _____
10. understand _____

NAME _____ DATE _____

INSTRUCTOR _____ CLASS TIME _____

Linking Verbs

Linking verbs do not show action. Instead, they do exactly what their name says. **Linking verbs** *connect* or *link* the words on one side of the verb with the

TABLE 1.1	*Common Linking Verbs*
am	feel
are	appear
is	sound
was	taste
were	smell
be	look
been	get
being	grow
	seem

words on the other. The word or words on the right side of a linking verb will either rename or describe the main noun on the left side. It would be impossible for you to memorize the thousands of action verbs available; however, because the list of all linking verbs is short, you can lock these words in your memory and recognize them as linking verbs when you see these words in a sentence. Table 1-1 lists the linking verbs you need to memorize.

The first group of linking verbs is called the *be* verbs because they refer to our state of being or our existence: *am, are, is, was, were, be, been, being.* In order to memorize these linking verbs, you may want to use helpful mental devices. For example, note that they are all short words, that the first two begin with *a,* that two others begin with *w,* that the last three actually have the word *be* in them. Whatever technique helps you, use it to memorize these linking verbs. And remember that the *be* verbs are not always used as linking verbs in a sentence, but can be used in various ways. You will see why this information is vital a little later.

In each of the following sentences, the linking verb is italicized.

I *am* a student in Springfield, Missouri.

We *are* teenagers from a school in Alabama.

Shaorong Huang *is* absolutely the best teacher in our school.

She *was* a delightful hostess.

Kwang and Sun Lee *were* the winners of the race.

Note: The verbs *be, been,* and *being* are forms of the *be* verb, but cannot be used without a helper. Helping verbs will be discussed later in the chapter.

The second group of the most commonly used linking verbs consists of nine different words, which also must be memorized: *feel, appear, sound, taste, smell, look, get, grow, seem.* We suggest you create a phrase from the first letter of each word in this group. By inserting one extra letter which does not represent one of the linking verbs, we can create the phrase FAST SLuGGS. The *u* is shown as lowercase because it is the letter not representing one of the linking verbs. You may want to use these beginning letters to create a different phrase that will have meaning for you. Whatever you come up with, it should help you be able to recall these nine words so that you are not merely attempting to memorize them. One important point about these nine verbs is that usually they are used as linking verbs, but not always. On occasion, they may be used as an action verb. For example, *smell* is a linking verb in the sentence: The roses smell fabulous. However, *smell* is an action verb in the sentence: The girls *smell* the roses.

In each of the following sentences, the linking verb is italicized:

F   1.   They *feel* good about their class schedule.

A   2.   Mother *appears* excited today.

S   3.   The songs on that tape *sound* great.

T   4.   Those pickles *taste* sour.

Note: The first letters of each verb listed above combine to spell FAST.

S   5.   The cookies in the oven *smell* wonderful.

Lu 6.   You *look* great in that outfit.

G   7.   She *gets* prettier every year.

G   8.   The weeds in our garden *grow* tall.

S   9.   Your parents *seem* understanding.

Note: The first letters of each verb listed above combine to spell SLuGGS (with the addition of lowercase *u*).

TRY-IT

EXERCISE

Underline the verbs in the sentences below and tell whether they are action (A) or linking (L) verbs.

_____   1.   The boy was very tired.
_____   2.   The girl feels tired too.
_____   3.   The doctor felt my hot forehead.
_____   4.   The men are happy about their jobs.
_____   5.   Carlos gets nervous before a new job.
_____   6.   He gets compliments from his employer.

The word *was* in the first sentence is a linking verb. It is a *be* verb and connects the right side of the sentence with the

© NTC/CONTEMPORARY PUBLISHING COMPANY

main noun on the left by describing *boy.* A good test to apply to check for a linking verb is to move the word on the left after the one on the right to see whether the sentence meaning changes. For example, you could say "the tired boy" and keep the same meaning. This is true for the next sentence as well. *Feels* is a linking verb because the word on the right, *tired,* describes the main word on the left, *girl.* Again, you could switch the words to "tired girl," and the sentence still makes sense. The word *are* in the fourth sentence is a linking verb. It is a *be* verb and connects *happy* to *men;* the word *gets* in the fifth sentence is a linking verb connecting *nervous* to *Carlos.* In each case, you can change the order to say "happy men" and "nervous Carlos" and the meaning doesn't change. The third and sixth sentences use one of the nine FAST SLuGGS verbs as an action verb, not a linking one. Note that the words on the right side of *felt* in the third sentence and *gets* in the sixth sentence do not describe the *doctor* or *He* on the left sides. The phrases "forehead doctor" and "compliments he" make no sense.

Another easy way to test whether one of these nine FAST SLuGGS verbs is used as a linking verb is to insert one of the *be* verbs in its place. If the sentence makes sense with the *be* verb, then the verb is a linking one. For example, if we replace *feels* in the second sentence with *is,* the sentence retains its meaning. Therefore, the second sentence uses a linking verb. However, if we replace *felt* with *is* in the third sentence, we have nonsense: *The doctor is my hot forehead.* Likewise, if we replace *gets* with *is* in the sixth sentence, the sentence becomes ridiculous: *He is many compliments from his employer.* This change in sentence meaning signals that the verb is not linking.

TRY-IT
EXERCISE

Underline the verbs in the sentences below and tell whether they are action (A) or linking (L) verbs.

_____ 1. The students feel exhausted.
_____ 2. The woman felt the fur coat.
_____ 3. The tortilla chips taste salty.
_____ 4. The cooks always taste the food.
_____ 5. The perfume smells very good.

_____   6. The customers smell the perfume.
_____   7. The children get easily bored.
_____   8. The man gets good money for his labor.
_____   9. The man grows overweight from junk food.
_____ 10. The family grows vegetables in their garden.

All the above verbs are first used as linking verbs and then used as action verbs; therefore, sentences 1, 3, 5, 7, and 9 have linking verbs (L), and sentences 2, 4, 6, 8, and 10 have action verbs (A).

© NTC/CONTEMPORARY PUBLISHING COMPANY

PRACTICE
EXERCISE 1-3

IDENTIFYING LINKING VERBS

Underline the linking verb in each sentence.

EXAMPLE: Natasha <u>is</u> a good cook.

1. Natasha <u>was</u> a winner of many awards at the state fair.
2. Her cakes <u>were</u> the best at the fair.
3. That cake with the blue ribbon <u>is</u> chocolate.
4. Natasha <u>is</u> not hungry anymore.
5. This <u>is</u> the winning recipe.
6. She <u>looks</u> very tired.
7. Her mother <u>seems</u> proud of her awards and ribbons.
8. Even her dad <u>feels</u> excited.
9. The cakes in the contest <u>taste</u> great.
10. The entire family <u>appears</u> pleased by her success.

NAME _____ DATE _____

INSTRUCTOR _____ CLASS TIME _____

PRACTICE	# USING LINKING VERBS
EXERCISE 1-4	

For each of the following, create a sentence. Each verb will be used in two separate sentences, first as a linking verb and then as an action verb.

EXAMPLE: sound (as linking) *The soccer players sound confident.*

sound (as action) *I sound the alarm.*

1.   taste (as linking) _____

2.   taste (as action) _____

3.   smell (as linking) _____

4.   smell (as action) _____

5.   get (as linking) _____

6.   get (as action) _____

7.   grow (as linking) _____

8.   grow (as action) _____

9.   feel (as linking) _____

10.   feel (as action) _____

NAME _____ DATE _____

INSTRUCTOR _____ CLASS TIME _____

© NTC/CONTEMPORARY PUBLISHING COMPANY

Helping Verbs

The third and last type of verb is called a **helping verb** because it is used with a main verb in a sentence to help establish when something happened. Another term meaning the same thing is *auxiliary verb.* A helping, or auxiliary, verb is used to make the meaning of the main verb more precise.

As before, we advise you to memorize helping verbs. You must be able to identify them as part of the verb. Be aware that they *can be used alone* and thus become the main verb.

TABLE 1.2 *Common Helping Verbs*

1. Any of the *be* verbs = *am, are, is, was, were, be, been, being*
2. *May, might, must* = 3 *M*s
3. *Do, does, did* = 3 *D*s
4. *Have, has, had* = 3 *H*s
5. *Can, could* = 3 pairs
   shall, should
   will, would

A strong understanding of helping verbs, coupled with what you now know about action and linking verbs, will equip you to understand the next component we discuss.

Use Table 1.2 to memorize the helping verbs. Note that items 2, 3, and 4 above contain three words, each series beginning with the same letter. The difference in item five is that there are three pairs, not three words. Remember: Any of the *be* verbs (*am, are, is, was, were, be, been, being*) can link, help, or stand alone.

An easy way to begin learning these helping verbs is to remember the sentence "Mothers dread having pairs." Note that *Mothers* begins with an *m* as does each of the words in the first set, *dread* begins with the same first letter as the next three words, and *having* represents the first letter of the last set of three. The word *pairs* in the above sentence shows that the last set of words contains three pairs of words, not just three words. Noting that the last word of each pair rhymes will help you memorize them.

In each of the following sentences, the helping verb is italicized:

*M*OTHERS = *may, must, might*

1. He *may* study his lesson.
2. He *must* study his lesson.
3. He *might* study his lesson.

*D*READ = *do, does, did*

1. I *do* study my lessons.
2. She *does* study her lessons.
3. They *did* study their lessons.

HAVING = *has, have, had*

1. He *has* studied his lessons.

2. They *have* studied their lessons.

3. She *had* studied her lessons.

PAIRS = *can/could, shall/should, will/would*

1. I *can* study each night.

   I *could* study each night.

2. I *shall* study each night.

   I *should* study each night.

3. I *will* study each night.

   I *would* study each night.

When two or more words make up the verb, we have a verb phrase rather than a single verb. **Verb phrases** consist of a main verb plus helping verb(s). Whenever there is a verb phrase, *only the last verb* in that phrase is the main verb. It may be either an action or a linking verb. The first part of the phrase is always helping.

Look at the following sentences:

> She *may find* peace of mind in solitude.
>
> Her face *does look* peaceful.
>
> She *may* frequently *find* peace of mind in solitude.

In the first sentence the verb phrase is *may find.* The helping verb is *may* and the main verb is *find,* an action verb. The helping verb in the second sentence is *does* and the main verb is *look,* a linking verb. Though the third sentence is similar to the previous two, there is a difference that could be deceptive. The third sentence has the word *frequently* between the helping verb *may* and the action verb *find.* Ignore any intervening words separating a helping verb from the main verb. The verb phrase still is *may find.*

The following words are never part of a verb phrase, even though they occur in the middle of one. They are **adverbs,** words that modify verbs. Adverbs usually answer the questions How? Where? When? Why? To what extent? and On what condition? They intervene between a helping verb and a main verb to describe

TABLE 1.3	*Common Adverbs*	
already	also	always
now	not	never
finally	fully	frequently
once	only	often
really	sometimes	usually

more precisely the verb phrase, but they are not part of the verb phrase. Use Table 1.3 to help you learn to identify adverbs.

TRY-IT
EXERCISE

In the following sentences, underline the helping verb(s) in the verb phrase and put parentheses around the intervening word that is *not* a verb.

1. We did not study last night.
2. They should never have taken that class.
3. She will often study at night.
4. They had already been working an hour.
5. I am always studying French.
6. He is usually reviewing his lessons.
7. Jacques will frequently make good grades.
8. I am now learning basic sentence skills.

In the first sentence, the verb phrase is *did study* and the intervening word is *not.* In the second sentence, the verb phrase is *should have taken* and the helping verbs are *should have;* the intervening word is *never.* In the third sentence, the verb phrase is *will study* and the intervening word is *often.* In the fourth sentence, the verb phrase is *had been working* and the helping verbs are *had been;* the intervening word is *already.* In the fifth sentence, the verb phrase is *am studying,* and the intervening word is *always.* In the sixth sentence, the verb phrase is *is reviewing* and the intervening word is *usually.* In the seventh sentence, the verb phrase is *will make* and the intervening word is *frequently.* In the eighth sentence, the verb phrase is *am learning* and the intervening word is *now.*

Using these sentences, we see that helping verbs help show when things happen. In the first sentence, the helping verb *did* tells that the action has been completed. In the second sentence, the helping verbs *should have* tell that the action has been completed. In the third sentence, the helping verb *will* tells that the action has not been completed, but will be in the future. In the fourth sentence, the helping verbs *had been* tell that the action has been completed. In the fifth sentence, the helping verb *am* tells that the action is in the present. In the sixth sentence, the helping verb *is* tells that the action is in the present. In the seventh sentence, the helping verb *will* tells that the action will be completed in the future. In the eighth sentence, the helping verb *am* tells that the action is in the present.

PRACTICE
EXERCISE 1-5

IDENTIFYING HELPING VERBS

Underline the verb phrase in each sentence below and write a label (H) above the helping verb(s).

                    H
EXAMPLE: Manuel <u>will be</u> two years old in March.

1.   Manuel has been walking for a year.

2.   His parents have not relaxed for the entire year!

3.   I have often followed a toddler all day.

4.   You may have cared for your baby brother or sister.

5.   Two-year-olds do ask numerous questions.

6.   Manuel can constantly talk.

7.   His favorite words must be "no" and "why."

8.   They might have been his first words.

9.   He can already walk to the neighbors' house.

10.   His parents are now wanting a sister for Manuel.

NAME _____ DATE _____

INSTRUCTOR _____ CLASS TIME _____

PRACTICE
EXERCISE 1-6
USING HELPING VERBS

Create a sentence using the listed helping verb with either an action or a linking verb.

EXAMPLE: must *I must go grocery shopping soon.*

1. had _____

2. can _____

3. does _____

4. should _____

5. did _____

6. was _____

7. may _____

8. would _____

9. were _____

10. been _____

© NTC/CONTEMPORARY PUBLISHING COMPANY

NAME _____ DATE _____

INSTRUCTOR _____ CLASS TIME _____

SUBJECTS

We began our study of the basics by examining verbs. When breaking down a sentence, the verb is the first thing you should locate. You must have a clear understanding of verbs in order to find the subject, the next important component of a sentence.

The **subject** is that element of a sentence (usually a noun or pronoun) which, if the verb is an action verb, *performs* the action of that main verb. If the verb is linking, it *links* the words on each side of it. The easiest way to identify the subject of a sentence is first to find the verb and then to ask "Who or what _____?" Fill in the blank with the verb you found. The "who" or the "what" is the subject. You can see now why it is so important to know how to find the verb first in breaking down a sentence. The subject is always found second. Although some people may say they prefer to find the subject first, they can never be certain they are correct until they check it with the verb.

For example, consider the following sentence:

Students study literature.

The action verb of this sentence is *study*. Once you identify the verb, you simply ask, "Who or what study?" The answer is the subject of the sentence. In this sentence the subject is *students*.

The sentence "Students study literature" is a fairly easy sentence to analyze both because it is short and because it is an example of the most common sentence order in the English language: subject first, verb second. Not all sentences follow this simple pattern, however. In some instances, groups of words can come between the subject and verb, or even before the subject. In other sentences, the subject may follow the verb. The subject might not even be named, but become something called an understood subject. Let's examine these exceptions to the typical subject-verb sentence pattern.

Words Between the Subject and the Verb: Prepositional Phrases

In many sentences there are words between the subject and verb, yet these words do not become the subject of the sentence. Find the verb in the following sentences. Ask "Who or What___?" and identify the subject of each sentence.

People in this beautiful city are polite and friendly.

Restaurants on the city's magnificent river serve numerous people.

Drivers within Cincinnati quickly yield to other drivers.

Residents from other congested cities are shocked by this thoughtfulness.

Thoughtfulness in any city of any state is wonderful.

© NTC/CONTEMPORARY PUBLISHING COMPANY

In the first sentence, *are* is the main verb and *people* is the subject. The prepositional phrase *in this beautiful city* does not change the subject. In the second sentence, *serve* is the main verb and *restaurants* is the subject. The prepositional phrase *on the city's magnificent river* does not change the subject. In the third sentence, *yield* is the main verb and *drivers* is the subject. The prepositional phrase *within Cincinnati* does not change the subject. In the fourth sentence, *are* is the main verb and *residents* is the subject. The prepositional phrase *from other congested cities* does not change the subject. In the fifth sentence, *is* is the main verb and *thoughtfulness* is the subject. The prepositional phrases *in any city of any state* do not change the subject.

TRY-IT
EXERCISE

First, underline the main verb in each sentence. Next, ask "Who?" or "What?" and circle the subject of the following sentences.

1. Students in this large school study literature.
2. Students with scholarships study literature.
3. Students near graduation day study eagerly.
4. Students down the hall from us study math.
5. Students like Chang Jin and Hae study constantly.
6. Students during a quarter of chemistry study many hours each day.

In these sentences we know the verb is *study,* so we ask our key question to find the subject: "Who or what study?" The answer still is *students.* Beware, however, of choosing as the subject words that come immediately before the verb. Give every verb the "Who? What?" test, and you'll have little trouble identifying the correct subject. Furthermore, if you identified *school, scholarships, day, us, Hae,* or *chemistry* as the subject, the reason may be that you have not learned to recognize prepositions in a sentence. This recognition is vital to your finding the correct subject of any sentence.

PREPOSITIONS. A **preposition** shows the position (pre*position*) of one word in relation to another. For example, take the word *student* and think of a preposition that shows the position of the student in relation to other objects.

The student is *across* the room.

The student is *around* the corner.

The student is *at* school.

The student is *beside* the desk.

The student is *by* the fountain.

The student is *in* the library.

Each of the italicized words is a preposition. Notice that *room, corner, school, desk, fountain,* and *library* all are nouns. This noun following the preposition is called the *object of a preposition;* the group of words together is called a *prepositional phrase.* Remember, however, that *no word in a prepositional phrase will be the subject of the sentence.* When identifying the subject of a sentence, then, it is sometimes helpful to put parentheses around all prepositional phrases first, and then go back to locate the verb and the subject. The subject will never be included in the parentheses.

Consider the following sentence:

Many of the students study literature.

We still have a sentence similar to our first one, but now the answer to "Who or what study?" changes. The answer and the subject is *Many,* not students. Though you may have said *students* and read some sense into the chosen subject and verb combination, *students* cannot be the subject because it is part of an intervening prepositional phrase between the real subject and verb. The word *of* is a preposition, and the first noun following it is *students.* Thus, if you put parentheses around the prepositional phrase *of the students* and eliminate it as subject, the answer to "Who or what study?" is *many,* the correct subject.

The most common prepositions are listed below in Table 1.4. Although you are not required to memorize them, you do need to review the list carefully

TABLE 1.4 *Common Prepositions*

about	below	in	under
above	beneath	into	until
across	beside	like	up
after	between	of	upon
against	beyond	off	with
along	by	on	within
among	down	over	without
around	during	past	at
except	through	before	for
to	behind	from	toward

three or four times so that you can recognize a preposition when you encounter one in your writing.

Remember that a prepositional phrase is a preposition followed by a noun or pronoun, so mentally place parentheses around all prepositional phrases in a sentence and ignore them when identifying the subject of the sentence.

Words Before the Subject and Verb

Although the subject can be the first word in a sentence, it does not have to be. In fact, any group of words can come before the subject. The most common are prepositional phrases, main verbs, and helping verbs.

PREPOSITIONAL PHRASES BEFORE THE SUBJECT. A nontypical subject position occurs when a sentence begins with one or more prepositional phrases:

In this beautiful city, people are polite and friendly.

On the city's magnificent river, restaurants serve numerous people.

Within Cincinnati, drivers quickly yield to other drivers.

From other congested cities, residents are shocked by this thoughtfulness.

In any city of any state, thoughtfulness is wonderful.

In the first sentence, the main verb is *are* and the subject is *people*. In the second sentence, the main verb is *serve* and the subject is *restaurants*. In the third sentence, the main verb is *yield* and the subject is *drivers*. In the fourth sentence, the main verb is *are* and the subject is *residents*. In the fifth sentence, the main verb is *is* and the subject is *thoughtfulness*. None of the prepositional phrases at the beginning change the subject of the sentence.

TRY-IT
EXERCISE

Put parentheses around all prepositional phrases. Then underline the subject in each of the following sentences.

1. In this large school, students study literature.
2. In the library of this school, students study literature.
3. Near graduation day, students study eagerly.
4. Down the hall from us, students study math.
5. Like Chang Jin and Hae, students study constantly.

6. During a quarter of chemistry, students study many hours a day.

In sentence one, the prepositional phrase that you should have enclosed in parentheses is *in this large school;* in sentence two the prepositional phrases are *in the library of this school;* in sentence three, the prepositional phrase is *near graduation day;* in the fourth sentence, the prepositional phrases are *down the hall from us;* in the fifth sentence, the prepositional phrase is *like Chang Jin and Hae;* in the sixth sentence, the prepositional phrases are *during a quarter of chemistry.* Since you will not find your subject inside a prepositional phrase, exclude that phrase from your search. Now answer the question, "Who or what study?" *Students* is the answer for each sentence.

VERB BEFORE THE SUBJECT.   Although the majority of sentences have the subject first and the verb second, some sentences do not follow this pattern. For example, sentences that begin with *there, here,* and *where* have the verb before the subject.

There were numerous friends at Meena's party.

Here are Taylor's last three essays.

Where is Myrtle's new bicycle?

In the first sentence, the main verb is *were* and the subject is *friends.* In the second sentence, the main verb is *are* and the subject is *essays.* In the third sentence, the main verb is *is* and the subject is *bicycle.*

TRY-IT

EXERCISE

Underline the subject in each of the following sentences.

1. There are students in the library.
2. Here is my English test.
3. Where is my test?
4. There is a good-looking shirt for Omar.
5. Here is the bill for that last purchase.
6. Where are those packages?

You should recognize these verbs as forms of the *be* verb. In the first sentence, the answer to "Who or what are?" is *students*, not *there*. Therefore, *students* is the subject of the sentence. The answer to "Who or what is?" in the second sentence is *test*. Therefore, *test* is the subject, as it is also the subject in the third sentence. The subject of the fourth sentence is *shirt;* the subject of the fifth sentence is *bill;* the subject of the sixth sentence is *packages*. The words *there, here,* and *where* are not even nouns and, therefore, cannot ever be the subject of a sentence. When searching for the subject, ignore these words and look for the subject elsewhere in the sentence.

HELPING VERB BEFORE THE SUBJECT.   Another nontypical subject position occurs in a question, where a helping verb comes before the subject.

May I go to the dance on Saturday night?

Would you go with me to the dance on Saturday night?

When will Ricardo ask Lauren for a date?

Whom might Lauren ask to the movie?

In the first two sentences, the main verb is *go*. In the first sentence, the helping verb is *may,* and in the second sentence the helping verb is *would*. In the next two sentences, the main verb is *ask*. In the third sentence, the helping verb is *will,* and in the fourth sentence, the helping verb is *might*. In sentences that ask questions, the helping verb comes before the subject.

TRY-IT
EXERCISE

Underline the verb in each of the following sentences.

1. Will students study literature in English class?
2. Should students study literature at home?
3. Do teachers of your classes work on their lesson plans?
4. Can teachers at your school work two jobs at one time?
5. Should men in Japan cook meals for the family?
6. Would men in your family cook meals?

In the first two sentences, the main verb is *study*. In the first sentence the helping verb is *will* and in the second sentence it is *should*. In the next two sentences, the main verb is

© NTC/CONTEMPORARY PUBLISHING COMPANY

work. In the third sentence the helping verb is *do* and in the fourth sentence it is *can*. In the last two sentences, the main verb is *cook*. In the fifth sentence the helping verb is *should* and in the sixth sentence it is *would*. Notice that in sentences that ask questions, the helping verb comes before the subject.

In order to easily identify the verb and the subject in a question, first turn the question into a statement without adding or deleting words.

▼ **Question:** Do students study literature?
▲ **Statement:** Students do study literature.

Note that the question is easier to break down into recognizable parts when it is transformed because the helping verb (*do*) and the main verb (*study*) are together in the statement. By asking our usual question "Who or what do study?" we determine the subject is *students.* Although the verb and the subject are the same for the question as for the statement, in the question the verb phrase *do study* is split by the subject.

Understood Subject

Often when a person makes a request or tells someone to do something, the subject is not stated but is understood. Whenever the subject is understood, it will be the word *you.* Grammatically the *understood you* is as much the subject of the sentence as if it were printed on the page or stated verbally.

Study this chapter carefully.

Study your Japanese textbook.

In both sentences the verb is *study.* Who or what study? If you want to answer *chapter* or *textbook,* realize that it does not make any sense because a chapter and a textbook cannot study anything. The answer is *you,* which is the understood subject in both sentences. Four characteristics should help you recognize an understood subject:

1. The sentence is a statement.
2. It is a request or command.
3. The sentence makes sense when spoken to someone.
4. By inserting the word *you* at the front of the sentence, you retain its intended meaning.

TRY-IT

EXERCISE

Determine the subject in each of the following sentences.

1. Close the door.
2. Brush your teeth after each meal.
3. Ask the teacher for an appointment.
4. Drive carefully on the highway.
5. Look at that beautiful sunset.

Because each sentence is a request or command, the subject is understood. If you ask "Who?" or "What?" should *close, brush, ask, drive,* or *look,* the answer is "you." Therefore, *you* is the subject of all of these sentences.

© NTC/CONTEMPORARY PUBLISHING COMPANY

| PRACTICE | # IDENTIFYING SUBJECTS |
| EXERCISE 1-7 | |

In each of the sentences, underline the subject of the sentence.

EXAMPLE: Summer <u>days</u> bring happiness.

1. Days of summer fun are finally here.

2. The fun of summer days is related to warm weather.

3. At the first sign of summer, I am lying in the sun.

4. There are many very warm days in May.

5. Do you enjoy warm weather?

6. Come inside after an hour in the hot sun.

7. Before knowledge about skin cancer, people spent hours in the sun.

8. Several teens in our neighborhood play tennis during the warm days of May.

9. Where is your favorite place for sunbathing?

10. Beside the lake in northern New Hampshire, we get a good tan.

NAME _____ DATE _____

INSTRUCTOR _____ CLASS TIME _____

PRACTICE
EXERCISE 1-8
USING SUBJECTS

Write a complete sentence using the verb or verb phrase listed.

EXAMPLE: liked *Jan liked the present from Tom.*

1. offered _The office offered me a job_
2. suggested _Jul suggested a good idea_
3. discover _____
4. are _____
5. do have _____
6. wants _____
7. were _____
8. is _____
9. talked _____
10. should try _____

NAME _____ DATE _____

INSTRUCTOR _____ CLASS TIME _____

FAKE VERBS

There are three groups of words that act and look so much like verbs that students often identify them as the main verbs of sentences. These words, however, are not verbs, so you will want to learn to recognize these fakes. They are verbals, rather than verbs.

Verbals

Verbals are words that are formed from a verb and look like a verb, but are used as either a noun or an adjective. **Nouns** name people, places, things, and ideas, such as *Michelle, Mexico, book,* and *love.* **Adjectives** are words that modify (limit, clarify, or describe) a noun or pronoun, such as *thoughtful* Michelle, *beautiful* Mexico, *exciting* book, and *genuine* love. Neither nouns nor adjectives can replace main verbs, yet students often mistakenly identify verbals as main verbs.

Since verbals usually are either a *verb* + *-ing* or *to* + a *verb,* you need to recognize them because they are the ones most commonly mistaken for the main verb. One rule you must remember is this: If a verb has an *-ing* ending, it is never going to be a sentence's main verb unless it has a helping verb to accompany it. Note that any of the *be* verbs can be used as helpers, and recall our learning aid for the other helpers: *Mothers Dread Having Pairs.* The second rule you must remember is that *to* + a *verb* is never the main verb of a sentence. Look at how *walking* is used in each of these following sentences:

Walking cultivates health.

Walking is a verbal; *cultivates* is the main verb.

To walk cultivates health.

To walk is a verbal; *cultivates* is the main verb.

People in a family *should be walking* for improvement of their health.

Walking is the main verb; *should be* are helpers.

VERB + -ING: ADJECTIVE. One of these groups of fake verbs consists of words that are formed from a verb, but are used as adjectives. Rather than being the main verb of a sentence, they modify a noun. In each of the following sentences the verb + *-ing* is italicized.

Studying at the kitchen table, Juanita learned Arabic.

The verbal *studying* is used as an adjective and modifies the word *Juanita.*

Working each night, Jason was often tired.

The verbal *working* is used as an adjective and modifies the word *Jason.*

VERB + -ING: NOUN.   Not only can a verb + *-ing* word serve as an adjective, it also can serve as a noun. As a noun, verbals fill many slots in a sentence. They can be subject, complement, or object of the preposition. Still, our original rule holds true: If there is no helping verb, the *-ing* word is not part of the verb. In the following sentence the verb + *-ing* is italicized:

Studying is a good habit.

Studying is used as a noun and is the subject of the verb *is.*

Working takes self-discipline.

Working is used as a noun and is the subject of the verb *takes.*

TO + VERB.   The last group of these fake verbs consists of the word *to* in front of a verb. *To work, to ski, to study,* and *to be* are examples of this type of verbal, which can serve as an adjective or a noun. In the following sentences the *to* + a verb is italicized:

She has enough ability *to succeed.*

The verbal *to succeed* is used as an adjective and modifies the word *ability.*

To succeed is her goal.

The verbal *To succeed* is used as a noun and serves as the subject of the verb *is.*
   Verbal contains the word *verb,* and, indeed, at first glance it looks like a verb. It may end in *-ing* but have no helper verb, or it may have *to* in front of it. In these cases it does not function as a verb, but rather as a noun or an adjective. Later, you will identify these verbals as present participles, gerunds, and infinitives. Making these distinctions is not necessary at this time, however.

TRY-IT

EXERCISE

In each of the following sentences, underline the main verb (or verb phrase) and put parentheses around the subject. Remember that verbals are not main verbs.

© NTC/CONTEMPORARY PUBLISHING COMPANY

1. Studying his book, the student underlined important ideas.
2. The student, studying hurriedly, learned very little.
3. Studying is good self-discipline.
4. To study requires self-discipline.
5. We will be studying each night.

In the first sentence, it looks like we might have two verbs, but remember: In order to be a main verb, any verb ending in *-ing* must have a helper verb, or it is not a verb at all. Since *studying* has no helper, we can eliminate it as a main verb possibility. Moving on in this sentence, we find the word *underlined* is the main verb. And by asking the "who or what" question, we find the subject to be *student.*

In the second sentence, the *-ing* verb is again *studying,* and there is no helping verb to go with it. Again, you must look elsewhere for your main verb. The main verb is *learned* and the subject is *student.*

In the third sentence, the verb *is* is linking and from the *be* verb group. The subject in the third sentence is *studying.* It can be a main verb only if accompanied by a helping verb. When an *-ing* form of the verb is used as an adjective or a noun, it cannot also be a verb.

In the fourth sentence, the main verb is the word *requires.* The answer to our "who or what" question is *to study,* the subject of the sentence. Remember that *to* + a verb can be the subject of a sentence.

In the fifth sentence, the word *studying* has helping verbs in front of it, so it is part of the verb. These three verbs—*will be studying*—are called a verb phrase. The subject is *we.*

Verbal Phrases

When a verbal has any modifiers attached to it, it is labeled a **verbal phrase**. A *modifier* is any word, or group of words, used to qualify, describe, or limit another word. Like verbals, verbal phrases can be used as either adjectives or nouns.

VERB + -ING PHRASE. A verbal phrase is a verbal with modifiers. The verbal with *-ing,* plus modifiers, is one type of verbal phrase.

Rushing to class on the third floor, Antonio is exhausted.

Rushing to class on the third floor is exhausting.

Before *rushing to class on the third floor,* Antonio quickly parked his car.

In all three sentences, the verbal phrase is *rushing to class on the third floor*. In the first sentence, the verbal phrase serves as an adjective and modifies the word *Antonio*. In the second sentence, the verbal phrase serves as a noun and is the subject of the verb *is*. In the third sentence, the verbal phrase serves as a noun and is direct object of the preposition *before*. Be aware that within verbal phrases can be prepositional phrases: *to class* and *on the third floor*.

TRY-IT
EXERCISE

Underline the verbal phrase in each of the following sentences.

1. Writing essays in English, Juan uses his grammar and punctuation skills.
2. Writing essays in English takes effort.
3. After writing essays in English, Juan is drained.
4. Reviewing basic rules of the language, Lauren feels self-confident.
5. Reviewing basic rules of the language requires time and effort.
6. Before reviewing basic rules of the language, Lauren was confused.

In the first three sentences the verbal phrase is *writing essays in English*. In the first sentence, the verbal phrase serves as an adjective and modifies the word *Juan*. In the second sentence, the verbal phrase serves as a noun and is the subject of the verb *takes*. In the third sentence, the verbal phrase serves as a noun and is the object of the preposition *after*. Notice that within the verbal phrase is the prepositional phrase *in English,* which modifies the word *essays*. In the last three sentences, the verbal phrase is *reviewing basic rules of the language*. In the fourth sentence, the verbal phrase serves as an adjective and modifies the word *Lauren*. In the fifth sentence, the verbal phrase serves as a noun and is the subject of the verb *requires*. In the sixth sentence, the verbal phrase serves as a noun and is the object of the preposition *Before*. Notice that within the verbal phrase is the prepositional phrase *of the language*.

In the following sentences, the verbal is *studying.* The verbal phrase is the verbal plus modifiers. The verbal phrase is italicized:

Studying in her quiet bedroom, Martina could learn new skills.

The verbal phrase is used as an adjective and modifies the word *Martina.*

Studying for English requires time and effort.

The verbal phrase is used as a noun and is the subject of the verb *requires.*

Before *studying her calculus,* Martina took a nap.

The verbal phrase is used as a noun and is the object of the preposition *Before.*

TO + A VERB PHRASE. Another common verbal phrase consists of *to* + a verb, plus modifiers. Like all the other verbal phrases, *to* + a verb fills various functions in a sentence.

Mariko lacks the desire *to rush to classes.*

To rush to classes destroys her peace of mind.

The verbal phrase in both sentences is *to rush to classes.* In the first sentence, the verbal phrase serves as an adjective and modifies the word *desire.* In the second sentence the verbal phrase serves as a noun and is the subject of the verb *destroys.* Be aware that prepositional phrases can be within verbal phrases.

TRY-IT
EXERCISE

Underline the verbal phrase in each of the following sentences.

1. Choon has no time to study for tomorrow's test.
2. To study for tomorrow's test will take time.
3. Itamar hopes to major in computer science.
4. To major in computer science is one of Itamar's dreams.
5. Many people want to obtain a satisfying job.
6. To obtain a satisfying job was Cassandra's dream.

The verbal phrase in the first and second sentences is *to study for tomorrow's test.* In sentence one, the verbal phrase serves as an adjective and modifies the word *time.* In sentence two, the verbal phrase serves as a noun and is the subject of the verb phrase *will take.* The verbal phrase in the third and fourth sentences is *to major in computer science.* In sentence three, the verbal phrase serves as a direct object. In sentence four, the verbal phrase serves as the subject of the verb *is.* The verbal phrase in the fifth and sixth sentences is *to obtain a satisfying job.* In sentence five, the verbal serves as a direct object. In sentence six, the verbal serves as the subject of the verb *was.*

In the following sentences phrases consisting of *to* + a verb are italicized. The verbal in each is *to earn:*

She has enough ability *to earn a high grade in English.*

The verbal phrase above serves as an adjective and modifies the word *ability.*

To earn a satisfying job is her goal.

The verbal phrase above serves as a noun and is the subject of the verb *is.*

| PRACTICE | # IDENTIFYING VERBAL PHRASES |
| EXERCISE 1-9 | |

Underline the verbal phrase in each of the following sentences. In each sentence, check the word that follows each *to*. If it is a verb, you have a verbal. If it is a noun or pronoun, you have a prepositional phrase. Verbal phrases can, of course, have prepositional phrases within them.

EXAMPLE: <u>Making sense of verbal phrases</u> is hard work.

1. Laughing at Jan's jokes, Tom nearly choked.

2. Studying early in the evening is a good habit.

3. A big step in maturity is balancing work and play.

4. Earning good grades takes self-discipline.

5. Many people feel awkward after laughing at themselves.

EXAMPLE: <u>To understand the rules of English</u> requires effort.

6. To graduate from college will be wonderful.

7. The seniors plan to get a job in their field of study.

8. The students had many questions to ask their history teacher.

9. The teacher was able to answer their questions on the Civil War.

10. To give clear answers to questions is not easy.

NAME _____   DATE _____

INSTRUCTOR _____   CLASS TIME _____

PRACTICE	# USING VERBAL PHRASES
EXERCISE 1-10	

Use either a verbal or a verbal phrase to complete the following sentences. In these five sentences, use a verb + *-ing*.

EXAMPLE: *Admitting the difficulty of the material*, the teacher suggested extra class sessions.

1. _____ , the students gained a better understanding of the subject matter.

2. _____ helped them know the format for the actual quiz.

3. A student can insure success by _____.

4. A major problem for many students results from _____.

5. Some students resist _____.

Use either a verbal or a verbal phrase to complete the following sentences. In these five sentences use *to* + a verb.

6. If you sign the first contract that is offered, you may have _____.

7. Informing your prospective employer that you are mobile can help ___.

8. It would be a mistake _____.

9. If you have serious reservations about a job, do not accept it just _____.

10. The most important criterion for a job is _____.

NAME _____ DATE _____

INSTRUCTOR _____ CLASS TIME _____

© NTC/CONTEMPORARY PUBLISHING COMPANY

| PRACTICE | **IDENTIFYING VERBS AND**
| EXERCISE 1-11 | **SUBJECTS**

Underline every verb and each subject in the following sentences. Then add a label above each word you underlined to identify it as an action verb (A), a linking verb (L), a helping verb (H), or a subject (S).

                              S   H   L
EXAMPLE: The most expensive <u>car</u> <u>may</u> not <u>be</u> the most efficient.

1. Parents of several children are often strict with their first child.

2. In a very large family, each child feels ignored at some time.

3. Jealousy within the family structure may frequently occur.

4. Many parents, trying to be fair, create problems.

5. Many of us may have sometimes wished for a better childhood.

6. Think about this possibility.

7. Attempting to treat every one of their children alike, parents may experience frustration.

8. Neither of the parents may have been given love.

9. Loving is the most important aspect of child-rearing.

10. Receiving unconditional love, children can grow self-confident.

NAME _____ DATE _____

INSTRUCTOR _____ CLASS TIME _____

USING VERBS AND SUBJECTS

PRACTICE
EXERCISE 1-12

For items 1 through 5, create a subject and a *linking* verb before the listed words. *Do not use a verb or subject more than once.*

EXAMPLE: _Miranda looked_ _____ tired.

1. _____ very busy.
2. _____ sunny.
3. _____ a studious person.
4. _____ loud.
5. _____ fragrant.

For items 6 through 10, create a subject and an *action* verb before the listed words. *Do not use a verb or subject more than once.*

6. _____ the car.
7. _____ an apartment.
8. _____ a vacation.
9. _____ some time.
10. _____ homework.

NAME _____ DATE _____

INSTRUCTOR _____ CLASS TIME _____

© NTC/CONTEMPORARY PUBLISHING COMPANY

COMPLEMENTS

In grammar, a **complement** is a group of words on the right side of the verb that completes the meaning of the sentence. (Note that the spelling of the grammatical *complement* differs from the spelling of the *compliment* you would pay to a friend whose sweater you admired.) To remember the meaning associated with grammar, note that the word *complement* seems to derive from the word *complete.* The English language has four common types of complements: direct objects, indirect objects, predicate nominatives, and predicate adjectives.

Direct Objects

Basically, a **direct object** is a word that receives the action of the verb. But there are some very important points you must commit to memory so that you know whether you have a direct object. First of all, the verb *must* be an action verb, with the word on the right side of that verb receiving the action. (There is an exception involving the passive voice of a verb, but we are going to ignore it until you have a strong understanding of direct objects.) Whenever you have a direct object, the verb is never a linking verb.

There are four basic steps to follow when testing for the presence of a direct object, and they must be done in the order listed below:

1. Find the main verb of the sentence and determine whether it is an ACTION verb.
2. *If the verb is action,* find the subject next.
3. Now repeat the subject and the verb and ask "whom or what?"
4. If the answer to the question directly receives the action of the verb, you have a direct object.

Here is the way the four steps would work in the sentence "Students study literature."

1. The main verb of the sentence is *study;* it is an action verb.
2. Because it is an action verb, the next step is to find the subject by asking "Who or what study?" We find that the subject is *students.*
3. We repeat the subject and verb and ask, "Students study whom or what?"
4. The noun on the right side of the verb directly receives the action, so *literature* is the direct object. The direct object is a very common complement and one you must learn to identify readily.

Indirect Objects

Indirect objects are the least important of the four complements. Although we think you should recognize them, we want you to realize that they are not as important as direct objects.

An **indirect object** tells *to whom* or *for whom* something is done. In order to have an indirect object within a sentence, however, you must first have a direct object. As a result, a problem that students frequently experience is confusing the indirect object with the direct object.

Remember the following points to avoid this mix-up:

1. The indirect object comes *before* the direct object.

2. To test for an indirect object, you can place either *to, for,* or *of* before it and it will make sense. None of these words will ever be stated in the sentence; they will always be understood.

3. You must locate a direct object in order for an indirect object to be possible.

In each of the following sentences, the indirect object is italicized. Note how each one fulfills the three criteria.

Miguel gave *Maria* a kiss.

I'll bring *you* the notes I took in class.

They bought their *baby* her first shoes.

Mindy threw *Tom* the basketball.

They awarded *Mr. Patel* the honor.

TRY-IT
EXERCISE

Underline the direct object in each of the following sentences. Put parentheses around each prepositional phrase. If either sentence has an indirect object, put brackets around it.

1. My teacher gave the test to me.
2. My teacher gave me the test.
3. Marika handed the baby to Raisa.
4. Raisa handed Marika the baby.
5. Tom bought flowers for Jan.
6. Tom bought Jan flowers.

7. Keisha sent some love letters to Jamal.
8. Keisha sent Jamal some love letters.

In the first sentence you may enclose in parentheses *to me* because it is a prepositional phrase. That leaves *gave* as the action verb, *teacher* as the subject, and *test* as the direct object. There is no word in front of the direct object, so there is no indirect object.

In the second sentence, however, there is no prepositional phrase to enclose. The verb and subject are the same as in the first sentence. Is *me* or *test* the direct object? What did the teacher actually hand over? The answer is *test,* which is the direct object. Note that there is a word before the direct object—one of the requirements for an indirect object. Can you insert *to, for,* or *of* before the word *me* and have it make sense? The word *to* could be inserted, and it is not overtly stated. Therefore, *me* is the indirect object.

In sentence three, *handed* is the action verb, *Marika* is the subject, and *baby* is the direct object. There is no indirect object. In sentence four, *handed* is the action verb, *Raisa* is the subject, *baby* is the direct object, and *Marika* is the indirect object. In sentence five, *bought* is the action verb, *Tom* is the subject, and *flowers* is the direct object. There is no indirect object. In sentence six, *bought* is an action verb, *Tom* is the subject, *flowers* is the direct object, and *Jan* is the indirect object. In sentence seven, *sent* is the action verb, *Keisha* is the subject, *letters* is the direct object. There is no indirect object. In sentence eight, *sent* is the action verb, *Keisha* is the subject, *letters* is the direct object, and *Jamal* is the indirect object.

| PRACTICE | IDENTIFYING DIRECT OBJECTS |
| EXERCISE 1-13 | AND INDIRECT OBJECTS |

Underline each direct object in the sentences below. If the sentence has both a direct object and an indirect object, put brackets around the indirect object. If a sentence has no direct object, write NONE.

EXAMPLE: My brothers give their [parents] sports <u>equipment</u> on special occasions.

1. I ride a stationary bicycle for exercise.

2. My dad plays golf for his exercise.

3. Mom will buy Dad golf clubs for his birthday.

4. Mom thinks positive thoughts for her exercise!

5. Nevertheless, she agrees with Dad about the importance of health.

6. They define *health* differently.

7. My brother and I gain fitness from sports.

8. I give my brother praise for his self-discipline and stamina.

9. He blushes at my comments.

10. However, he enjoys the praise.

NAME _____ DATE _____

INSTRUCTOR _____ CLASS TIME _____

PRACTICE	# USING DIRECT OBJECTS AND
EXERCISE 1-14	INDIRECT OBJECTS

Using the action verb listed, write a complete sentence with a direct object. Put parentheses around each direct object.

EXAMPLE: hit *Samantha hit (the ball) out of the park.*

1. saw _____

2. found _____

3. requested _____

4. followed _____

5. bet _____

6. learned _____

Using the action verb listed, write a complete sentence with a direct object and an indirect object. Put parentheses around the direct object and brackets around the indirect object.

7. baked _____

8. sent _____

9. asked _____

10. buy _____

NAME _____ DATE _____

INSTRUCTOR _____ CLASS TIME _____

© NTC/CONTEMPORARY PUBLISHING COMPANY

Predicate Nominatives

Complements on the right side of the verb that point back to the subject on the left side of the verb and rename it are called **predicate nominatives**. The word *nominative* is sometimes called *noun* because that is what you need in order to rename the subject. Note that the noun on the right side of the verb is linked by a linking verb to the subject on the left. Hence, you *must* have a linking verb present to have a predicate nominative.

Jean is a delightful, understanding mother.

Richard was a successful fisherman for years.

Mark has been a skillful construction worker.

Connie was a student at Purdue University.

The *be* verb (*is*) in the first sentence is a linking verb, the subject is *Jean,* and the word *mother* on the right of the linking verb points back and renames the subject. Therefore, the word *mother* is a predicate nominative. The *be* verb (*was*) in the second sentence is a linking verb, the subject is *Richard,* and the word *fisherman* on the right of the linking verb points back and renames the subject. Therefore, the word *fisherman* is a predicate nominative. The *be* verb (*been*) in the third sentence is a linking verb, the subject is *Mark,* and the word *worker* on the right of the linking verb points back and renames the subject. Therefore, the word *worker* is a predicate nominative. The *be* verb (*was*) in the fourth sentence is a linking verb, the subject is *Connie,* and the word *student* on the right of the linking verb points back and renames the subject. Therefore, the word *student* is a predicate nominative.

TRY-IT
EXERCISE

Underline the predicate nominative in each of the following sentences.

1. My cousin is a baseball player for the Chicago Cubs.
2. Her mother has been an attorney for ten years.
3. Kathy will always be an excellent teacher.
4. Dennis is Kathy's husband.
5. My nephews are both fathers.
6. My niece is a college student and a dental assistant.

The *be* verb (*is*) in the first sentence is a linking verb, the subject is *cousin,* and the word on the right of the linking verb (*player*) does point back and rename the subject, so *player* is a predicate nominative. The second sentence contains a form of the linking verb *be; has* is a helping verb for *been*. The subject is *mother,* and the predicate nominative is *attorney,* which points back and renames the subject. The third sentence contains the linking verb *be* and the helping verb *will.* The subject is *Kathy,* and the predicate nominative is *teacher.* The fourth sentence contains the linking verb *is.* The subject is *Dennis,* and the predicate nominative is *husband.* The fifth sentence contains the linking verb *are.* The subject is *nephews,* and the predicative nominative is *fathers.* The sixth sentence contains the linking verb *is.* The subject is *niece,* and the predicate nominatives are *student* and *assistant.*

Predicate Adjectives

The last type of complement we are going to discuss is similar to the predicate nominative. Note that these last two terms contain the word *predicate.* Like a predicate nominative, a predicate adjective must have a linking verb. The word on the right of the verb will again point back to the subject. The one characteristic setting it apart from a predicate nominative is that a predicate adjective *describes* the subject; it does not *rename* it. Thus, the word on the right side of the verb is not going to be a noun. Instead, it will be an adjective—a word that describes a noun or pronoun.

That Greek pastry tastes delicious.

The physics test seemed difficult.

The boys grew tired near the end of the race.

Those men in the first row are very smart.

The linking verb in the first sentence is *tastes,* the subject is *pastry,* and the predicate adjective is *delicious.* The linking verb in the second sentence is *seemed,* the subject is *test,* and the predicate adjective is *difficult.* The linking verb in the third sentence is *grew,* the subject is *boys,* and the predicate adjective is *tired.* The linking verb in the fourth sentence is *are,* the subject is *men,* and the predicate adjective is *smart.* Often, you can put the predicate adjective in front of the subject and it will make sense. For example, you could say *delicious pastry, difficult test, tired boys,* or *smart men.*

TRY-IT

EXERCISE

Underline the predicate adjective in each of the following sentences.

1. The students appear sleepy.
2. Leroy feels exhausted.
3. Hae seems very sensitive.
4. Rachel will always be self-confident.
5. Jamal was extremely active.
6. Tiffany is very delightful.

The linking verb in the first sentence is *appear,* the subject is *students,* and the predicate adjective is *sleepy.* The second sentence contains the linking verb *feels,* the subject *Leroy,* and the predicate adjective *exhausted.* The third sentence contains the linking verb *seems,* the subject *Hae,* and the predicate adjective *sensitive.* The fourth sentence contains the linking verb *be,* the helping verb *will,* the subject *Rachel,* and the predicate adjective *self-confident.* The fifth sentence contains the linking verb *was,* the subject *Jamal,* the predicate adjective *active.* The sixth sentence contains the linking verb *is,* the subject *Tiffany,* and the predicate adjective *delightful.* Frequently, you can check the predicate adjective by putting it in front of the subject to test its meaning. In these sentences, *sleepy students, exhausted Leroy, sensitive Hae, self-confident Rachel, active Jamal,* and *delightful Tiffany* repeat the meaning intended.

| PRACTICE |
| EXERCISE 1-15 |

IDENTIFYING PREDICATE ADJECTIVES AND PREDICATE NOMINATIVES

To check your understanding of the relationship between linking verbs, predicate adjectives, and predicate nominatives, underline the predicate adjective (PA) or predicate nominative (PN) of these sentences you did previously in Practice Exercise 1-3 on page 13. Identify each of the following as PA or PN.

EXAMPLE: Natasha is a good <u>cook</u>.   PN

_____ 1. Natasha was a winner of many awards at the state fair.

_____ 2. Her cakes were the best at the fair.

_____ 3. That cake with the blue ribbon is chocolate.

_____ 4. Natasha is not hungry anymore.

_____ 5. This is the winning recipe.

_____ 6. She looks very tired.

_____ 7. Her mother seems proud of her awards and ribbons.

_____ 8. Even her dad feels excited.

_____ 9. The cakes in the contest taste great.

_____ 10. The entire family appears pleased by her success.

NAME _____ DATE _____

INSTRUCTOR _____ CLASS TIME _____

PRACTICE	# USING LINKING VERBS, PREDICATE ADJECTIVES, AND PREDICATE NOMINATIVES
EXERCISE 1-16	

For each of the following, create a sentence using the verb as a linking verb followed by either a predicate nominative or a predicate adjective. Note that the first nine verbs derive from FAST SLuGGS, our memory device for linking verbs.

EXAMPLE: become *Hannah's twin sisters become excited at the surprise party.*

1. feel _____

2. appear _____

3. sound _____

4. taste _____

5. smell _____

6. look _____

7. get _____

8. grow _____

9. seem _____

10. was _____

© NTC/CONTEMPORARY PUBLISHING COMPANY

NAME _____ DATE _____

INSTRUCTOR _____ CLASS TIME _____

PRACTICE	# VERBS AND SUBJECTS
EXERCISE 1-17	

Circle the verb(s) and label each one by type (A = action, L = linking, H = helping). Then underline the subject for each sentence.

EXAMPLE: The <u>boy</u> (must)ᴴ (have)ᴴ (been)ᴸ unhappy with the situation.

1. The classroom exercises seemed difficult.

2. Problems with English are spotted more easily through the use of exercises.

3. Spending very little time on assignments, a few of the students barely pass the class.

4. Students studying many hours find success through their hard work.

5. Ask the teacher questions about any unclear assignments.

6. Teachers will usually help you in any way possible.

7. Do you feel hesitant during classroom discussion?

8. In this case, your shyness may create a problem.

9. Of all the available teachers, I must have luckily chosen a good one.

10. Some teachers will give students positive feedback.

NAME _____ DATE _____

INSTRUCTOR _____ CLASS TIME _____

PRACTICE
EXERCISE 1-18

COMPLEMENTS

Using these sentences from the previous exercise, underline each complement and indicate whether it is used as a direct object (DO), an indirect object (IO), a predicate nominative (PN), or a predicate adjective (PA). If there is no complement, write NONE.

EXAMPLE: The boy must have been <u>unhappy</u> with the situation.   PA

_____ 1. The classroom exercises seemed difficult.

_____ 2. English is learned through the use of exercises.

_____ 3. A few of the students barely pass the class.

_____ 4. Several find success through their hard work.

_____ 5. Ask the teacher questions about any unclear assignments.

_____ 6. Teachers will usually help you in any way possible.

_____ 7. Do you feel hesitant during classroom discussions?

_____ 8. In this case, your shyness will be a problem.

_____ 9. Of all the available teachers, I must have chosen a good one.

_____ 10. Some teachers will give students positive feedback.

NAME _____ DATE _____

INSTRUCTOR _____ CLASS TIME _____

COMPOUNDS

The final area we need to cover in this chapter involves the concept of **compound subjects, verbs,** or **complements** in a sentence. You may have learned in chemistry or physics that mixing two or more elements can result in a compound. The principle is similar in English. Connecting two or more words with a joining word (called a *conjunction*) results in a compound unit. There are various connectives we can use, but for now let's keep it simple and look at the most common conjunction—*and*.

Look at the sentences below. The compound element is the italicized words, the label in parentheses at the end of the sentence is how the compound is used in the sentence, and the conjunction *and* falls in between.

1. The energetic boy *bounced* the ball against the house and *caught* it. (compound verb)

2. The hesitant *father* and his eager *daughter* prepared for a camping trip in the forest. (compound subject)

3. There are Coke *cans* and candy *wrappers* all over campus. (compound subject)

4. *Studying* and *relaxing* need to be balanced in order to gain the most from each. (compound subject)

5. My German shepherd goes *to* and *from* school every day. (compound preposition)

6. You probably go home after *work* and *school.* (compound object of the preposition)

7. The thief knocked the elderly *man* and *woman* off their feet. (compound direct object)

8. The college offered the *valedictorian* and *salutatorian* four-year scholarships. (compound indirect object)

9. Rosie O'Donnell is an *actor* and a *singer.* (compound predicate nominative)

10. You are now *knowledgeable* and *comfortable* about learning the language. (compound predicate adjectives)

As you can see, any part of a sentence can become a compound.

© NTC/CONTEMPORARY PUBLISHING COMPANY

PRACTICE EXERCISE 1-19 — IDENTIFYING COMPOUND ELEMENTS

Underline any compound elements in the following sentences. Then identify *which element* is compound: verb (V), subject (S), direct object (DO), indirect object (IO), predicate nominative (PN), predicate adjective (PA), preposition (P), or object of preposition (OP).

EXAMPLE: The <u>coaches</u> and their <u>players</u> have a good relationship.   S

_____ 1. In order to finish his chores, Spencer mowed the lawn before and after his ballgame.

_____ 2. Fulfilling obligations could not be accomplished without thinking and planning in advance.

_____ 3. The coach chose Dwayne for the starting lineup and then took him out.

_____ 4. The parents asked the coach and his assistant some questions about the change.

_____ 5. They were calm and collected in their response.

_____ 6. They are and always have been fair men.

_____ 7. Ranting and raving would only have hampered the situation.

_____ 8. The parents thanked the coach and his assistant for their positive behavior.

_____ 9. The results of the game were a win and a spot in the semifinals.

_____ 10. The players, the coaches, and the parents celebrated after the game.

NAME _____   DATE _____

INSTRUCTOR _____   CLASS TIME _____

PRACTICE
EXERCISE 1-20
USING COMPOUND ELEMENTS

Create a single sentence from each pair given, making the words that differ into a compound element. Then, beside your new sentence, identify the compound as verb (V), subject (S), direct object (DO), indirect object (IO), predicate nominative (PN), predicate adjective (PA), preposition (P), or object of preposition (OP).

EXAMPLE: I like pie. I like cake. _*I like pie and cake. (DO)*_

1. The boys laughed at the jokes. The girls laughed at the jokes.

    _____

2. Angela announced her engagement. Angela announced her wedding

    date. _____

3. Miguel gave Rachel a gift. Miguel gave Nathan a gift.

    _____

4. Choon is a professor. Choon is an author.

    _____

5. Jill feels secure. Jill feels content. _____

6. Leon irons his sheets. Leon patches his sheets.

    _____

7. The horse jumped over the fence. The horse jumped over the bushes.

    _____

8. Joe goes above the call of duty. Joe goes beyond the call of duty.

    _____

9. The milk tastes sour. The milk smells sour.

    _____

10. Drinking can be dangerous. Driving can be dangerous.

    _____

NAME _____ DATE _____

INSTRUCTOR _____ CLASS TIME _____

© NTC/CONTEMPORARY PUBLISHING COMPANY

© NTC/CONTEMPORARY PUBLISHING COMPANY

REVIEW	**PREPOSITIONAL PHRASES,**
EXERCISE 1-1	**VERBS, AND SUBJECTS**

DIRECTIONS: Put parentheses around each prepositional phrase. Next, in the left-hand blank under the sentence, write the verb or verb phrase. Finally, in the right-hand blank write the simple subject.

1. Students study English in the first-period class.

   _____   _____

2. Students in this college should review English skills each night.

   _____   _____

3. Many of the students are often reviewing skills in English.

   _____   _____

4. I am a good student in English class.

   _____   _____

5. We have been studying the types of verbs in common English sentences.

   _____   _____

6. Very few students would remember these verbs without a review.

   _____   _____

7. The girl in the front row of our class has known the rules for years.

   _____   _____

8. Several of these skills could have been learned in middle school.

   _____   _____

9. Improving my skills in English, I study each night.

   _____   _____

10. From my point of view, our teacher seems patient during class.

   _____   _____

NAME _____ DATE _____

INSTRUCTOR _____ CLASS TIME _____

11.   Did you work the exercises on verbs in our assignment?

    _____   _____

12.   I must not have finished the assignments in our workbook until
    midnight last night.

    _____   _____

13.   Jim did not start on the exercises until late at night.

    _____   _____

14.   Study earlier on the next assignment.

    _____   _____

15.   Neither of those classes in math has been easy.

    _____   _____

16.   Tomorrow's assignment in history sounds difficult.

    _____   _____

17.   The class across the hall from us might be one in psychology.

    _____   _____

18.   Many of the classes on my schedule for next quarter look interesting.

    _____   _____

19.   Many students in this class appear knowledgeable about basic English.

    _____   _____

20.   In the room above us, the teacher has been talking loudly for the entire
    hour.

    _____   _____

REVIEW EXERCISE 1-2 IDENTIFYING VERBS, SUBJECTS, AND COMPLEMENTS

DIRECTIONS: In the left-hand blank under the sentence, write the verb or verb phrase. Next, in the middle blank, write the subject(s). Finally, in the right-hand blank, write the complement(s) and identify each as direct object (DO), indirect (IO), predicate nominative (PN), or predicate adjective (PA). If a sentence has no complement, write NONE.

1. *TV Guide* lists the latest shows.

    _____ _____ _____

2. The talk shows during the day and the game shows in the early evening are very popular.

    _____ _____ _____

3. Cable television has hurt the ratings of the three major networks.

    _____ _____ _____

4. This new addition has given some unwanted competition to the networks.

    _____ _____ _____

5. Many people are renting movies for their videocassette recorders.

    _____ _____ _____

6. During the week some good shows are shown on PBS.

    _____ _____ _____

7. Some classic movies on PBS grow better with time.

    _____ _____ _____

8. Before television, people must have found other methods of entertainment.

    _____ _____ _____

NAME _____ DATE _____

INSTRUCTOR _____ CLASS TIME _____

9. Books, movies, and sports might have been an important part of people's lives before television.

_____ _____ _____

10. Do you watch television every night of the week?

_____ _____ _____

Continue following the above directions, but remember that verbals and verbal phrases can serve as subjects.

11. Being a single parent takes time and energy.

_____ _____ _____

12. Balancing classes and work, Darlene feels overwhelmed.

_____ _____ _____

13. Paying the bills seems very difficult.

_____ _____ _____

14. Darlene and her baby have been living by themselves.

_____ _____ _____

15. Going to school during the day, she works and studies at night.

_____ _____ _____

16. To pay her tuition, she needs a good job.

_____ _____ _____

17. She will be studying her English lessons at night.

_____ _____ _____

18. Lacking time and energy, Darlene grows tired and impatient.

_____ _____ _____

19. Parenting causes frustration and joy.

_____ _____ _____

20. To be a good mother is Darlene's goal.

_____ _____ _____

© NTC/CONTEMPORARY PUBLISHING COMPANY

© NTC/CONTEMPORARY PUBLISHING COMPANY

REVIEW	**VERBS, SUBJECTS,**
EXERCISE 1-3	**COMPLEMENTS, AND**
	COMPOUNDS

DIRECTIONS: In the left-hand blank under the sentence, write the verb or verb phrase. Next, in the middle blank, write the subject(s). Finally, in the right-hand blank, write the complement(s) and identify each as direct object (DO), indirect (IO), predicate nominative (PN), or predicate adjective (PA). If a sentence has no complement, write NONE.

1.   Many of the students at our college work each night.

   _____   _____   _____

2.   The students and teachers usually review homework before class.

   _____   _____   _____

3.   Before each test, both of the classes get a review of grammar.

   _____   _____   _____

4.   Attending the 11:00 class, the teacher and students get very hungry.

   _____   _____   _____

5.   French is my best class.

   _____   _____   _____

6.   Learning can bring pleasure to people of all ages.

   _____   _____   _____

7.   The chapters in English grow harder and longer each week.

   _____   _____   _____

8.   During this year of school, I am a student and a waitress.

   _____   _____   _____

9.   Do you know the tuition and book fees of the best school in this state?

   _____   _____   _____

NAME _____   DATE _____

INSTRUCTOR _____   CLASS TIME _____

10. Here are books with information about the tuition and a chart explaining the book fees at the school.

    _____ _____ _____

11. Thousands of students feel exhausted after their first quarter in college.

    _____ _____ _____

12. Sleepy eyes and tired bodies are characteristics of the typical college student.

    _____ _____ _____

13. Our night class met at 6:20 and adjourned at 9 P.M.

    _____ _____ _____

14. Bruce and my sister will soon be the best students in their class.

    _____ _____ _____

15. Several of our professional people attended and graduated from college.

    _____ _____ _____

16. Earning a college degree, I will need self-discipline and determination.

    _____ _____ _____

17. The teacher asked Josh and me some unexpected questions during class.

    _____ _____ _____

18. That new boy in the back row looks tall and thin.

    _____ _____ _____

19. He may have been a basketball player in high school.

    _____ _____ _____

20. On the way to class, Melinda lost her notes and textbook.

    _____ _____ _____

CHAPTER QUIZ 1-1 VERBS, SUBJECTS, COMPLEMENTS, AND COMPOUNDS

DIRECTIONS: In the left-hand blank under the sentence, write the verb or verb phrase. Next, in the middle blank, write the subject(s). Finally, in the right-hand blank, write the complement(s) and identify each as direct object (DO), indirect object (IO), predicate nominative (PN), or predicate adjective (PA).

1. Studying each night, Mike is now making much better grades.

   _____ _____ _____

2. Studying and thinking take time and effort.

   _____ _____ _____

3. Both of the men are intelligent and charming.

   _____ _____ _____

4. Neither of those students will fail this course.

   _____ _____ _____

5. Many of the teachers at our school have finished four years of graduate work.

   _____ _____ _____

6. There are some good students and some poor teachers in every school.

   _____ _____ _____

7. With the arrival of television, people are reading fewer books.

   _____ _____ _____

8. Reading more books, teens can widen their horizons.

   _____ _____ _____

NAME _____ DATE _____

INSTRUCTOR _____ CLASS TIME _____

9. One of the national surveys has recently shown a trend of less reading by teens.

   _____ _____ _____

10. Do you read many books?

   _____ _____ _____

11. Reading brings a person enjoyment and knowledge.

   _____ _____ _____

12. The men and women sitting in the library read their books and take notes.

   _____ _____ _____

13. Hundreds of people study in our library each evening.

   _____ _____ _____

14. On Saturday afternoon, several sports fans were cheering the team at the football game.

   _____ _____ _____

15. Several of the cheering fans marched down Main Street before the game.

   _____ _____ _____

16. After the game, the coach gave the team praise for a good job.

   _____ _____ _____

17. The good playing of the team pleased the crowd.

   _____ _____ _____

18. The team practiced in the afternoons and played during the weekends.

   _____ _____ _____

19. Mail these tickets to my family.

   _____ _____ _____

20. Our coach is the best friend of many of his players.

   _____ _____ _____

<table>
<tr><td>CHAPTER</td><td rowspan="2"># VERBS, SUBJECTS,
COMPLEMENTS, AND
COMPOUNDS</td></tr>
<tr><td>QUIZ 1-2</td></tr>
</table>

CHAPTER QUIZ 1-2

VERBS, SUBJECTS, COMPLEMENTS, AND COMPOUNDS

DIRECTIONS: In the left-hand blank under the sentence, write the verb or verb phrase. Next, in the middle blank, write the subject(s). Finally, in the right-hand blank, write the complement(s) and identify each as direct object (DO), indirect object (IO), predicate nominative (PN), or predicate adjective (PA).

1. The music is enjoyable and sounds marvelous.

   _____   _____   _____

2. Buy us three of the most popular songs on the charts.

   _____   _____   _____

3. The trumpets and drums playing in the background are terrific.

   _____   _____   _____

4. With great care I chose the best tape and paid the waiting clerk.

   _____   _____   _____

5. Listening to the music, I found peace and contentment.

   _____   _____   _____

6. That girl standing by the stereo is Melissa.

   _____   _____   _____

7. Wanting relaxation and rest, I will be playing this song many times.

   _____   _____   _____

8. After the concert, we were tired and happy.

   _____   _____   _____

NAME _____ DATE _____

INSTRUCTOR _____ CLASS TIME _____

9. Children, teens, and adults enjoy music of high quality.

_____ _____ _____

10. Christopher has been recording many hit songs this year.

_____ _____ _____

11. Recording is his favorite hobby.

_____ _____ _____

12. Chris will frequently write a new song.

_____ _____ _____

13. Several of his friends write and work closely with him and his company.

_____ _____ _____

14. There were two hits and two failures last year.

_____ _____ _____

15. From this side of the room, the sound seems distorted.

_____ _____ _____

16. Move the speaker to the left and listen to the bass.

_____ _____ _____

17. Moving the speaker to the left, I can hear the stereo more clearly.

_____ _____ _____

18. Standing over there, I can distinctly hear the bass and the treble.

_____ _____ _____

19. Following the rules of his contract, Chris will be recording another song next month.

_____ _____ _____

20. He has been following his natural musical ability and his teacher's suggestions.

_____ _____ _____

© NTC/CONTEMPORARY PUBLISHING COMPANY

CHAPTER 2

SENTENCE ERRORS

© NTC/CONTEMPORARY PUBLISHING COMPANY

Effectiveness in composition begins with clearly written sentences. A sentence, as you have just learned, has a main verb and a subject, and communicates a completed thought. This definition seems simple enough, yet many students have trouble applying it in their own writing. If you are one of these students, this chapter will be helpful.

In order to write well, you'll want to avoid making sentence errors. The best strategy for eliminating these errors from your writing is to build a thorough understanding of independent and dependent clauses.

INDEPENDENT CLAUSES

An **independent clause** has the same three qualities as a sentence: a main verb, a subject, and a completed thought. This is often called the *main clause* of the sentence. If an independent (main) clause stands alone between a capital letter and some end punctuation mark (period, question mark, or exclamation point), it is called a sentence. If, however, it is written as *part* of a sentence, it is called a clause.

Consider the following sentences:

College life is exciting and fun.

I spend most of my free time in the library.

College life is exciting and fun, but I spend most of my free time in the library.

The first and second sentences are both independent clauses and sentences. The third sentence, however, is one sentence containing two independent clauses: on both sides of the word *but* are a main verb, a subject, and a completed thought.

Every sentence you write will have at least one independent clause. This all-important main clause will serve as the skeleton for any sentence variation you create. Further, because every punctuation rule you learn will be based on identifying independent clauses in a sentence, the material in the first two chapters of this book is vitally important. In short, if you can't identify main verbs and subjects, you can't find independent clauses; if you can't find independent clauses, you'll have trouble punctuating sentences correctly.

DEPENDENT CLAUSES

Both independent and dependent clauses have a main verb and a subject. A **dependent clause**, however, is a group of words that *does not* express a completed thought and *cannot* stand alone. Just as a dependent child must lean on an independent adult, a dependent clause must lean on an independent clause and be attached to it. Another term for a dependent clause is *subordinate,* meaning to put something in a position of less importance. Because a dependent clause is subordinate to an independent clause, it gets its meaning from the independent clause. Therefore, it is always a *part* of a sentence—never a sentence by itself. Consider the following sentences:

As cars quickly fill the parking lot beside the school.

Students walk into the building and talk eagerly with each other.

Classes will start exactly on time.

If students and teachers rapidly park their cars and walk into the building.

The first and fourth groups of words are neither independent clauses nor sentences. Rather, each is a dependent clause. Each gets its meaning from being attached to the independent clause below or above it. Attaching the dependent clause in the first group of words to the independent clause below it, we create an acceptable sentence: *As cars quickly fill the parking lot beside the school, students walk into the building and talk eagerly with each other.* Attaching the dependent clause in the fourth group of words to the independent clause above it, we create another acceptable sentence: *Classes will start exactly on time if students and teachers rapidly park their cars and walk into the building.*

© NTC/CONTEMPORARY PUBLISHING COMPANY

TRY-IT
EXERCISE

Identify whether these clauses are independent (IC) or dependent (DC).

_____ 1. Many people want a college degree.
_____ 2. Few students finish the course work.
_____ 3. Although many people want a college degree.

Although the clause in the third item has a main verb and a subject, it does not express a completed thought. It is, therefore, a dependent clause. In contrast, sentences one and two, as indepenent clauses, express a completed thought and can stand alone.

Two independent clauses can be joined to create a well-written sentence. For example, the independent clauses in sentences one and two could be joined as follows:

Many people want a college degree, but few students finish the course work.

Also, a dependent clause can be joined to an independent clause to create a well-written sentence. For example, attaching the dependent clause (in italics) in item three above to one of the independent clauses creates an acceptable sentence:

Although many people want a college degree, few students finish the course work.

Subordinate Conjunctions

Dependent clauses can begin with either relative pronouns or subordinate conjunctions, but at this point we will concentrate only on subordinate conjunctions. The term *subordinate conjunction* is appropriate. If you are subordinate to your boss, you need your boss for instructions and guidance. You are dependent on him or her for your job and your salary. A **subordinate conjunction** introduces a clause that is dependent on an independent clause for its meaning.

Look at the following sentences:

When I am crossing a busy street, I am careful.

As I cross a busy street at 5:00, I use caution.

The group of words before the comma in each sentence above is a dependent clause. These words cannot stand alone and make sense. Therefore, the dependent clauses have meaning only when attached to independent clauses.

Study the subordinate conjunctions listed in Table 2.1. Use this table to help you learn to recognize subordinate conjunctions.

TRY-IT
EXERCISE

Underline the dependent clause in each of the following sentences and circle the subordinate conjunction that causes the clause to be dependent.

1. After we left the football game on Saturday, Tony and I went to Maria's house.
2. Tony rented a video before we drove to her house.
3. Although Tony had already seen the movie, he wanted Maria and Raoul to see it.
4. As Raoul opened the front door, he grabbed the video from Tony's hand.
5. Raoul and Tony started the movie while Maria and I served the pizza.

The dependent clause in each sentence begins with a subordinate conjunction. In the first sentence the subordi-

TABLE 2.1 *Common Subordinate Conjunctions*	
after	since
although	though
as	unless
because	until
before	when
if	where
once	while

nate conjunction is *after*. In the second sentence it is *before*. In the third sentence it is *although*. In the fourth sentence it is *as* and in the fifth it is *while*.

Many subordinate conjunctions also serve as prepositions. For example, in the first sentence the word *after* is a subordinate conjunction because it is followed by a group of words that has a verb and a subject. If, however, it had been followed by a noun or a pronoun, it would serve as a preposition. If the sentence read "After the football game, Tony and I went to Maria's house," *after* would be a preposition, and "after the football game" would become a prepositional phrase.

PRACTICE
EXERCISE 2-1

DEPENDENT CLAUSES BEGINNING WITH A SUBORDINATE CONJUNCTION

Underline the dependent clause in each of the following sentences.

EXAMPLE: <u>After they have watched TV for many years,</u> teenagers may see life from a distorted view.

1. Because TV often gives a false image of life, many viewers become confused.

2. Before TV told viewers how to look, think, and act, people followed their own consciences.

3. If TV stars become role models, our next generation will have some twisted values.

4. Once a person sees six killings a night, watching death becomes commonplace and less horrifying.

5. The brutality of taking another's life has been diminished since death can be watched on TV over 24 times a week.

6. Although TV violence distorts viewers' values, slim TV actresses also cause problems for the viewing public.

7. While girls watch the lean, beautiful women on TV, their own bodies seem unattractive in comparison.

8. Some women get an unrealistic view of themselves when they mistake TV's reflection of life for reality.

9. TV images cause some women to diet until they are ill from anorexia.

10. Unless viewers maintain open minds, TV can distort their view of reality.

NAME _____ DATE _____

INSTRUCTOR _____ CLASS TIME _____

| PRACTICE EXERCISE 2-2 | # USING DEPENDENT CLAUSES BEGINNING WITH A SUBORDINATE CONJUNCTION |

The following independent clauses contain a subordinate conjunction followed by a blank. Use the subordinate conjunction shown to create a dependent clause that will be subordinate to the independent clause.

EXAMPLE: Students were in the mood for celebration as *the last week of classes approached*.

1. After _____, everybody is going to meet at a pizza parlor.

2. Although _____, Mary cannot go.

3. She has to go home because _____.

4. Since _____, she decided to have a party at her place the next month.

5. Unless _____, all the guests said that they were free and would be there.

6. She sent invitations and enclosed directions telling where _____.

7. Until _____, Mary will not be able to plan the details.

8. Mary will know how much to buy when _____.

9. While _____, she will have someone volunteer to grill the hot dogs.

10. If _____, they would have to stay inside.

NAME _____   DATE _____

INSTRUCTOR _____   CLASS TIME _____

Your understanding of dependent and independent clauses will serve as the foundation for the next step in your learning: elimination of sentence errors.

The three most common sentence errors are comma splices, fused sentences, and sentence fragments. A comma splice occurs when you join two independent clauses with a comma and no conjunction. A fused sentence comes from joining two independent clauses without putting any punctuation mark between them. Finally, when a part of a sentence is handled as if it were a complete sentence, a sentence fragment is the result.

COMMA SPLICES AND FUSED SENTENCES

Comma splices and **fused sentences** (also known as *run-on sentences*) are errors that occur when you fail to put a *stop sign* between two independent clauses. All punctuation marks help the reader by telling him or her to stop or to slow down. The strongest stop sign in the English language is a period, and the next strongest is a semicolon. There are various other ways to tell the reader to stop, and we will consider some of these in the next chapter. Right now, however, our emphasis is on detecting common sentence errors. Correction will come later.

You will be able to detect these sentence errors if you understand the meaning of the words *splice* and *fused*. *Splice* means to join or unite ends by weaving them together. *Fuse* means to join together by melting. By placing only a comma between two independent clauses (a comma splice), you are joining them in such a way that the reader slows down, but does not stop. By putting no punctuation mark between two independent clauses (a fused sentence), you are confusing the readers by "melting" the clauses into one glob. In doing so, you are urging your reader to move forward rather than to stop or slow down.

Look at these sentences:

Some students never study.

Others study all the time.

Some students never study others study all the time.

Some students never study, others study all the time.

It is easy to recognize that when the first and second sentences are joined into the third, a fused sentence is created and the meaning gets lost. Obviously, in the third sentence a stop sign is needed after the word *study*. In the fourth sentence, a comma splice error is created. The comma does not say stop; it says slow down. Since you want the reader to stop, you need something stronger than a comma between these two independent clauses.

This will be your first chance to see the relationship between independent clauses, dependent clauses, verbal phrases, prepositional phrases, and punc-

© NTC/CONTEMPORARY PUBLISHING COMPANY

tuation marks. As you complete the exercise that follows, remember that if there is a phrase or a dependent clause before an independent clause, you do *not* have a comma splice.

TRY-IT

EXERCISE

Identify each of the following as comma splice (CS), fused sentence (FS), or correct (C).

_____ 1. Teaching is not easy. Hours of work go into each lesson.

_____ 2. Teaching is not easy hours of work go into each lesson.

_____ 3. Teaching is not easy, hours of work go into each lesson.

_____ 4. Although teaching seems easy, hours of work go into each lesson.

_____ 5. Working hours on each lesson, a teacher prepares for class.

_____ 6. During the hours after supper, a teacher reviews the next day's lessons.

The first example consists of two sentences, so it is correct. The stop sign after each is a period, which is needed. But in the second and third sentences, the needed end punctuation is not provided, thus creating major errors. The two sentences that are correct individually in the first example are fused in the second example and spliced in the third. The fourth, fifth, and sixth examples, however, are not comma splices because two independent clauses have not been spliced together. In the fourth example, there is a dependent clause before the comma and an independent clause after. In the fifth example, there is a verbal phrase before the comma and an independent clause after. In the sixth example, there are prepositional phrases before the comma and an independent clause after.

© NTC/CONTEMPORARY PUBLISHING COMPANY

To summarize, the following list indicates the types of clauses found in the previous Try-It exercise and the punctuation in each of these six sentences.

1. Independent Clause. Independent Clause.
2. Independent Clause Independent Clause. (fused sentence)
3. Independent Clause, Independent Clause. (comma splice)
4. Dependent Clause, Independent Clause.
5. Verbal Phrase, Independent Clause.
6. Prepositional Phrase, Independent Clause.

Note that sentences one, four, five, and six are correct. Only the second and third sentences have sentence structure errors.

PRACTICE	IDENTIFICATION OF FUSED
EXERCISE 2-3	SENTENCES AND COMMA
	SPLICES

If any of the sentences contain a comma splice or a fused sentence, underline where the error occurs. Identify each underlined error as a CS (comma splice), FS (fused sentence), or identify the sentence as C (correct) in the blank provided.

EXAMPLE: I saw his <u>light, it</u> was shining in the east window.   CS

_____ 1.   Observe those around you, an awareness of others' actions will teach you a great deal.

_____ 2.   Students should not get nervous before a test extreme nervousness may lower their grades.

_____ 3.   If the door to the classroom is locked, go back to the car and wait for me.

_____ 4.   Bob and I went to class early, we wanted to review our notes before the test.

_____ 5.   The exams were not difficult, I could pass them with ease.

_____ 6.   When a student reads the material each night, tests are no threat.

_____ 7.   Working on lessons each night, a student feels confident at test time.

_____ 8.   It's almost spring, I can tell by the change in the weather.

_____ 9.   Although the weather feels like spring, it is still winter.

_____ 10.   Spring is here I can tell by the weather.

NAME _____   DATE _____

INSTRUCTOR _____   CLASS TIME _____

© NTC/CONTEMPORARY PUBLISHING COMPANY

PRACTICE	IDENTIFICATION OF FUSED
EXERCISE 2-4	SENTENCES AND COMMA
	SPLICES

IDENTIFICATION OF FUSED SENTENCES AND COMMA SPLICES

PRACTICE EXERCISE 2-4

In the following sentences, if there is a comma splice, underline the comma where the error occurs. If there is a fused sentence, underline the point where the sentence is fused.

EXAMPLE: While standing in line to register for classes, Marcia fainted, the boy behind her called the ambulance.

1. Before going to the grocery, you should make a list if you make a habit of planning first, you won't buy unneeded items.

2. Looking at similar products, a shopper will notice that they are packaged very much alike, it is easy to pick up the wrong item.

3. Because companies compete with one another, each tries to outdo the other in placement of a product, location influences the consumer.

4. If the claims by the manufacturer are true, I do not mind attempts to get me to buy a product, false claims tend to anger me though.

5. When a product sounds too good to be true, it very well is just that, lots of people have wasted money hoping to get a bargain.

6. Even though the government attempts to prosecute advertisers who make false claims, it cannot catch all who exaggerate a product's ability, there would be fewer products on the market if it could.

7. If you have been cheated, you can call the Better Business Bureau if the problem is more serious, you can go through small claims court.

8. Because of the number of cases waiting to go to trial, the court process may be slow, it may also be the most effective means of stopping the company from doing further harm.

9. Without consumers who are willing to get involved, unknowing buyers are harmed other buyers are saved from frustration by consumers who are willing to get involved.

10. Since a person rarely gets something for nothing, perhaps it would be wise not to try, a person usually gets what he or she pays for.

NAME _____ DATE _____

INSTRUCTOR _____ CLASS TIME _____

SENTENCE FRAGMENTS

A **sentence fragment**, the third major sentence error, consists of a group of words between a capital letter and end punctuation that does not express a complete thought. Between every capital letter and end punctuation mark, you must have at least one independent clause. Attached to that independent clause can be numerous modifiers, phrases, or dependent clauses. Because these modifiers, phrases, and dependent clauses are fragments (parts) of sentences—not complete sentences—they must never stand alone.

Having learned to identify dependent clauses, verbal phrases, and prepositional phrases, now you are ready to easily identify and eliminate sentence fragments in your own writing. The most common sentence fragments that students write are verbal phrase fragments (verb + -ing and to + verb), prepositional phrase fragments (preposition plus noun or pronoun), or dependent clause fragments (clauses that begin with subordinate conjunctions). Each of these is perfectly acceptable when attached to an independent clause. When placed between a capitol letter and end punctuation, however, a sentence fragment error results.

You can eliminate numerous fragments if you remember that subordinate conjunctions (listed in Table 2.1) introduce dependent clauses. We call these words "fragment catchers" because they introduce fragments of a sentence, groups of words that can never stand alone between a capital and a period. When you see a fragment catcher, look carefully at the words that follow it.

Look at the following groups of words:

When I walk down the street.

Walking down the street.

To walk down the street.

On the street near the river.

None of these groups of words is a complete sentence. The first is a dependent clause. The second and third are verbal phrases. The fourth is two prepositional phrases. Each of these is a sentence fragment error as now written. But if attached to an independent clause, each would become an acceptable sentence.

For example, consider the following sentences made using the above fragments:

When I walk down the street, I feel great.

Walking down the street, I feel great.

To walk down the street makes me feel great.

On the street near the river, I see lots of people.

Do a mechanical check whenever you are in doubt about a group of words being a sentence. Looking at the words between the capital letter and the end punctuation, ask yourself the following questions:

1. Is there a main verb?

If there is not a main verb, you immediately know the words are not a clause and, therefore, they cannot be a sentence.

2. If there is a main verb, is there a subject?

If there is a main verb and a subject, the words form a clause. At this point you must determine whether it is a dependent or an independent clause.

3. If it is a clause, does it begin with a subordinate conjunction?

If it does, it probably is a dependent clause.

4. Does it express a completed thought?

If it has a main verb, a subject, and expresses a completed thought, it is a sentence, not a fragment. One of the most common errors that students make is writing a fragment that should have been attached to the sentence before or after it.

Consider the following:

I was excited and scared. When graduation day finally arrived.

After I'd spent four years studying and working. Graduation day finally arrived.

Going out in the world on my own. I found a whole new set of challenges.

In each example above, one of the groups of words will not stand alone between a capital letter and end punctuation. The following examples show how each could be corrected by attaching the fragment to the sentence:

I was excited and scared when graduation day finally arrived.

After I'd spent four years studying and working, graduation day finally arrived.

Going out in the world on my own, I found a whole new set of challenges.

Be aware that although you are unlikely to see a fused sentence in magazines or books, you *will* encounter both comma splices and sentence fragments. Professional writers use both for an informal, conversational effect. Copywriters for advertisements use them to get their reader's attention. Without exception, however, student writers should avoid writing comma splices and sentence fragments in their academic work. In the academic world, such sentence structure errors quickly label a writer as uneducated. Likewise, in the standard, formal English used in the business world, these sentence structure errors are equally unacceptable.

TRY-IT
EXERCISE

Identify each of the following as a complete sentence (S) or a sentence fragment (F).

_____ 1. Unless students do their homework each night of the week.
_____ 2. Lessons will be difficult and frustrating in every class.
_____ 3. Studying each evening at home in the kitchen after supper.
_____ 4. Maria became very skilled in sentence structure.

The first and third items are sentence fragments. The first item is a dependent clause incorrectly placed between a capital and a period. Number three is a verbal phrase incorrectly placed between a capital and a period. Numbers two and four are complete sentences.

PRACTICE EXERCISE 2-5 IDENTIFICATION OF SENTENCE FRAGMENTS

Underline any group of words that is a sentence fragment. If the numbered item does not include a sentence fragment, identify it as correct (C) in the blank provided.

EXAMPLE: <u>Studying languages in college with two different teachers</u>. I work many hours each night.

_____ 1. I've spent four years studying Spanish. To get the major I want.

_____ 2. Mastering Spanish and English at the same time. I spend hours on homework.

_____ 3. Studying Spanish with Ms. Brod and English with Ms. Hellyer.

_____ 4. I learned Spanish and English while they were my teachers.

_____ 5. Working in the language lab each night, I quickly learned the basics of Spanish.

_____ 6. When I took my test in English. I knew that I'd learned the rules.

_____ 7. After I finish these classes in Spanish and English. I'll have a double major.

_____ 8. My goal is to be an interpreter in the business world. On the stock market in New York or at a company like General Electric.

_____ 9. People who know two languages are in demand. In many fields such as transportation, business, or teaching.

_____ 10. I might teach in Florida. Because they are begging for teachers who know both English and Spanish.

NAME _____ DATE _____

INSTRUCTOR _____ CLASS TIME _____

| PRACTICE EXERCISE 2-6 | # CORRECTION OF SENTENCE FRAGMENTS |

Make each of the following fragments into sentences by writing an independent clause either before or after the fragment.

EXAMPLE: Because learning to use the language takes time.

Because learning to use the language takes time, you should study English each night.

1. If you have problems with punctuation or grammar.

_____

2. When writing essays or creating paragraphs.

_____

3. Since language concepts are grasped by repeated use.

_____

4. While taking classes in both Spanish and English.

_____

5. Trying to understand the structure of the English language.

_____

6. To understand the structure of the English language.

_____

7. Wanting desperately to pass this English test.

_____

8. Facing the biggest challenge of her life.

_____

9. After John received the student loan.

_____

10. Down the hall on the third floor near the drinking fountain.

_____

NAME _____ DATE _____

INSTRUCTOR _____ CLASS TIME _____

Having learned to recognize and avoid fused sentences, comma splices, and sentence fragments—three major errors in sentence structure—you are now ready to identify and correct faulty parallelism and dangling modifiers. Faulty parallelism occurs when the parts of a sentence are not in the same grammatical form. Dangling modifiers occur when a phrase or clause does not modify the correct word. Although these two errors in sentence structure are not considered as major as the first three discussed, your sentences will be more effective if you rid them of such errors.

FAULTY PARALLELISM

A sentence is coherent when all its words, phrases, and clauses fit smoothly together and relate in a clear, logical way. One error that occurs commonly and interferes with the coherence of sentences is a lack of parallelism.

Parallelism in a sentence structure refers to a pattern of writing in which words or phrases used in a sentence are similar in form. In life, we make things parallel without even thinking about it. For example, if you lost one of the hubcaps from your car, you would buy another to match the three that you still had, or you would buy four that matched. You instinctively know that you don't want a spoked hubcap on one tire and unspoked hubcaps on the other three. The same principle applies when you are writing items in a series. You want the parts of the sentence to share the same grammatical form:

Studying, dating, and working take all my time.

I like to study, to date, and to work.

My girlfriend is understanding, generous, and intelligent.

She takes classes, studies the lessons, and helps her parents.

In the first sentence *studying, dating,* and *working* share the same grammatical form. All three are *-ing* verbals. All are subjects of the verb *take*. In the second sentence, *to study, to date,* and *to work* are in the same grammatical form. All three are *to- + -a-verb* verbals. All are direct objects of the verb *like*. In the third sentence, *understanding, generous,* and *intelligent* are in the same grammatical form. All three are adjectives serving as predicate adjectives describing *girlfriend*. In the fourth sentence, *takes classes, studies the lessons,* and *helps her parents* are in the same grammatical form. All three are verbs with direct objects.

TRY-IT

EXERCISE

Underline the three parallel elements in each sentence.

1. She likes reading, sewing, and cooking.
2. She is cheerful, intelligent, and creative.
3. Reading, sewing, and cooking are her hobbies.

In the first sentence, all the verbals act as direct objects of the verb *likes*. All are parallel. In the second sentence, all the predicate adjectives of the verb *is* are parallel. In the third sentence, all the subjects are parallel.

If a student wrote the direct objects in the following sentences so they were *not* in the same identical grammatical form, he or she would be guilty of faulty parallelism:

▼ CORRECT: She likes reading, sewing, and cooking.
▲ INCORRECT: She likes reading, to sew, and cooks great meals.

▼ CORRECT: She is cheerful, intelligent, and creative.
▲ INCORRECT: She is full of cheer, intelligent, and likes to create things.

▼ CORRECT: Reading, sewing, and cooking are her hobbies.
▲ INCORRECT: Reading, to sew, and being a good cook are her hobbies.

In each of the examples above, notice that there is always a "break" point where you can test a sentence for clear parallel structure. The first sentence pair breaks after *likes*, the second after *is*, and the third before *are*. For example, after the word *likes* in the first sentence, you can test every element that follows. Your ear will tell you whether the structure is right. When you say *likes reading, likes sewing,* and *likes cooking,* you can hear that these elements are parallel. In contrast, in reading aloud the sentence that has faulty parallelism—*She likes reading, to sew, and cooks great meals*—you say *likes reading, likes to sew, likes cooks great meals.* Your ear can readily hear the lack of parallelism in that sentence.

| PRACTICE | # IDENTIFICATION OF FAULTY |
| EXERCISE 2-7 | # PARALLELISM |

Put parentheses around those words that keep the sentence from having parallel structure.

EXAMPLE: What do teachers know about making good grades, pleasing parents, and (part-time jobs)?

1. Fred wants to play tennis, practice clarinet, and he dates Rachel.

2. Fred likes to tease his brother, watching TV, and eating popcorn.

3. He jogs to lose weight, stay healthy, and it's fun.

4. Jogging, swimming, and his bike rides keep him busy.

5. He finds time for exercise by making a schedule, staying on it, and self-discipline.

6. Some people have free time, abundant energy, and are very determined.

7. Driving to work, running errands, and school take time.

8. During the summer he plans to mow lawns, paint the house, and he'll play some softball.

9. Softball helps him exercise, relax, and it's free.

10. He is a man with a variety of interests, a good personality, and who has many friends.

NAME _____ DATE _____

INSTRUCTOR _____ CLASS TIME _____

PRACTICE EXERCISE 2-8 | CORRECTION OF FAULTY PARALLELISM

Put parentheses around the words that keep the sentence from having parallel structure and then rewrite the sentence using parallelism.

EXAMPLE: Brad is handsome, personable, and (has lots of money).
Brad is handsome, personable, and rich.

1. I want to go swimming at Eastfork State Park, hiking at the Cincinnati Nature Center, and bicycle ride at the Loveland bike trail.

   _____

2. Marie went to work prepared to type reports, with a good personality for answering the phone, and to file contracts.

   _____

3. The students claimed to have learned the rules, worked the exercises, and they had tried to study the text.

   _____

4. Moving is a task requiring organization, time, and it is hard work.

   _____

5. My favorite desserts are cherry pie with ice cream, chocolate cake with chocolate icing, and I also like whipped cream on pumpkin pie.

   _____

6. By walking to campus, riding an exercise bike, and since I play basketball, I manage to get my aerobic exercise.

   _____

7. After taking the final exam, the students handed in a self-addressed card, were wanting to have a party, and filled out evaluation forms.

   _____

8. Many people fear traveling by plane, by bus, or getting on a train.

   _____

9. The farm was filled with the sounds of newborn animals: the mooing of calves, the bleating of lambs, and there were several baby pigs squealing.

   _____

10. I don't like movies that are violent, use profanity, and that have scary scenes.

    _____

NAME _____ DATE _____

INSTRUCTOR _____ CLASS TIME _____

DANGLING MODIFIERS

Another error that interferes with the coherence of sentences is **dangling modifiers.** Introductory phrases should modify the subject of the following clause; otherwise, the introductory phrase dangles. This subject should be the first noun or pronoun following the introductory phrase.

In the following sentence, the introductory modifying phrase is italicized:

Smelling the hay in the barn, my childhood memories came back to me.

Following the modifying phrase is the subject *memories.* The problem is that the phrase is not really describing *memories.* Memories cannot smell hay. Thus, the modifier is said to be misplaced or to be dangling because the subject is not the word being described by this phrase.

In order to correct the above dangling modifier, we must create a subject that the introductory phrase correctly modifies:

Smelling the hay in the barn, I was overcome by my childhood memories.

Now the introductory phrase is no longer a dangling modifier because it correctly modifies the subject *I.*

TRY-IT
EXERCISE

Put parentheses around each dangling modifier in the following sentences. Underline the word(s) that the modifier was meant to modify.

1. Studying the lesson, the punctuation rules were learned by the student.
2. After reading for hours, the novel finally made some sense to Melissa.
3. To be well cooked, you should stew chicken for over an hour.

In each sentence above, the verbal phrase at the beginning does *not* modify the subject of the independent clause. It is not the punctuation that is studying, but the student; it is not the novel that is reading, but Melissa; it is not you who will be well cooked, but the chicken. Each of these introductory phrases is a dangling modifier.

PRACTICE	# IDENTIFICATION OF DANGLING
EXERCISE 2-9	# MODIFIERS

Each of these sentences contains a dangling modifier. Underline the word(s) that the modifier was meant to modify.

EXAMPLE: Feeling inadequate in the kitchen, my mother taught <u>me</u> to bake cookies.

1. After studying for hours, the answers to the algebra problems were clear to Juan.

2. Wearing shorts and a polo shirt, the new car was washed by my brother.

3. To be well done, you should grill hamburgers 15 minutes.

4. Having a fabulous sun roof, my sister purchased the car.

5. Administering the needed vaccine, the babies received shots from the doctors.

6. Standing at the end of the table, the turkey was carved by my dad.

7. Being made out of sturdy plastic, the Patels enjoy their new picnic dishes.

8. After being fertilized and watered, the homeowner had to mow the thick grass.

9. Unable to understand grammar, our English teacher gave Itamar help.

10. Losing their insulation seal, the McGrews must replace the old windows.

NAME _____ DATE _____

INSTRUCTOR _____ CLASS TIME _____

PRACTICE EXERCISE 2-10	# CORRECTION OF DANGLING MODIFIERS

The following sentences are from the previous exercise. Rewrite each sentence, making the modifier modify the word it logically should.

EXAMPLE: Feeling inadequate in the kitchen, my mother taught me to bake.

Feeling inadequate in the kitchen, I was taught how to bake by my mother.

1. After studying for hours, the answers were clear to Juan.

    _____

2. Wearing shorts and a polo shirt, the new car was washed by my brother.

    _____

3. To be well done, you should grill hamburgers 15 minutes.

    _____

4. Having a fabulous sun roof, my sister purchased the car.

    _____

5. Administering the vaccine, the babies received shots from the doctors.

    _____

6. Standing at the end of the table, the turkey was carved by my dad.

    _____

7. Being made out of sturdy plastic, the Patels enjoy their new dishes.

    _____

8. After being fertilized and watered, Beth had to mow the thick grass.

    _____

9. Unable to understand grammar, our English teacher gave Itamar help.

    _____

10. Losing their insulation seal, the McGrews must replace the old windows.

    _____

NAME _____ DATE _____

INSTRUCTOR _____ CLASS TIME _____

© NTC/CONTEMPORARY PUBLISHING COMPANY

REVIEW EXERCISE 2-1 | IDENTIFICATION OF COMMA SPLICES, FUSED SENTENCES, AND SENTENCE FRAGMENTS

DIRECTIONS: Some of the following items are fused or spliced sentences, some are fragments, and some are correct sentences. Underline the error and then identify each item as a comma splice (CS), a fused sentence (FS), a sentence fragment (FRAG), or correct sentence (C).

_____ 1. Mike is one of the best students in our English class, he learned punctuation and grammar rules when he was in high school.

_____ 2. When my English grade was slipping, I asked Mike to help me.

_____ 3. Our teacher threatened to give failing grades to papers with sentence fragments many students were just being careless.

_____ 4. Studying takes many hours each evening. To read all the assignments in my four classes and take notes on each of them.

_____ 5. Driving to school each morning at 7:30, I am in the morning rush hour.

_____ 6. I drive east down Montgomery Road, then I turn north on Interstate 71.

_____ 7. When I drive down Kenwood Road, I am amazed at the new buildings. On both sides of the street and in the lot behind the old Kenwood Plaza.

_____ 8. As we watched the lazy days of summer turn into the crisp days of fall.

_____ 9. As the lazy days of summer dwindled, I realized fall was coming, classes would soon begin.

_____ 10. The fall trees are lovely. Magnificent shades of golden red.

_____ 11. One day this fall when the leaves were turning vibrant shades of scarlet and the air was crisp and chilly.

NAME _____   DATE _____

INSTRUCTOR _____   CLASS TIME _____

_____ 12. Turning various shades of scarlet, the leaves were beautiful.

_____ 13. The lovely blue sky was filled with gorgeous clouds. Drifting over the horizon and creating beautiful patterns of white in the azure background.

_____ 14. Because of light traffic and beautiful weather, I enjoyed my drive to school.

_____ 15. This school year will go quickly, then it will be spring.

_____ 16. Blooming all over campus, the tulips bring loveliness and the promise of warm weather, spring is just around the corner.

_____ 17. Since the tulips started blooming all over campus. I've been studying outside on the lawn behind the English building.

_____ 18. It's almost spring, I see tulips, crocuses, and daffodils blooming all over our campus.

_____ 19. Blooming along the drive on the north side of campus. The daffodils bring color and beauty.

_____ 20. Walking slowly to my first class of the day, I am thrilled at the spring flowers on our campus.

| REVIEW EXERCISE 2-2 | IDENTIFICATION OF COMMA SPLICES, FAULTY PARALLELISM, AND DANGLING MODIFIERS |

DIRECTIONS: Identify each item as an example of one of the following: faulty parallelism (FP), dangling modifier (DM), comma splice (CS), or correct (C).

_____ 1. Reading books, writing lessons, and the papers she types keep her busy.

_____ 2. Having been guilty of driving while intoxicated, the judge suspended the man's license.

_____ 3. Rita took the job at the grocery, she didn't want to spend her life at the factory. Working at the grocery brought more satisfaction.

_____ 4. Leaving the job at the factory, Rita felt much better about her future. Having a new baby to care for, she did not want to work evenings.

_____ 5. The day was rainy, cloudy, and it seemed the humidity was oppressive.

_____ 6. Jamal has a new dependent on his taxes, his wife had a baby last spring. After this addition to the family arrived, Jamal has more bills.

_____ 7. Spending countless hours each day with the baby, Jamal's wife is busy, tired, and happy.

_____ 8. To support her family, Rita needs her job at the grocery.

_____ 9. Driving down Interstate 275, the orange barriers blocked my lane of traffic.

_____ 10. Cookies should be soft, chewy, and flavorful.

_____ 11. Walking rapidly and dashing across the terminal, the airport in Atlanta was navigated by the passengers.

NAME _____ DATE _____

INSTRUCTOR _____ CLASS TIME _____

_____ 12.   The Corvette is fast, sleek, and it costs a lot of money.

_____ 13.   Containing soybeans and costing very little, our company will produce a new, low-calorie meat patty.

_____ 14.   She is slim, pretty, and she always seems gracious.

_____ 15.   I wonder if dreams come true, I certainly hope that they do.

_____ 16.   Believing in the value of goals, I continue to make them a part of my plans.

_____ 17.   Some people's dreams are illusions, others' dreams are anchored in reality.

_____ 18.   Sean's stories are hard to believe, some of them sound farfetched to me.

_____ 19.   Juan is fat, short, and his hair is getting thin.

_____ 20.   Having reached the age of three, Juan enrolled his son in nursery school.

REVIEW EXERCISE 2-3

COMMA SPLICES, FUSED SENTENCES, SENTENCE FRAGMENTS, FAULTY PARALLELISM, AND DANGLING MODIFIERS

DIRECTIONS: Identify each of the following items as comma splice (CS), fused sentence (FS), sentence fragment (FRAG), faulty parallelism (FP), dangling modifier (DM), or correct sentence (C).

_____ 1.   Daydreaming in class, partying at night, and a full-time job can cause a person to earn low grades.

_____ 2.   Walking in Northgate Mall by the store displays, one of the mannequins had fallen over.

_____ 3.   Sandra has her mind made up, nothing will change it.

_____ 4.   When she spoke to Manuel about the matter, Sandra was aware of her frustration.

_____ 5.   Speaking with both Manuel and Sandra, their lawyer settled the case out of court. Keeping a divorce simple is not easy.

_____ 6.   I feel sorry for animals in captivity life will never be the same for them.

_____ 7.   Studying her notes and reviewing the textbook, Juanita realized her weaknesses in grammar.

_____ 8.   Having a leaking roof and needing repair, the man purchased the house.

_____ 9.   Gary is tall, pleasant, and he makes a good appearance.

_____ 10.   Many women want to date him, his wife doesn't appreciate his admirers.

NAME _____   DATE _____

INSTRUCTOR _____   CLASS TIME _____

_____ 11. We decided to divide the work, I'll mow the lawn each week.

_____ 12. Working in the lawn behind our house, I became very tired.

_____ 13. To mow that lawn in less than an hour with an old lawnmower, and to finish the job before my mother has supper ready.

_____ 14. Playing jacks in the driveway by our house, and skipping rope under the elm tree in the back yard.

_____ 15. Playing jacks and skipping rope in the driveway, I quietly watch my children from the upstairs window.

_____ 16. Playing jacks and skipping rope are fun. While playing these games, children let their imaginations roam.

_____ 17. Sincere love demands giving many people cannot give easily.

_____ 18. The basis of love is communication, love is a never-ending conversation.

_____ 19. Relaxing by the lake and talking quietly, the flickering campfire was watched by the couple.

_____ 20. Because loving is the greatest risk in the world, many people choose the safety of empty lives.

CHAPTER	IDENTIFICATION OF COMMA
QUIZ 2-1	SPLICES, FUSED SENTENCES, AND SENTENCE FRAGMENTS

IDENTIFICATION OF COMMA SPLICES, FUSED SENTENCES, AND SENTENCE FRAGMENTS

DIRECTIONS: Identify each of the following items as comma splice (CS), fused sentence (FS), sentence fragment (FRAG), or correct (C).

_____ 1. Although the stores were very crowded, Mother and I went shopping at the mall last Friday night.

_____ 2. I usually choose what I like, then Mother decides if we can afford it. She and I seldom disagree on major purchases.

_____ 3. The other day when I bought three new shirts and paid for them with my own money. I had a great deal of trouble.

_____ 4. The stores were packed with people. The same hustle and bustle of every city during the hectic, pre-Christmas rush.

_____ 5. Driving around town to see the Christmas decorations, and choosing the most beautiful display in the neighborhood. We had a great time.

_____ 6. When we finally started home, it was very late in the evening. After our drive through the neighborhood, we were tired.

_____ 7. Last summer I went water-skiing at a lake in northern Florida, it was one of the best summers of my life.

_____ 8. I liked my vacation at the lake, it was a beautiful place to read and think.

_____ 9. Spending two weeks at the lake, I water-skied every day of the vacation. It was a marvelous escape from my problems.

_____ 10. Reading in the morning, skiing in the afternoon, and playing tennis in the evening, I had a great vacation, I could have stayed the entire summer.

_____ 11. Riding on the waves with the wind and the water in my face, soaring through the air like a carefree bird.

NAME _____ DATE _____

INSTRUCTOR _____ CLASS TIME _____

_____ 12. Because it made me feel free and young like a child, I enjoyed waterskiing.

_____ 13. Soaring through the air like a bird on its first flight, skimming over the water at top speed. I felt free.

_____ 14. Although I had a great time and made new friends at the lake in Florida last summer. I am planning a vacation in Colorado next year.

_____ 15. I would not like to play tennis and water-ski every day of the week it would get monotonous after a few months.

_____ 16. The stereo plays pleasant music, listening gives me peace and calmness.

_____ 17. While I listen to the beat of the music, I feel good, my problems disappear as the music relaxes me.

_____ 18. Especially when a problem is taking all my time and attention, making life a tangled mess of confusion.

_____ 19. Listening to the music coming from the stereo in the family room, and relaxing in the calmness of the moment. Life seems very good.

_____ 20. After a very difficult day at school, I listen to pleasant music.

CHAPTER
QUIZ 2-2

IDENTIFICATION OF COMMA SPLICES, FUSED SENTENCES, SENTENCE FRAGMENTS, FAULTY PARALLELISM, AND DANGLING MODIFIERS

DIRECTIONS: Identify each of the following items as comma splice (CS), fused sentence (FS), sentence fragment (FRAG), faulty parallelism (FP), dangling modifier (DM), or correct (C).

_____ 1. Walking to the table in the dining room, the chocolate cake was dropped by my sister.

_____ 2. The day slipped quickly away from me, then I wished for less work or more hours. This quick passage of time shocks me.

_____ 3. Blowing softly in the April breeze, we watched the swaying willows.

_____ 4. When I sit in front of a crackling fire, I like to play soft music, it is my way of relaxing.

_____ 5. Watching the flames of a roaring fire, I enjoy cold nights.

_____ 6. I enjoy watching a burning fire. In the early spring and late fall when the days are cold with just a hint of winter in the air.

_____ 7. Because a fire has a magical quality about it, causing peaceful meditation, making inner peace and contentment within my reach.

_____ 8. Some teachers require essays for tests, other teachers rely on objective tests. Some give both kinds.

_____ 9. Once in the early fall and once during spring quarter when everyone is taking final exams. The library is packed.

_____ 10. Running upstairs at breakneck speed, the books fell from my arms.

NAME _____   DATE _____

INSTRUCTOR _____   CLASS TIME _____

_____ 11. The best students have self-discipline, good minds, and they are organized.

_____ 12. To deal with the problem of their students' lack of writing skills, and to help with the understanding of basic grammar. The teachers decided on a new curriculum.

_____ 13. Taking notes in math as fast as I could without stopping, trying to understand the teacher's rapid lecture. I was exhausted.

_____ 14. Studying three hours every night and reviewing notes each morning, my parents were pleased with my good grades.

_____ 15. Teachers and students need schedules, then they get things finished on time.

_____ 16. The students working on the exercises for today's lesson, and the teacher grading yesterday's tests in sentence structure.

_____ 17. An effective teacher knows the subject matter, enjoys teaching, and it helps if he or she can relate well with students.

_____ 18. When we went to the shopping center near the freeway and drove the crowded streets at 5 o'clock on Friday night. The traffic was terrible.

_____ 19. Shopping at the Forest Fair Mall and the Kenwood Towne Center, the sweater was finally found by my sister.

_____ 20. Before paying the clerk or buying the sweater, my sister asked if they accepted Visa credit cards.

PUNCTUATION

CHAPTER 3

PUNCTUATION JOINING INDEPENDENT CLAUSES

L earning to use punctuation correctly will help you communicate effectively with your reader. When speaking, you use hand gestures, eye movement, and voice intonation to convey your ideas, but when writing, you must rely on punctuation to tell the reader when to slow down, stop, or emphasize. Correct punctuation increases your reader's understanding of and interest in your writing.

If you are like many students who are unsure of punctuation rules, you probably punctuate when you pause. You should not rely on the "punctuate when you pause" guideline, however, because it doesn't always work. For example, if you were to ask four classmates to read the same sentence, chances are that each would pause at a different place. Although the pause principle has value—and guessing sometimes works—you need more clearly defined punctuation guidelines than pausing or guessing. This chapter will give you these needed guidelines.

Students who don't know where to punctuate tend to do one of two things: write short, simple sentences that require no punctuation, or write longer sentences that have punctuation marks scattered randomly throughout. These same students wouldn't dream of using a semicolon, and they use commas as if they were sprinkling them out of a salt shaker. Those who write short sentences do so at the cost of sounding choppy and childlike; likewise, those who sprinkle punctuation liberally through long sentences do so at the cost of confusing the reader. Fortunately, you can avoid these problems and gain confidence in using punctuation by learning a few basic principles.

A sentence composed of two or more independent clauses is called a *compound* sentence. There are four common methods of joining two (or more) independent clauses. We will discuss all four methods in this chapter. If you thoroughly understand these four punctuation rules, you will be able to write compound sentences with ease. In addition, your writing will sound more mature and, hence, more effective.

As in the previous chapters, we will present only the most basic rules for you to master. All of these have exceptions and variations, but you need to master the rules that apply 95 percent of the time before you concern yourself with the exceptions that are involved in the other 5 percent. Therefore, this chapter will focus on rules that work for the majority of the sentences that you will write.

JOINING WITH COORDINATING CONJUNCTIONS AND CONNECTIVES

In Chapter 1, we learned that *and* is a conjunction that creates a compound. Now let's look at a more extensive list of conjunctions: *and, but, for, or, nor, so,* and *yet.* Always use a comma before these words when they join independent clauses. The first five words are coordinating conjunctions, and the last two are connectives. Although the first five (*and, but, for, or, nor*) always serve as coordinating conjunctions, the last two (*so, yet*) don't always neatly fit, having exceptions and variations. For now, ignore those exceptions. By calling these words connectives, you will be aware that the first five and the last two are technically different. To keep this rule simple, learn that all seven connect equal grammatical parts. Thus the term *coordinating* makes sense, meaning equal or matching. If you coordinate your shirt and slacks, you make them match. Coordinating conjunctions connect words of equal grammatical parts: words to words, phrases to phrases, independent clauses to independent clauses. If you remember that *coordinate* means equal, you will always check to see that the constructions on each side of these seven words are similar.

We want you to memorize the famous 5 + 2: *and, but, for, or, nor,* plus *so, yet.* Of the first five, *and* and *but* are probably the most common and the easiest to remember. The next three contain the word *or,* differing only in their first letter. The last two are less common than the others but follow the same rules. You can use a comma between two independent clauses *only* if one of these seven words follows that comma. Think of the comma and the word as one unit. If you use a comma without the word, you will have created a comma splice, which we discussed in the previous chapter. Do not, however, add a comma every time you see one of these words. First, check to be sure that there is an independent clause on each side of the word. If in doubt, mentally cover up the connecting word and examine the words on each side of it; then ask yourself, "Is that a sentence?"

Look at the following sentences:

On cold mornings the old car would not start.

We had to buy a new battery.

These two sentences can be joined into a new sentence: *On cold mornings the old car would not start, and we had to buy a new battery.* When these are joined, they form a compound sentence: a sentence consisting of two or more independent clauses.

TRY-IT
EXERCISE

Look at the following sentences. Underline the word that joins the two independent clauses.

1. The old car was dented, and we took it to the body shop for repairs.
2. The old car was dented, but it ran well and required little gas.
3. The old car was dented, for my brother is a very careless driver.
4. The old car must start today, or I will be very angry.
5. The old car is not beautiful, nor is it economical.
6. The old car still runs well, so I will drive it many more miles.
7. The old car has dents and rust, yet it runs smoothly and burns little gasoline.

Notice that every sentence above has an independent clause on each side of the connecting word. Be aware that the second and seventh sentences have a compound main verb in the independent clause on the right side of the connecting word. Therefore, there is *no* comma before the *and* in the right-hand clause of either of these sentences. The second sentence has the compound verb *ran* and *required.* The seventh sentence has the compound verb *runs* and *burns.*

Confusing a compound sentence and a compound verb is the biggest problem students have with this rule of punctuation. Look at the following sentences:

We tested all the old cars in the lot, and we bought the best one.

We tested all the old cars in the lot and bought the best one.

In the first sentence, there is an independent clause on each side of *and;* hence, a comma is used before the *and.* You can test each sentence by covering the *and* and reading the words on each side. If you do this test on the second sentence, the words on the right are *bought the best one.* This, of course, is not an independent clause because there is no subject. The second sentence, therefore, is a simple sentence with a compound verb: *tested* and *bought.* Before placing a comma in any sentence, always check the words to the right of a connecting word to be certain that they form an independent clause.

It is important to remember that you *never* place a comma between two independent clauses unless that comma is followed by either *and, but, for, or, nor, so,* or *yet.* Placing a comma between two independent clauses that do not have a joining word creates a comma splice error, as explained in the previous chapter.

© NTC/CONTEMPORARY PUBLISHING COMPANY

PRACTICE COORDINATING CONJUNCTIONS
EXERCISE 3-1

Decide where the comma should be placed (or whether it is needed at all) in each sentence below. Write the last word of the first independent clause, add the comma, and then write the word that would follow the comma. If no comma is needed, identify the sentence as correct (C).

EXAMPLE: night, and I went shopping for a new shirt last night and the prices were much too high.

1. I wanted a new pair of shoes but each pair I tried was the wrong size.

    _____

2. I bought a shirt with blue and red plaid on a navy background so now I need a new pair of navy slacks.

    _____

3. I found the new slacks in that store near the shopping mall and bought them before I changed my mind.

    _____

4. I need another blue shirt and the store at the mall has one I'd like.

    _____

5. I am buying too many clothes and spending too much money.

    _____

6. I must take a close look at what I have spent this month or my income will not cover my bills.

    _____

7. My job doesn't pay for my basic expenses or unneeded luxuries.

    _____

8. I will not have enough money for my car payment nor will I have money for savings.

    _____

9. I enjoy shopping at the mall yet shopping with Hae is more fun.

    _____

10. Hae and I have a good time for we eat and talk between purchases.

    _____

NAME _____   DATE _____

INSTRUCTOR _____   CLASS TIME _____

| PRACTICE | # WRITING COMPOUND |
| EXERCISE 3-2 | SENTENCES |

Combine the sentences in 1–5 to form a single compound sentence.
Use a *different* coordinating conjunction for each sentence.

EXAMPLE: The boy went to the emergency room. He had stepped on a
rusty nail.

The boy went to the emergency room, for he had
stepped on a rusty nail.

1. The employees stayed after normal working hours. They also came in
    early the next morning.

    _____

2. Ricardo ordered frozen yogurt for dessert. He really wanted ice cream.

    _____

3. Shayna missed her appointment. She had gotten lost.

    _____

4. He might want a bowl of chili. He might be in the mood for pizza.

    _____

5. Learning punctuation is confusing at first. It soon becomes simple.

    _____

Items 6–10 list a conjunction. Create a compound sentence with an independent clause on each side of the conjunction given.

EXAMPLE: yet

Ben was hungry, yet he found nothing to eat.

6. nor _____

7. for _____

8. or _____

9. so _____

10. but _____

NAME _____ DATE _____

INSTRUCTOR _____ CLASS TIME _____

JOINING WITH NO CONNECTIVE WORD

Independent clauses can also be joined with a semicolon. With a semicolon, no connective word is necessary. Consider this sentence:

Sean got a high grade on the test; Shannon's grade was not as good.

This compound sentence has two independent clauses with no connective word. In order to tell the reader to stop, we placed a semicolon after *test*. A semicolon is a weak period. If you look carefully at this punctuation mark, you will see that it consists of a comma with a period over it. This combination is very logical because a semicolon tells readers to slow down more than they would for a comma and less than they would for a period. A semicolon is literally halfway between a comma and a period and, thus, serves a unique function that neither a comma nor a period can serve. Yet students carefully avoid this useful punctuation mark. This avoidance results from not knowing how to use semicolons correctly. After this chapter, you will feel comfortable using a semicolon because you will know when to use it and why it is appropriate.

One way to add sophistication and effectiveness to your writing is to use semicolons to join two independent clauses that have no joining word between them. If these two independent clauses are closely connected in thought, you don't need to use any connective word between them. A period, of course, is always correct, but, using only short sentences will make your writing sound choppy and immature.

In the previous section, we used coordinating conjunctions and connectives to join independent clauses, and we put a comma before these joining words, as in the following example:

On cold mornings the old car would not start, and we had to buy a new battery.

This compound sentence could have been written as follows:

On cold mornings the old car would not start; we had to buy a new battery.

In this example, the semicolon actually is a better choice than the period because it tells the reader to make a half stop, not a full stop. Too many full stops within a paragraph lead to choppiness.

© NTC/CONTEMPORARY PUBLISHING COMPANY

TRY-IT
EXERCISE

Insert semicolons between the independent clauses in the following sentences.

1. My new Volvo was parked in the driveway her old Buick was in the garage.
2. Every car in the lot was used each had over 60,000 miles on it.
3. Some cars constantly need repair others run well and never cause problems.
4. Leroy recently purchased a used Toyota his sister bought a new Honda.
5. The Kims have three cars the Harrises have two cars and want a van.

In the first sentence, the semicolon would be after *driveway;* in the second, it would be after *used;* in the third, it would be after *repair;* in the fourth, it would be after *Toyota;* in the fifth, it would be after *three cars.* Notice that every sentence has an independent clause on each side of the semicolon, but there are no connective words joining the clauses. Also be aware of the compound main verb in the second clause of the third sentence: *run* and *cause.* Because this is a compound verb, there is no comma before *and.* In the fifth sentence, the second clause has the compound verb *have* and *want.* Because this is a compound verb, there is no comma before *and.*

| PRACTICE | # JOINING INDEPENDENT CLAUSES |
| EXERCISE 3-3 | WITH NO JOINING WORD |

In the blank for each numbered item, write the last word of the first independent clause, a semicolon, and the word that begins the second clause.

EXAMPLE: <u>mess; tomorrow</u>   Today was a mess tomorrow has to be better.

_____ 1. Doug is often late to our class he usually misses the unannounced quizzes.

_____ 2. His schedule is lousy he comes at 8:00 and stays until 4:00.

_____ 3. Ability alone does not make a good student self-discipline and hard work are equally important.

_____ 4. Many of your essays were well written others showed a total lack of preparation.

_____ 5. The grades on this test were amazing they went from 99 to 36.

_____ 6. Most 8:00 classes are filled with listless students our class is an exception to the rule.

_____ 7. Test day is filled with tension today was no exception.

_____ 8. There is no doubt about her final grade she has earned nothing but As this quarter.

_____ 9. The chemistry test was a shock I thought I'd walked into the wrong room.

_____ 10. Some tests are too difficult others seem too easy.

NAME _____   DATE _____

INSTRUCTOR _____   CLASS TIME _____

| PRACTICE EXERCISE 3-4 | # WRITING COMPOUND SENTENCES WITH NO CONNECTING WORD |

The unpunctuated compound sentences below contain coordinating conjunctions. Keeping the sentence compound in structure, remove any coordinating conjunction that separates two independent clauses and replace it with a semicolon.

EXAMPLE: Raoul planned a surprise party for his mom and dad's anniversary and the big event was a total success.

Raoul planned a surprise party for his mom and dad's anniversary; the big event was a total success.

1. I wanted a new pair of shoes but each pair I tried on was the wrong size.

    _____

    _____

2. I bought a shirt with blue and red plaid on a navy background so now I need a new pair of navy slacks.

    _____

    _____

3. I need another blue shirt and the store at the mall has one I'd like.

    _____

    _____

4. I am spending too much money so I must budget more carefully.

    _____

    _____

5. Keisha and I have fun at the mall for we eat and talk between purchases.

    _____

    _____

NAME _____ DATE _____

INSTRUCTOR _____ CLASS TIME _____

© NTC/CONTEMPORARY PUBLISHING COMPANY

JOINING WITH CONJUNCTIVE ADVERBS AND SENTENCE MODIFIERS

Conjunctive adverbs and sentence modifiers are useful tools that join two or more independent clauses. These words join words, sentences, and paragraphs—not just clauses. Conjunctive adverbs and sentence modifiers have the unique ability both to *join* two independent clauses and to *interrupt* the flow of an independent clause. First, we will learn how they join or connect.

TABLE 3.1	*Common Conjunctive Adverbs*
also	moreover
anyway	nevertheless
besides	otherwise
consequently	still
furthermore	therefore
hence	thus
however	then (Do not use a comma after this conjunctive adverb.)
indeed	
instead	(These are single words.)

Because both conjunctive adverbs and sentence modifiers make good transitions, they are words worth knowing. Once again, their names describe their function. *Conjunctive* means "to join together." Conjunctive adverbs and sentence modifiers join the clauses on each side of them. They modify the independent clause they introduce and join it to the independent clause that went before it. The major difference between them is that conjunctive adverbs consist of one word, while sentence modifiers consist of short phrases. Becoming familiar with Table 3.1, which gives the most common conjunctive adverbs, and Table 3.2, which gives the most common sentence modifiers, will make it easier to use them correctly.

TABLE 3.2	*Common Sentence Modifiers*
	as a result
	for example
	in addition
	on the other hand
	in fact
	in other words
	on the contrary
	(Note that these are phrases.)

If you write two independent clauses and join them with any of the words in Tables 3.1 or 3.2, put a semicolon before the word. But before you use the semicolon, check to be sure that there is an independent clause on each side of the conjunctive adverb or sentence modifier.

Look at the following sentence:

On cold mornings our car would not start; therefore, we had to buy a new battery.

Notice that there is a semicolon before the conjunctive adverb *therefore* and a comma after it. Teachers and texts disagree about the need for the comma after a conjunctive adverb. There is never anything wrong with using it; indeed, there are times that many educated people would consider it wrong to omit it. To avoid confusion, make a habit of inserting the comma after any conjunctive adverb that joins two independent clauses. (The only exception to this practice is when using the conjunctive adverb *then.*) Although the need for a comma after a conjunctive adverb is debated, the need for a semicolon before it is not in question.

Look at the following sentence:

The new car was expensive; as a result, I am now making large payments.

Notice that there is a semicolon before the sentence modifier *as a result* and a comma after it. The use of this comma is agreed upon by the majority of teachers and texts; therefore, make a habit of putting a comma after any sentence modifier that joins two independent clauses.

Every time you write a conjunctive adverb or a sentence modifier, don't automatically place a semicolon before it. Use a semicolon (or a period) only if there is an independent clause on each side of the conjunctive adverb or the sentence modifier. These words not only serve as connectives; they also serve as interrupters. This is a quality that conjunctive adverbs and sentence modifiers do not share with coordinating conjunctions, which cannot be used as interrupters.

Interrupters

There are numerous kinds of interrupters, but we will concentrate on the three most common: conjunctive adverbs, sentence modifiers, and parenthetical expressions. Use commas to set off all interrupters. An interrupter is a group of words that interrupts the normal flow of a sentence. Such expressions are not essential to the meaning of the sentence and can be lifted out without significantly changing the meaning.

Conjunctive adverbs and sentence modifiers serve a slightly different function from parenthetical expressions, so we'll discuss them first. Before you punctuate a sentence with a conjunctive adverb or a sentence modifier, you must determine whether the word or phrase is *joining* two independent clauses or *interrupting* the flow of an independent clause.

SENTENCE MODIFIERS AND CONJUNCTIVE ADVERBS RULE. Use commas to set off sentence modifiers and conjunctive adverbs of two or more syllables when they are used as interrupters within a sentence.

When these words are used within a sentence, they need a comma on each side of them. The most common student error concerning the punctuation of

© NTC/CONTEMPORARY PUBLISHING COMPANY

interrupters is failure to put a comma on both sides of the interrupter. Perhaps you can avoid this error if you remember that the purpose of putting commas around interrupters is to set them off from the normal flow of the sentence. Think of drawing a circle around the interrupter, so that it is no longer a part of the sentence. Rather than actually drawing a circle, put a comma on each side of the interrupter. You can think of the commas as handles; if you can lift the word out without changing the meaning of the sentence, you should insert a comma on each side of the interrupter.

TRY-IT
EXERCISE

In the following sentences, set off the interrupter by inserting a comma on each side of it.

1. Many students for example work nights while attending school.
2. Some of them as a result are too tired to concentrate during class.
3. Many of these tired students nevertheless make excellent grades.
4. Some students however lack time for their homework.
5. Patrick on the other hand carefully balances time at school and at work.

In the first sentence, the interrupter is *for example;* in the second, the interrupter is *as a result;* in the third, the interrupter is *nevertheless;* in the fourth, the interrupter is *however;* in the fifth, the interrupter is *on the other hand.* All five are set off by inserting a comma on each side of the interrupter. All five could be lifted out without changing sentence meaning.

PARENTHETICAL EXPRESSIONS RULE.   There are many common parenthetical expressions that are used as interrupters. The most significant difference between sentence modifiers, conjunctive adverbs, and parenthetical expressions is that parenthetical expressions can smoothly flow into the sentence and, therefore, might *not* join or interrupt. For example, look at the parenthetical expressions *to tell the truth* and *I regret to say* in each of the following sentences:

A person must try to tell the truth.

She is, to tell the truth, a remarkable person.

TABLE 3.3 *Common Parenthetical Expressions*

generally speaking	surprisingly enough
to tell the truth	to our dismay
in my opinion	to be sure
to summarize	of course
quite frankly	first
first of all	he says
as a matter of fact	I believe
I think	I hope
I am certain	I regret to say
I am afraid	

I regret to say that we can't attend the party.

We can't, I regret to say, attend the party.

In two of these four sentences, the parenthetical expression is neither an interrupter nor a joiner. It flows into and is a part of the sentence. Parenthetical expressions become interrupters if they are inserted so that they break the sentence flow. In the first sentence, there is no interrupter. *To tell the truth* is a verbal phrase serving as the direct object of the verb phrase *must try;* the subject is *person.* In the second sentence, *to tell the truth* has become an interrupter. In the third sentence there is no interrupter; the main verb is *regret,* the subject is *I,* and the direct object is the verbal *to say.* In the second and fourth sentences, the words become interrupters simply because they break the natural flow of the sentence. Becoming familiar with Table 3.3, which gives the most common parenthetical expressions, will make learning to use them easier. This table is not a complete list of parenthetical expressions, of course, but knowing these will help you identify others.

TRY-IT
EXERCISE

In each of the following sentences, set off the interrupter by inserting a comma on each side of it.

1. Students in this class generally speaking must balance work and school.
2. Many of the best students I am certain get less than seven hours of sleep each night.

3. These same students as a matter of fact are often single or married mothers.
4. Single mothers in this class surprisingly enough are some of the best students.
5. These mothers in my opinion want a good future for themselves and their children.

In sentence one, the parenthetical expression is *generally speaking;* in sentence two, it is *I am certain;* in sentence three, it is *as a matter of fact;* in sentence four, it is *surprisingly enough;* in sentence five, it is *in my opinion.* All should be set off by inserting a comma on each side of the interrupter. Finally, all five could be lifted out without changing sentence meaning.

TRY-IT
EXERCISE

As you have learned in this chapter, two independent clauses joined by either a conjunctive adverb or a sentence modifier require a semicolon before the connective and a comma after; however, when either of these interrupts the flow of the sentence, commas are inserted on each side. For each of the following sentences, decide whether the conjunctive adverb or sentence modifier is used as a joiner or an interrupter. Insert semicolons and commas where needed.

1. This car is a good one for example I have had no major repairs in five years.
2. This car for example has had no major repairs in five years.
3. This car is a good one however it needs paint and body work.
4. This car however needs paint and body work.
5. My parents' car does not need repair work on the contrary it's in excellent condition.
6. My parents' car on the contrary is in excellent condition.
7. Our mechanic is honest nevertheless his prices for body work are very high.
8. Our mechanic's prices for body work nevertheless are very high.

9. My parents' car seldom needs repairs as a result it is rarely in the mechanic's garage.
10. Their car as a result is seldom in the mechanic's garage.

In the first sentence, *for example* joins two independent clauses and should have a semicolon before it and a comma after. In the third sentence, *however* joins two independent clauses and should have a semicolon before it and a comma after. In the fifth sentence, *on the contrary* joins two independent clauses and should have a semicolon before it and a comma after. In the seventh sentence, *nevertheless* joins two independent clauses and should have a semicolon before it and a comma after. In the ninth sentence, *as a result* joins two independent clauses and should have a semicolon before it and a comma after. In the second, fourth, sixth, eighth, and tenth sentences, the conjunctive adverb or sentence modifier falls in the middle of an independent clause and does not join two clauses; therefore, it is an interrupter and should have a comma inserted on each side of it.

This completes our discussion of the three most common types of interrupters and their appropriate punctuation.

To help you review the punctuation rules discussed in this chapter, refer to Table 3.4 on page 129.

PRACTICE EXERCISE 3-5
CONJUNCTIVE ADVERBS AND SENTENCE MODIFIERS

For each of the following, decide where punctuation should be inserted in the sentence. Write the last word of the first independent clause, insert the semicolon, write the conjunctive adverb or sentence modifier, and add the punctuation following it. If the sentence modifier is used within an independent clause, insert commas on each side of it.

EXAMPLE: My old car may not be modern and beautiful nevertheless it is

always very dependable.

beautiful; nevertheless,

EXAMPLE: It has always for example started on cold mornings.

, for example,

1. My new car costs too much money furthermore it needs constant repairs and burns too much gas.

2. My old car is not beautiful in fact it has patches of rust all over it.

3. I wanted a new sports car however I had to settle for a used sedan.

4. My new car uses too much gas in addition it constantly needs repairs.

5. Russell says that his car will last only one more year on the contrary I know it has more miles left in it than that.

NAME _____ DATE _____

INSTRUCTOR _____ CLASS TIME _____

6. Letitia's car on the contrary will not run through this next winter.

   _____

7. Cars like hers on the other hand have been known to run fifteen years.

   _____

8. I have driven my old Ford for twelve years consequently I am now looking for a new model.

   _____

9. I hope that my parents will give me the down payment for my car otherwise I must get a loan from the bank.

   _____

10. On cold mornings my car refuses to start hence I am getting a new battery before next winter.

   _____

© NTC/CONTEMPORARY PUBLISHING COMPANY

PRACTICE
EXERCISE 3-6

WRITING COMPOUND SENTENCES

Each of the following items contains two separate independent clauses. Combine these into a compound sentence using the type of connective indicated at the beginning of each line. Punctuate correctly.

EXAMPLE: The squirrels walked up to Sarah. She fed them some of her popcorn.

CC (Coordinate Conjunction): *The squirrels walked up to Sarah, so she fed them some of her popcorn.*

SM (Sentence Modifier): *The squirrels walked up to Sarah; as a result, she fed them some of her popcorn.*

CA (Conjunctive Adverb): *The squirrels walked up to Sarah; consequently, she fed them some of her popcorn.*

1. Itamar lost his driver's license. He had to apply for a new one.

CC: _____

_____

SM: _____

_____

CA: _____

_____

NAME _____ DATE _____

INSTRUCTOR _____ CLASS TIME _____

2. The police thought the accident was Amit's fault. It was Roger's.

CC: _____

_____

SM: _____

_____

CA: _____

_____

3. Maya was determined to work on the computer program until the lab closed. She might not finish by the deadline.

CC: _____

_____

SM: _____

_____

CA: _____

_____

4. The defendant confessed to stealing the bicycle from the garage. He did not confess to taking some jewelry from the bedroom.

CC: _____

_____

SM: _____

_____

CA: _____

_____

5. The grocery store was out of skim and 2% milk. She bought whole milk.

CC: _____

_____

SM: _____

_____

CA: _____

_____

TABLE 3.4 *Summary of Punctuation Patterns*

Four Punctuation Rules for Joining Two Independent Clauses

1. Two independent clauses can be joined by a semicolon if the ideas of each are closely related.
   IC; IC.
2. Two independent clauses can be joined by a coordinating conjunction (or a connective). This is the only time you can put a comma between two independent clauses.
   IC, (coordinating conjunction) IC.

and	so
but	yet
for	
or	
nor	

3. Two independent clauses can be joined by a semicolon followed by a conjunctive adverb and a comma.
   IC; (conjunctive adverb), IC.

also	moreover
anyway	nevertheless
besides	otherwise
consequently	still
furthermore	therefore
hence	thus
however	then
indeed	(Do not use a comma after
instead	this conjunctive adverb.)

4. Two independent clauses can be joined by a semicolon followed by a sentence modifier and a comma.
   IC; (sentence modifier), IC.

as a result	in fact
for example	in other words
in addition	on the contrary
on the other hand	

Punctuation Rule for Interrupters

An independent clause can be interrupted by any of the following. A comma would be placed on each side of each of these interrupters.
- conjunctive adverb of two or more syllables
- sentence modifier
- parenthetical expression

REVIEW	# COORDINATING CONJUNCTIONS
EXERCISE 3-1	

DIRECTIONS: Punctuate the following sentences. Do not change the word order or insert words; do not make two simple sentences. If no punctuation is needed, write *none* in the blank provided.

_____ 1. The old car sitting in our driveway has been wrecked and the previous owner sold it to me for a good price.

_____ 2. The car is noisy when I first start it in the morning but it quiets down when the engine gets warmed up.

_____ 3. We sifted the flour for the angel food cake and measured it in our new plastic measuring cups.

_____ 4. Flour for an angel food cake must be sifted three times so we took turns with the flour sifter.

_____ 5. The taxpayer with a late return may claim a shortage of money or he may blame his accountant for the lateness.

_____ 6. The taxpayer with a late return may claim a shortage of money or blame his accountant for the lateness.

_____ 7. The girls do not have a game tonight nor do they have one tomorrow.

_____ 8. The pizza recipe called for cheddar cheese and ground beef mixed with onions.

_____ 9. The pizza recipe called for cheddar cheese and I found none in our refrigerator.

_____ 10. The rural areas have a pleasant atmosphere and give me a feeling of peace.

_____ 11. The rural areas have a pleasant atmosphere and they give people a peaceful feeling.

_____ 12. She went through the textbook hurriedly but her comprehension of the material was amazing.

NAME _____ DATE _____

INSTRUCTOR _____ CLASS TIME _____

_____ 13. She went through the textbook carefully and had an amazing comprehension of the material.

_____ 14. Three of the editors argued against the article and voted to reject its publication in the newspaper.

_____ 15. You can correct your weaknesses in English by yourself or you can get a tutor at the writing lab.

_____ 16. Synthetic fabrics should be washed in cool water and dried on the gentle cycle of the clothes dryer.

_____ 17. Synthetic fabrics should be washed in cool water and they should be dried on the gentle cycle of the clothes dryer.

_____ 18. Brandon dated one girl from his high school and another from his brother's college in Mississippi.

_____ 19. Brandon married his high school sweetheart and they moved from Mississippi to a town in Georgia.

_____ 20. Brandon and his new wife moved to Atlanta in June and started working for a national phone company in July.

REVIEW EXERCISE 3-2 — CONJUNCTIVE ADVERBS, SENTENCE MODIFIERS, AND INTERRUPTERS

DIRECTIONS: Punctuate each of the following sentences. Do not change the word order or insert words; do not make two simple sentences.

1. Your firm has not given us good service during the last month however we have previously been pleased and hope for improved relations.

2. I am not however canceling my last order.

3. I don't believe that I have seen Jan's new haircut on the other hand I may have seen it last week.

4. I like Jan's hair cut short her boyfriend on the other hand likes long hair.

5. The accountant found the error in the figures in fact her firm received a bonus.

6. The accountant found the error in the figures her firm in fact received a bonus for her help.

7. The jet is faster than many planes and is thought in addition to be safer than most.

8. The jet is faster than many planes in addition it is thought to be safer than most.

9. Homework should be done each night of the week however some students procrastinate during the week and study only on Sunday afternoon.

10. Homework should be done each night of the week students may however use the weekend for review of their class notes.

11. I have a lot of homework for example I have spent four hours on accounting each night this quarter.

NAME _____ DATE _____

INSTRUCTOR _____ CLASS TIME _____

12. Last night for example we had one problem which took over an hour.

13. I opened my accounting book and started studying the assigned chapter then I realized that my calculator was at home.

14. For ten weeks I studied accounting every night as a result I scored a 96 percent on the last test and earned a high grade in that class.

15. I studied accounting every night and as a result scored a 96 percent on the test.

16. Wendy and Wilma are identical twins hence they often share opinions.

17. Wilma thought the play was very long nevertheless she enjoyed the witty dialogue and the excellent acting.

18. Wendy thought the play was very long she enjoyed nevertheless the witty dialogue and the excellent acting.

19. My vacation last summer was wonderful indeed it was nearly perfect.

20. I want to recapture my experience of last summer thus I will go back to the same town and live in the same house for a few weeks.

REVIEW EXERCISE 3-3 — PUNCTUATION OF COMPOUND SENTENCES

DIRECTIONS: Punctuate the following sentences. Do not change the word order or insert words; do not make two simple sentences. If no punctuation is needed, write *none* in the blank provided.

_____ 1. The snow was very deep he could not drive his car to school.

_____ 2. The snow was very deep and he could not drive his car to school.

_____ 3. The snow was very deep therefore he could not drive his car to school.

_____ 4. The snow was very deep he did however get his car out of the garage and into the driveway.

_____ 5. The snow made driving hazardous nevertheless most students were planning to drive to the concert.

_____ 6. He could not drive his car to school for the battery was dead and would not start.

_____ 7. He could not even start the car for his neighbors across the street.

_____ 8. He shoveled the neighbor's driveway and pushed two stranded cars out of snowdrifts.

_____ 9. He must get his car started then he can attend his classes and run errands on the way home.

_____ 10. The snow was very deep and wet moreover the temperature stayed near zero all day.

_____ 11. The snow was very deep and wet the temperature moreover stayed near zero all day.

_____ 12. His new car would not start consequently he asked a neighbor for a ride to school and left his car in the garage all day.

_____ 13. His new car would not start furthermore the windshield was covered with two inches of snow and a very thin sheet of solid ice.

NAME _____ DATE _____

INSTRUCTOR _____ CLASS TIME _____

_____ 14. His new car would not start in other words the battery was dead.

_____ 15. He could not start his car the battery in other words was dead.

_____ 16. The beautiful snow was wet and heavy it was perfect for making a snowman.

_____ 17. The beautiful snow was wet and heavy thus it was perfect for making a snowman.

_____ 18. The beautiful snow was wet and heavy so the neighbor's children were making a snowman.

_____ 19. The beautiful snow was wet and heavy many children as a result were making snowmen.

_____ 20. I spent the entire day inside by the fire and watched the beauty of the falling snow.

CHAPTER QUIZ 3-1 PUNCTUATION OF COMPOUND SENTENCES

DIRECTIONS: Punctuate the following sentences. Do not change the word order or insert words; do not make two simple sentences. If no punctuation is needed, write *none* in the blank provided.

_____ 1. A college education gives people new insights into themselves and shows them the ideas and attitudes of other people.

_____ 2. Going to college takes determination and requires a great deal of self-discipline.

_____ 3. Going to college is wise for some people yet it is unnecessary for others.

_____ 4. Miguel must attend some college in Indiana next year or he will not receive a scholarship from that state.

_____ 5. Shayna is not going to college next year nor will she be returning soon.

_____ 6. Alana on the other hand is attending college next year she is preparing for a job in computer programming.

_____ 7. He is quitting his job at the factory and going to college factory work generally speaking is not giving him satisfaction.

_____ 8. Dave will return to graduate school next fall he must as a result save some money during the coming months.

_____ 9. Jamal will return to college for a degree in business administration however he has had very little previous experience in business.

_____ 10. Lin-Wen will return to a technical college in September she will however transfer to a four-year college during her junior year.

_____ 11. Dave attended a good liberal arts college in West Virginia and received excellent preparation for graduate school.

NAME _____ DATE _____

INSTRUCTOR _____ CLASS TIME _____

_____ 12. The women will finish college in June then they will search for jobs in computer programming and business administration.

_____ 13. College students gain knowledge about their major area of study and learn self-discipline in the use of time and money.

_____ 14. The brothers will soon be attending college they will spend their time wisely or fail the difficult and demanding courses.

_____ 15. They will try in other words to keep a balance between social and academic life many students waste time and money before they achieve this balance.

_____ 16. Many bright people as a matter of fact do not attend any college their goals can be reached without a bachelor's degree.

_____ 17. College is not necessary for all people thus each person must decide whether a degree should be included in his or her future.

_____ 18. College is not necessary for everyone on the contrary many people do not need a college degree to obtain a satisfying job.

_____ 19. College is not necessary for everyone many adults live fulfilled lives and have no college degree.

_____ 20. Satisfying jobs often do not require a college degree in fact the majority of people do not need a bachelor's or master's degree.

© NTC/CONTEMPORARY PUBLISHING COMPANY

CHAPTER QUIZ 3-2   PUNCTUATION OF COMPOUND SENTENCES

DIRECTIONS: Punctuate the following sentences. Do not change the word order or insert words; do not make two simple sentences. If no punctuation is needed, write *none* in the blank provided.

_____ 1. Finding meaning in life is difficult and takes all of a person's effort.

_____ 2. Many parents make it difficult for their teenagers yet they do not realize this.

_____ 3. Adults in society give students a great deal of advice they often I regret to say are only repeating worn-out phrases.

_____ 4. Each person must set his or her own goals for no one can give peace of mind to someone else.

_____ 5. Many people seek contentment in wealth few people find it there.

_____ 6. Power, prestige, and money are often presented by adults as the keys to success and many teenagers blindly follow this example.

_____ 7. Two of our friends wanted to attend a well-known university so they sent applications to Harvard and Yale.

_____ 8. They attended classes that they disliked and learned subjects that they detested then they were surprised to find their lives were meaningless and joyless.

_____ 9. These friends earned large salaries after college and disliked every aspect of the jobs bringing them this income.

_____ 10. Students must trust their common sense or they will spend their lives in unsatisfying jobs and discover the frustration of wasted dreams.

_____ 11. Many teenagers surprisingly enough have neither interest nor ability in academic subjects and should not attend college.

NAME _____ DATE _____

INSTRUCTOR _____ CLASS TIME _____

_____ 12. College takes a great amount of time and money and is not a wise choice for everyone attending college does not guarantee personal satisfaction.

_____ 13. Thousands of people have satisfying jobs on the other hand many of them do not have a college degree.

_____ 14. Many people with satisfying jobs on the other hand do have a college degree.

_____ 15. A college degree does not assure high wages on the contrary many skilled workers earn more than college graduates.

_____ 16. A college degree does not assure high wages many skilled workers as a matter of fact earn more than college graduates.

_____ 17. Going to college often brings a student personal growth therefore many gains are not financial.

_____ 18. A college degree does not assure high wages the degree can however promote personal growth and increase self-discipline.

_____ 19. A college degree does not assure high wages however it can promote personal growth and increase self-discipline.

_____ 20. Some people need a college education others will never need one.

4

PUNCTUATION SEPARATING ELEMENTS IN A SENTENCE

Whenever you have ideas in your mind and want to communicate them to the mind of another person, you either talk to or write to that person. The ability to write clear sentences and to punctuate them correctly is essential to communication. Now that you know how to punctuate compound sentences and interrupters, you'll want to learn how to punctuate introductory elements and items in a series. Remember that punctuation marks are for your reader's benefit, making it easier for him or her to know what is in your mind and for you to communicate effectively through writing.

SEPARATING INTRODUCTORY ELEMENTS

An introductory element is a group of words that comes before the independent clause in a sentence. The most common introductory elements are dependent clauses, prepositional phrases, and verbal phrases. These introductory elements are usually separated from the independent clause with a comma.

Dependent Clause Before an Independent Clause

As you have learned, a dependent clause has a verb and a subject, but it can't stand alone. When standing alone between a capital letter and end punctuation, a dependent clause becomes a sentence fragment, a major error to be avoided in standard written English. Yet, when this same dependent group of words is attached to an independent clause, it becomes a complete, well-written sentence.

Dependent clauses begin with either subordinating conjunctions or relative pronouns. We are going to emphasize the punctuation of clauses that begin

TABLE 4.1	*Common Subordinating Conjunctions*	
after	since
although	though
as	unless
because	until
before	when
if	where
once	while

with subordinating conjunctions (see Table 4.1), for they are the ones that you, as a beginning writer, need to master first.

These subordinating conjunctions join parts of a sentence that have unequal value, in contrast to coordinating conjunctions, which join parts of a sentence that are of equal value. Therefore, subordinating conjunctions introduce clauses that are dependent on the independent clause for their meaning.

Look at the following:

When I am crossing a busy street, I am very careful.

As I cross a busy street at 5:00, I use caution.

As you have learned, the group of words before the comma in each sentence above is a dependent clause. It cannot stand alone and make sense. For example, you could not write *When I am crossing a busy street.* Neither could you write *As I cross a busy street at 5:00.* Therefore, the meaning for the above sentences comes only when the dependent clause is attached to an independent clause.

Most instructors and texts tell students to use a comma to set off long introductory dependent clauses that come before an independent clause. Inevitably, the first question students ask is: "How long is *long?*" It is a sensible question with no easy answer. But to help your understanding, consider any dependent clause five words or longer to be long enough to require a comma after it. Using this rule as a guide, you will seldom place commas where they are not needed. Note that it is never wrong to use a comma after a dependent clause, regardless of its length; however, failing to put commas after long introductory dependent clauses confuses the reader. Therefore, the rule can read: Use a comma to set off long (five words or more) introductory dependent clauses.

If a dependent clause follows an independent clause, however, it seldom has to be set off with a comma. Therefore, we will apply the rule that dependent clauses that follow independent clauses do not usually have to be set off with

© NTC/CONTEMPORARY PUBLISHING COMPANY

commas. Of course, there are exceptions to this rule, but these exceptions can be learned more easily later in your composition education.

Look at the following sentences:

I am very careful when I am crossing a busy street.

I use caution as I cross a busy street at 5:00.

I always slow down before I cross a busy street at 5:00.

Because these dependent clauses follow independent clauses, there is no comma after *careful, caution,* or *down.*

PRACTICE	# INTRODUCTORY DEPENDENT
EXERCISE 4-1	CLAUSES

Decide where the comma should be inserted (if at all) in each of the following sentences. In the blank provided, write the word before each comma, the comma, and the word after it. Place a C in the blank if the sentence is correct.

EXAMPLE: _day, we_ Although it had been raining all day we went to the football game.

_____ 1. As we left the house for the trip to the football game the rain drenched us.

_____ 2. After we left the house for the trip to the football game the wind started blowing.

_____ 3. The wind started blowing after we left the house for the game.

_____ 4. It started raining as we left the house for the game.

_____ 5. While we were driving to the game it started raining.

_____ 6. When the wind was blowing and the rain was pouring we almost went back home.

_____ 7. We almost returned home when the rain began coming down in sheets.

_____ 8. Because this game was an important one for the team we ignored the wind and rain.

_____ 9. If our team could win this important game we would get into the play-offs.

_____ 10. Before we won the football game the sun came out.

NAME _____ DATE _____

INSTRUCTOR _____ CLASS TIME _____

| PRACTICE | **USING DEPENDENT CLAUSES** |
| EXERCISE 4-2 | |

In this exercise, you will create ten sentences. Five will have the dependent clause *before* the independent clause, and five will have the dependent clause *after* the independent clause. In each sentence use the listed subordinate conjunction at the beginning of the dependent clause and attach that dependent clause to an independent clause. Correctly punctuate your sentences.

EXAMPLE: When *I answered the phone, the caller hung up.*

In these five sentences, put the dependent clause *before* the independent clause.

1. Although _____

2. Since _____

3. Unless _____

4 While _____

5. Until _____

In the next five sentences, put the dependent clause *after* the independent clause.

6. _____ when _____

7. _____ after _____

8. _____ if _____

9. _____ whenever _____

10. _____ before _____

NAME _____ DATE _____

INSTRUCTOR _____ CLASS TIME _____

Prepositional Phrase Before an Independent Clause

Use a comma to set off a long series (five words or more) of introductory prepositional phrases or one long introductory prepositional phrase.

Consider the following sentences:

In the basement of our home on McKinley Street, my mother stored fruit.

In our convenient, huge, cool, dark basement, my mother stored fruit.

In the first sentence, the three prepositional phrases are italicized; the comma goes after the *last* prepositional phrase in the series. In the second sentence, the prepositional phrase is italicized; the comma goes after the last word of the long introductory prepositional phrase.

Since prepositional phrases consist of prepositions followed by nouns or pronouns, you will want to review the list of prepositions given in Table 1.4 on page 23. Notice that some of these prepositions also serve as subordinating conjunctions; therefore, they might introduce either a prepositional phrase or a dependent clause. Beware of *after, as, before, since,* and *until,* which can be used as both. To see how these words can function as both prepositions and subordinating conjunctions, consider these sentences:

After my very difficult test *in* Chinese, I was exhausted.

After I took my very difficult test in Chinese, I was exhausted.

Before the day *of* my very difficult test *in* calculus, I studied.

Before I took my very difficult test in calculus, I studied.

In the first and third sentences, the prepositions are italicized. The first sentence has two prepositional phrases before the independent clause, and the last phrase is followed by a comma. The third sentence has three prepositional phrases before the independent clause, and the last phrase is followed by a comma. In contrast, the second and fourth sentences have a dependent clause before the independent clause; each is followed by a comma.

TRY-IT

EXERCISE

Identify each introductory element in the following sentences as a prepositional phrase (PP) or a dependent clause (DC).

1. After the game at the stadium, we ate at McDonald's.
   After we went to the game at the stadium, we ate at McDonald's.

2. Before the game with the toughest team in town, our school was unbeaten.
   Before we played the toughest team in town, our school was unbeaten.

3. Since the game with our biggest rivals, our school has only one defeat.
   Since we lost the game with our biggest rivals, we have only one defeat.

4. Until conference play in January, our teams will not meet again.
   Until we play them during conference in January, our teams will not meet again.

The first sentence in each pair has a series of prepositional phrases for an introductory element, and the second sentence in each pair has a dependent clause. All these introductory elements should be followed by a comma.

© NTC/CONTEMPORARY PUBLISHING COMPANY

PRACTICE EXERCISE 4-3
IDENTIFICATION OF PREPOSITIONAL PHRASES

Underline the prepositions that introduce the prepositional phrases in the following introductory elements.

EXAMPLE: <u>Above</u> the picture <u>on</u> the wall <u>of</u> my bedroom, I saw a spider.

1. On a shelf in the closet of my bedroom, my shoes are easy to find.

2. In the kitchen after a dinner for ten people, Mother looked tired.

3. At the end of our driveway, the snowplow left piles of dirty snow.

4. Before my first test during finals week at college, I was nervous.

5. After my final test in English class, I felt great.

6. Under the car in our garage, our dog takes naps.

7. Behind the house across the street from us, Mrs. Wallace has a garden.

8. About halfway between our houses, a hedge of bushes blooms each spring.

9. With a jump rope in her hand, Mindy asked me to play.

10. Around nine o'clock at night on Mondays, I'm leaving class.

NAME _____ DATE _____

INSTRUCTOR _____ CLASS TIME _____

PRACTICE	# USING PREPOSITIONAL
EXERCISE 4-4	# PHRASES

The following exercise items have a preposition listed at the beginning. Create a sentence using the preposition in an initial prepositional phrase or a series of prepositional phrases (do not create a clause); attach these introductory phrases to a dependent clause and punctuate according to the rule.

EXAMPLE: Of _all the available styles, I like antique furniture the most._

1. Inside _____

2. Beside _____

3. Without _____

4. For _____

5. Within _____

6. Along _____

7. Above _____

8. Below _____

9. Between _____

10. Past _____

NAME _____ DATE _____

INSTRUCTOR _____ CLASS TIME _____

Verbal Phrase Before an Independent Clause

Both types of verbal phrases—verb + -ing and to + a verb—are set off by a comma when used at the beginning of a sentence to modify the independent clause. Use a comma to set off a long (five words or more) introductory phrase or a string of prepositional phrases (five words or more) that begin with a verb + -ing or to + a verb.

VERB + -ING PHRASE RULE.   The verb + -ing is one of the most common types of verbal phrases. We are dealing here with participial and gerund phrases, but at this stage in your learning, you do not need to know these terms. As discussed in Chapter 1, if you have a verb + -ing (and if it does not have a helping verb with it), you have a *verbal*, not a main verb. If that verbal has related words with it (and they are not helping verbs), you have a *verbal phrase*.

Look at the following sentences:

Looking for a major area of study, Geraldo considered business.

Making such a difficult decision, Geraldo felt confused.

Suffering the pangs of indecision, Geraldo talked to his dad.

In each of these sentences, the introductory element lacks a main verb; therefore, each is a verbal phrase. The verbals are *Looking, Making,* and *Suffering;* the verbal phrases are *Looking for a major area of study, Making such a difficult decision,* and *Suffering the pangs of indecision.* Remember that clauses have main verbs, but phrases do not.

Do not set off verbal phrases when they serve as the subject of the independent clause. Look at the following sentences:

Eating burritos, tacos, and rice, Maria enjoyed the dinner.

Eating burritos, tacos, and rice is enjoyable.

Cooking a huge dinner for a family of four, Maria had fun.

Cooking a huge dinner for a family of four takes a great deal of time.

The first and third sentences have an introductory verbal phrase before the independent clause; therefore, each of these verbal phrases is followed by a comma. In contrast, the second and fourth sentences have a verbal phrase used as the subject of the sentence. In the second sentence, *Eating burritos, tacos, and rice* serves as the subject of the main verb *is.* In the fourth sentence, *Cooking a huge dinner for a family of four* serves as the subject of the main verb *takes.*

TRY-IT

EXERCISE

Put brackets around each verbal phrase in the following sentences and parentheses around each dependent clause. If there is no verbal phrase or dependent clause, write *none* in the blank provided.

_____ 1. Selecting economics for his major, Luis felt confident that he'd be accepted into the MBA program.

_____ 2. Selecting economics for his major will be Luis's ticket into the MBA program.

_____ 3. A major in economics will be Luis's ticket into the MBA program.

_____ 4. Because Luis selected economics as his major, he should be accepted into the MBA program.

The verbal phrase in the first sentence is *selecting economics for his major.* This verbal phrase modifies the word *Luis,* which is the subject of the sentence. The verbal phrase in the second sentence is also *selecting economics for his major,* but this phrase does not modify the subject; rather, it is the subject of the entire sentence and is not set off by a comma. The verbal phrase in the second sentence is just as much the subject of the sentence as the word *major* is the subject of the third sentence. Both answer the question: "Who or what *will be?*" The third sentence, however, has no verbal phrase and no dependent clause. This sentence has the verb phrase *will be,* the subject *major,* and the direct object *ticket.* The introductory element in the fourth sentence is a dependent clause because it has a main verb and a subject and is introduced by a subordinating conjunction.

© NTC/CONTEMPORARY PUBLISHING COMPANY

PRACTICE	# IDENTIFYING VERB + -ING PHRASES
EXERCISE 4-5	

Put parentheses around the verbal that introduces any verbal phrase in the following sentences.

EXAMPLE: (Sitting) at the dinner table last Sunday, Mark announced his marriage.

1. I saw Mark sitting with Rachel at the game.

2. Sitting on our lawn chairs is relaxing.

3. Selecting Mrs. Lopez from many applicants, the principal hired a good teacher.

4. I saw the principal sorting the applications into piles.

5. Selecting a good teacher takes time.

6. Working on his car for over a month, Antonio found the problem.

7. I found Antonio working on his car.

8. Working on a car demands patience and skill.

9. Tiffany is the student getting all the correct answers.

10. Getting all the correct answers, Tiffany earned an A.

NAME _____   DATE _____

INSTRUCTOR _____   CLASS TIME _____

PRACTICE EXERCISE 4-6

USING VERB + ING PHRASES

The verbal phrase in each sentence below is the subject of the sentence. Rewrite the sentence making the verbal phrase an introductory element. To do this, copy the verbal phrase, placing it before your independent clause. This will require adding and/or rearranging words in your independent clause. Then punctuate the sentence.

EXAMPLE: Asking his teacher lots of questions helped John learn the material.

Asking his teacher lots of questions, John learned the material.

1. Watching a ball game live for the first time is thrilling for children.

2. Changing the oil in her own car saves Lia money.

3. Gazing at the sunset over the ocean was a beautiful sight to Nora.

4. Getting candid pictures of movie stars is a photographer's goal.

5. Shopping at flea markets around town saves money for some people.

6. Running up the stairs as fast as he can makes Jason tired.

7. Sending credit cards to graduates is considered a low risk by banks.

8. Skipping breaks on a long car trip is dangerous to me and to other drivers.

9. Playing tennis daily keeps Choon and Noh in shape.

10. Listening to soft music during surgery calms the doctors and nurses.

NAME _____ DATE _____

INSTRUCTOR _____ CLASS TIME _____

© NTC/CONTEMPORARY PUBLISHING COMPANY

T̲O̲ + A VERB PHRASE RULE.   Use a comma to set off a long (five words or more) introductory *to* + a verb phrase.

We are dealing here with infinitive phrases, but again you do not need to understand that term. Do not confuse *to* + a verb with prepositional phrases. If *to* is followed by a verb, it's a verbal phrase, but if it is followed by a noun or pronoun, it's a prepositional phrase.

Read the following sentences:

To study for my test in economics, I reviewed my class notes.

I took my books *to the study hall.*

To exercise on a daily basis, Connie and Dave get up early each morning.

Connie and Dave go *to the bike trail* on the river each morning.

The first and third sentences have a verbal phrase of *to* plus a verb at the beginning, and the second and fourth sentences have a prepositional phrase of *to* plus a noun in them.

Once again, as with *-ing* verbals, do not set off the verbal phrase when it serves as the subject of the sentence. Look at the following sentences:

To eat sushi, shrimp tempura, and rice for dinner, Sachi skipped lunch.

To eat sushi, shrimp tempura, and rice is enjoyable.

To cook dinner for a family of four, Sachi planned in advance.

To cook dinner for a family of four takes a great deal of time.

The first and third sentences have an introductory verbal phrase before the independent clause; therefore, each of these verbal phrases is followed by a comma. In contrast, the second and fourth sentences have a verbal phrase used as the subject of the sentence. In the second sentence, *To eat sushi, shrimp tempura, and rice* serves as the subject of the main verb *is.* In the fourth sentence, *To cook dinner for a family of four* serves as the subject of the main verb *takes.*

TRY-IT
EXERCISE

For each of the following sentences, put parentheses around each verbal phrase and underline each dependent clause. If there is no verbal phrase or dependent clause, write *none* in the blank provided.

————   1.   To make a better grade in economics, Aisha needs more study time at night.

© NTC/CONTEMPORARY PUBLISHING COMPANY

_____ 2. To make a better grade in economics is his goal.

_____ 3. A good grade in economics is Aisha's goal.

_____ 4. Although Aisha wants to make a good grade in economics, he does not study at night.

The first sentence begins with the verbal phrase *to make a better grade in economics* and is set off with a comma because it modifies the separately stated subject *Aisha.* In the second sentence the verbal phrase *to make a better grade in economics* is not a modifier but is the subject of the entire sentence and is not set off by a comma. The verbal phrase in the second sentence is as much the subject of the verb *is* as the word *grade* is the subject of the third sentence; however, the third sentence has no verbal phrase and no dependent clause. It consists of the main verb *is,* the subject *grade,* and the direct object *goal.* The introductory element in the fourth sentence is a dependent clause because it has a main verb and a subject and is introduced by a subordinating conjunction.

In summary, a comma is used to set off long (five words or more) introductory dependent clauses, prepositional phrases, and verbal phrases. Verbal phrases begin with both a verb + *-ing* and *to* + a verb.

PRACTICE	# IDENTIFICATION OF <u>TO</u> + A VERB
EXERCISE 4-7	# PHRASES

Put parentheses around any *to* + a verb that introduces any verbal phrase.

EXAMPLE: (To practice) for the contest, she gave the talk twenty times.

1. To graduate with honors in chemistry, Leon went to classes and took good notes.

2. To earn a bachelor's degree is an accomplishment.

3. Jong wants to borrow ten dollars, so he can go to the movies.

4. To earn his tuition for college, Tony works at King's Island in the summer.

5. To be a good employee at the amusement park, Tony goes to work early.

6. To work on his car is Ira's idea of a good time.

7. He actually likes to get his hands dirty.

8. To make good grades in literature classes, students go to the library for research.

9. To lend money is a risk to the lender.

10. Elaine wants to stop by the grocery store tonight.

NAME _____   DATE _____

INSTRUCTOR _____   CLASS TIME _____

PRACTICE	# USING <u>TO</u> + A VERB PHRASES
EXERCISE 4-8	

For each verbal phrase that follows, write two sentences. The first sentence should use the verbal phrase as the subject. The second sentence should use the verbal phrase as an introductory element. Circle the subject of each sentence.

EXAMPLE: To earn a college degree

(To earn a college degree) takes time and effort.

To earn a college degree, a (student) must spend time and effort.

1. To water the flowers in dry weather

   _____

   _____

2. To exercise on a regular basis

   _____

   _____

3. To watch television day and night

   _____

   _____

4. To volunteer to help in the Special Olympics

   _____

   _____

5. To own a pet dog or cat

   _____

   _____

NAME _____ DATE _____

INSTRUCTOR _____ CLASS TIME _____

SEPARATING ITEMS IN A SERIES

A series contains three or more parallel elements, and any of the coordinating conjunctions may be used to connect the last two.

▼ **RULE:** Use commas to separate words, phrases, or clauses in a series.

Consider the following sentences:

Texts, pamphlets, schedules, and notebooks were under the students' desks.

Students usually leave their texts, schedules, or notebooks under their desks.

Our teacher will give tests after the first unit, near midterm, and during finals.

Fulfillment comes when you have work to do, when you have goals to accomplish, and when you have someone to love.

The first two sentences are examples of words in a series. In the first sentence, *texts, pamphlets, schedules,* and *notebooks* are separated by commas. In the second sentence, *tests, schedules,* and *notebooks* are separated by commas. Note that the items in the first sentence are joined by *and,* but the items in the second sentence are joined by *or.* In the third sentence the prepositional phrases *after the first unit, near midterm,* and *during finals* are separated by commas. Finally, in the fourth sentence the independent clauses *when you have work to do, when you have goals to accomplish,* and *when you have someone to love* are separated by commas.

The comma before the coordinating conjunction is omitted by some writers, but its use may prevent misreading; therefore, the *U.S. Government Printing Office Style Manual* requires the comma. Using the comma will confuse no one; omitting it may. Always use the comma before the coordinating conjunction when there are three or more items in a series.

TRY-IT
EXERCISE

Look at the following sentences containing words in a series. Set off the items in the series by inserting commas where needed.

1. Keisha likes bowling golfing and swimming.
2. Their neighbors are engineers accountants or professors.

3. That sweat suit comes in aqua lavender or pink.
4. Trevor Abigail and Lindsey live next door.
5. For breakfast we had ham and eggs orange juice and muffins.

Each example has three items that need to be separated by commas. For example, in sentence one there should be one comma after *bowling* and another after *golfing*. In sentence two there should be one comma after *engineers* and another after *accountants*. In sentence three there should be one comma after *aqua* and another after *lavender*. In sentence four there should be one comma after *Trevor* and another after *Abigail*. Note that in sentence five, *ham and eggs* is one unit. Words used customarily in pairs are set off as one item: *bacon and eggs, bread and butter, profit and loss*. Therefore, in sentence five there should be a comma after *eggs* and another after *juice*.

TRY-IT
EXERCISE

Look at the following phrases in a series. Set off the phrases by inserting commas where needed.

1. The stream runs through the culvert over the backyard and down the hill.
2. He spent the hour explaining his proposal answering questions and defending his position.
3. Amber answered the phone reached for her calendar and wrote in her date book.
4. Fixing breakfast answering the phone and writing a grocery list can be done simultaneously.
5. The car swerved around the corner across the yard and into our mailbox.

Each item has three phrases that need to be separated. For example, in sentence one there should be a comma after *culvert* and after *backyard*. In sentence two, there should be one comma after *proposal* and another after *questions*. In sentence three, there should be a comma after *phone* and another after *calendar*. In sentence four, there should be a comma after *breakfast* and *phone*, but be sure you do not put

a comma after *list*. In sentence five, there should be a
comma after *corner* and another after *yard*.

TRY-IT
EXERCISE

Look at the following clauses in a series. Set off the
clauses by inserting commas where needed.

1. Life is great when you feel loved when you know you are
   valued and when you have good health.
2. Go to the bookstore buy the textbook and read the first
   chapter before Friday's class.
3. The doctor told Earlene that she should eat more slowly
   take a calcium supplement daily and exercise more
   often.
4. Good friends are those who listen to you who cheer for
   you and who cry with you.
5. Will you rinse the dishes fill the dishwasher and wipe
   the countertop before you leave the kitchen?

Each item has three clauses that need to be separated.
For example, in sentence one commas go after *loved* and
valued. In sentence two, commas go after *bookstore* and *textbook*. In sentence three, commas go after *slowly* and *daily*. In
sentence four, commas go after *to you* and *for you*. Finally, in
sentence five, commas go after *dishes* and *dishwasher*.

PRACTICE	# PUNCTUATION OF ITEMS IN A
EXERCISE 4-9	# SERIES

Insert the commas (if needed) where they should go in each sentence.

EXAMPLE: Our school is using team teaching for psychology, sociology, and philosophy.

1. I have enjoyed the psychology class that is taught by Dr. Hatch Ms. McQuire and Mr. North.

2. They plan the lessons invite the speakers hold discussions and grade papers.

3. I have found the lectures to be educational enjoyable and helpful.

4. Dr. Hatch is a short overweight cheerful teacher.

5. Each student must listen to lectures discuss the readings and write critiques.

6. The class requires skill in listening reading and writing.

7. Tests are given at the beginning of the quarter around midterm and during finals.

8. Mr. North told us to attend all lectures to write five critiques and to study for all tests.

9. Next year Miss McQuire will teach Psychology I in the fall Child Development II in the winter and Psychology of Aging in the spring.

10. Jamal Lia Chris and I have already enrolled in Psychology of Aging.

NAME _____ DATE _____

INSTRUCTOR _____ CLASS TIME _____

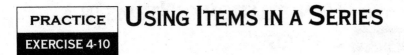

Each of the following numbers has a list of items. Create a sentence using the list and correctly punctuate it.

EXAMPLE:　paper pencils erasers

Having plenty of paper, pencils, and erasers is important during a test.

1.　hammer pliers screwdriver

2.　eating nutritiously exercising regularly relaxing mentally

3.　bacon and eggs toast and butter coffee and cream

4.　standing in a line sitting in a traffic jam waiting in a doctor's office

5.　deposit money in the bank purchase groceries buy gas for the car

6.　when I am tired when I am hungry when I am hot

7.　to wash to wax to buff

8.　the water the air the food

9.　fresh fruits garden vegetables whole wheat bread skim milk

10.　over the mountains through the forests across the deserts

NAME _____　DATE _____

INSTRUCTOR _____　CLASS TIME _____

© NTC/CONTEMPORARY PUBLISHING COMPANY

SUMMARY OF PUNCTUATION PATTERNS

Two Punctuation Rules for Separating Introductory Elements

Introductory dependent clauses are usually followed by a comma. Subordinating conjunctions often begin dependent clauses and are *dependent* clause signals; hence, they can be called *fragment catchers.*

(Subordinating Conjunction) DC, IC.

after	since
although	though
as	unless
because	until
before	when
if	where
once	while

Note: Usually no comma is needed if the dependent clause *follows* the IC.

Introductory phrases are usually followed by a comma.:

Prepositional Phrase, IC.

Verbal Phrase, IC.

    (Verb plus *-ing*)

    (*To* plus verb)

Three Punctuation Rules for Separating Items in a Series

Words, phrases, and **clauses** in a series of three or more items are separated by a comma.

word, word, and word

phrase, phrase, and phrase

dependent clause, dependent clause, and dependent clause

REVIEW	**PUNCTUATION OF**
EXERCISE 4-1	**INTRODUCTORY ELEMENTS**

DIRECTIONS: Punctuate the following sentences. If a sentence needs no punctuation, write *none* in the blank provided.

_____ 1. If I go on the trip to Atlanta next weekend I will tell him to write.

_____ 2. When I saw that there was going to be difficulty with a nonstop flight I withdrew my request.

_____ 3. I withdrew my request for a nonstop flight when I saw that there was going to be difficulty.

_____ 4. Because the last day for reservations was Friday I took an unwanted schedule.

_____ 5. After I had taken all that time and trouble I was glad to leave.

_____ 6. I was glad to leave after all the time and trouble.

_____ 7. While the flight attendants were fixing sandwiches the passengers got comfortable in their seats.

_____ 8. The passengers got comfortable in their seats while the flight attendants were fixing sandwiches.

_____ 9. As the plane rose into the sky above the airport I watched the fields on the ground below.

_____ 10. I watched the fields on the ground below as the plane rose into the sky above the airport.

_____ 11. Since I have returned to my hometown in Alabama I have been very happy.

_____ 12. I have been very happy since I returned to my hometown in Alabama.

_____ 13. Although the trip was exciting and educational home looked good to me.

NAME _____ DATE _____

INSTRUCTOR _____ CLASS TIME _____

_____ 14. In the woods behind our house daffodils were blooming when I returned.

_____ 15. Within the magnificent trees in our yard birds were singing loudly.

_____ 16. Having planned this trip several years in advance I am excited.

_____ 17. Suffering from the problem of overscheduling flights the airline is getting a bad reputation.

_____ 18. Watching flights from other airlines come into the airport people were getting impatient.

_____ 19. To eliminate the practice of standby flights the airline changed the rules.

_____ 20. To fully appreciate one's home and friends a person should take a trip.

REVIEW	PUNCTUATION OF
EXERCISE 4-2	INTRODUCTORY ELEMENTS AND ITEMS IN A SERIES

PUNCTUATION OF INTRODUCTORY ELEMENTS AND ITEMS IN A SERIES

DIRECTIONS: Punctuate the following sentences. If a sentence needs no punctuation, write *none* in the blank provided.

_____ 1. After her children were grown and required less care my neighbor entered college.

_____ 2. Having reared her three children she now had some free time for herself.

_____ 3. To obtain the type of job that she wanted she discovered that she needed a college education.

_____ 4. At the college on the other side of our town she enrolled in a business program.

_____ 5. Talking with her advisor filling out enrollment forms and finding her classrooms she spent three hours one afternoon.

_____ 6. Talking with her advisor filling out enrollment forms and finding her classrooms took three hours of her time.

_____ 7. When she took her first test in accounting she was nervous.

_____ 8. Quickly gaining her composure and control she took a deep breath and picked up her pencil.

_____ 9. Feeling confident about the material she finished the test proofread each question and handed it to the teacher.

_____ 10. Because she had thoroughly studied her notes the test seemed easy.

_____ 11. While she was proofreading her test and checking her answers many students picked up their books handed in their tests and left the room.

NAME _____ DATE _____

INSTRUCTOR _____ CLASS TIME _____

_____ 12. Being one of the last students in the room she again became nervous.

_____ 13. Although she was one of the last finished she took a deep breath reviewed her answers and found no errors.

_____ 14. After she handed the test to the teacher she went to Baskin-Robbins for an ice-cream cone.

_____ 15. When she earned the highest grade in the class she felt great.

_____ 16. She felt great when she earned the highest grade in the class.

_____ 17. Finishing her first quarter of college she was exhausted determined and pleased.

_____ 18. With her grown children in other cities she needed new interests challenges and goals.

_____ 19. Though college might not be good for everyone it was right for her.

_____ 20. After the hard test and the high grade her husband took her to a nice restaurant for a celebration dinner.

REVIEW	# SUMMARY OF PUNCTUATION
EXERCISE 4-3	# RULES

DIRECTIONS: This exercise will test all the punctuation skills you have learned. For each of the following: 1. Punctuate the sentence. 2. Do not change the word order or insert words; do not make two simple sentences. 3. If the sentence needs no punctuation, write *none* in the blank provided.

_____ 1. Fruits and vegetables give needed vitamins and they should be part of one's daily diet.

_____ 2. Fruits and vegetables give needed vitamins and should be part of a person's diet.

_____ 3. Although people need fruits and vegetables each day some teens substitute pizza and Pepsi for oranges and apples therefore these teens may lack balanced diets.

_____ 4. My mother taught us good manners she did not however insist on formality at all times.

_____ 5. My mother taught us good manners however she did not insist on formality.

_____ 6. Because my mother taught us good manners I feel comfortable when I am in public in fact good manners simplify my life.

_____ 7. The library has good sources for research and is as a matter of fact an excellent place to study.

_____ 8. The library has good sources for research indeed it is an excellent place to study read or relax.

_____ 9. If I am writing a research paper I check the library's reference room then I make a bibliography of possible sources.

_____ 10. The library closed early last night as a result I went home ate a sandwich and reviewed my notes.

NAME _____ DATE _____

INSTRUCTOR _____ CLASS TIME _____

_____ 11. Reviewing my class notes and reading new assignments I seldom have time to watch television many students I am certain are surprised by this lack of free time.

_____ 12. I left the library early nevertheless I managed my time and finished all my homework.

_____ 13. Students seldom lack ability they often I regret to say lack good study habits.

_____ 14. Students seldom lack ability on the contrary many are very bright and have good basic skills.

_____ 15. If students organize their time stick to a schedule and attend classes regularly they usually do well in school.

_____ 16. Studying every night at a specified time Brenda learned calculus.

_____ 17. Studying every night at a specified time is very difficult.

_____ 18. Students' grades improve as they acquire good study habits.

_____ 19. During the four years of Shayna's college education she worked each weekend and was on the dean's list each quarter.

_____ 20. While Shayna was in college she worked each weekend and was on the dean's list each quarter.

CHAPTER
QUIZ 4-1

SUMMARY OF PUNCTUATION RULES

DIRECTIONS: This quiz will test all the punctuation skills you have learned. For each of the following: 1. Punctuate the sentence. 2. Do not change the word order or insert words; do not make two simple sentences. 3. If the sentence needs no punctuation, write *none* in the blank provided.

_____ 1. After I get finished with my classes at school I work for four hours at McDonald's.

_____ 2. I work for four hours at McDonald's after I finish school.

_____ 3. I work at McDonald's after school and do my homework between 8 P.M. and midnight then I drop exhausted into bed and sleep soundly.

_____ 4. After attending classes doing homework and working at McDonald's I am often very tired nevertheless I am always pleased with my accomplishments.

_____ 5. Before the manager will dismiss me from work I must finish all my jobs and check my register.

_____ 6. I must finish my jobs and check my register before my manager will dismiss me from work.

_____ 7. Working the evening shift at McDonald's I have no time I regret to say for dates during the week.

_____ 8. Working the evening shift at McDonald's is ruining my social life.

_____ 9. Running to work every evening dashing to classes each morning and trying to study during the afternoon wears me out.

_____ 10. Running to work every evening dashing to classes each morning and trying to study during the afternoon I dream of a less hectic life.

NAME _____ DATE _____

INSTRUCTOR _____ CLASS TIME _____

_____ 11. Sitting in class and listening to discussion I often wish for time to study to review and to think.

_____ 12. Listening to the other students discuss the lesson depresses me.

_____ 13. When I listen to the other students' answers I sometimes quite frankly feel angry in fact I get very jealous of their free time.

_____ 14. While they are studying each night I am serving customers their hamburgers milk shakes and french fries.

_____ 15. To keep my high grade point average I must study early in the morning however getting out of bed at the crack of dawn is difficult.

_____ 16. Working fifty hours each week of summer vacation I will save money for next year's tuition then I can give my total attention to school and eliminate my frustration and anger.

_____ 17. Until the end of this spring quarter I must juggle school and work.

_____ 18. Until I save money from my summer job I must juggle school and work.

_____ 19. Because the money from this part-time job helps me pay my tuition I must work because summer vacation and a full-time job are three months away I must be patient.

_____ 20. Although many of my friends can study each week night I can't therefore I will live frugally and save money this coming summer.

© NTC/CONTEMPORARY PUBLISHING COMPANY

CHAPTER	**SUMMARY OF PUNCTUATION**
QUIZ 4-2	**RULES**

DIRECTIONS: This quiz will test all the punctuation skills you have learned. For each of the following: 1. Punctuate the sentence. 2. Do not change the word order or insert words; do not make two simple sentences. 3. If the sentence needs no punctuation, write *none* in the blank provided.

_____ 1. Studying requires a great deal of effort but knowledge gives a person satisfaction.

_____ 2. I work each night on my lessons as a result I don't get behind and feel trapped.

_____ 3. In English class this year at college we are learning rules for punctuation and the reasons for these rules many of us therefore are now writing better sentences.

_____ 4. Since we started college this quarter we have reviewed sentence structure punctuation and grammar therefore many of us are now writing better sentences.

_____ 5. After we have finished this rather long unit we will know how to punctuate we must of course practice these skills for the rest of our lives.

_____ 6. Doing the exercises reviewing notes and asking questions students in English will learn punctuation rules.

_____ 7. I now know the basic rules of punctuation writing essays consequently has become easier and less threatening.

_____ 8. As I realize my strengths and weaknesses I feel more confident about English consequently I am writing better essays.

_____ 9. My friend on the other hand is still making errors and feels insecure about English.

_____ 10. I am slowly eliminating my weaknesses in the punctuation of sentences on the other hand I am rapidly improving my use of thesis topic sentences and transitions.

NAME _____ DATE _____

INSTRUCTOR _____ CLASS TIME _____

_____ 11. When I finish this class in English I will not write comma splices fused sentences or sentence fragments.

_____ 12. Although I know the rules of punctuation I must apply them when I write paragraphs and essays.

_____ 13. Knowing the rules is a challenge applying them is even more difficult.

_____ 14. When I started this class a few weeks ago I knew little I have learned a great deal in a short amount of time.

_____ 15. I've learned a great deal in a few weeks indeed my writing as a result has improved significantly.

_____ 16. Reading the text and reviewing my class notes take a great deal of my precious time but I want a good grade on the next test.

_____ 17. Reading the text reviewing my class notes and participating in class discussion I learned basic rules.

_____ 18. Before I did this chapter on sentence structure I wrote short sentences however my sentence structure has improved a great deal since I finished the chapter and started correctly using phrases and clauses.

_____ 19. My essays always had short sentences in them short sentences however make an essay sound elementary and choppy.

_____ 20. Working for an hour every night at home I reviewed the rules of punctuation and studied my workbook.

GRAMMAR

CHAPTER

5

SUBJECT AND VERB AGREEMENT

Learning to make subjects and verbs agree in number will give you a powerful writing skill. Although it may seem unfair, failure to make subjects and verbs agree quickly labels a writer as uneducated. Once you have mastered these basic rules, however, your sentences will demonstrate your knowledge of the language.

In standard written English, a verb must agree in number with its subject. Two words agree in number when both are singular or both are plural. To minimize errors in subject-verb agreement, you must correctly identify the subject and determine whether that subject is singular or plural. This chapter will teach you how to achieve subject and verb agreement.

SINGULAR AND PLURAL SUBJECTS AND VERBS

Technically, only nouns—not verbs—can be singular or plural, but to simplify your learning, we are going to allow verbs to be described as singular and plural. Singular verbs take singular subjects; plural verbs take plural subjects:

▼ **SINGULAR SUBJECT AND VERB:** The boy reads.
▲ **PLURAL SUBJECT AND VERB:** The boys read.
▼ **SINGULAR SUBJECT AND VERB:** The girl walks
▲ **PLURAL SUBJECT AND VERB:** The girls walk.

Looking at the four sentences above, you can see that the *plural subjects* end in *s*, while the third-person *singular verbs* end in *s*. Remembering that *plural* subjects and *singular* verbs end in *s* will help you to avoid subject-verb agreement errors.

Singular and Plural Subjects

The most common way to make *nouns* plural is to add *s* or *es*. The vast majority of words in the English language become plural simply by adding an *s*. The plural of words ending in *s, sh, ch, z,* and *x,* however, is formed by adding *es*. This *es* ending allows for the extra syllable that is created in order for the word to be pronounced:

Singular	Plural
student	student*s*
teacher	teacher*s*
box	box*es*
class	class*es*

Singular and Plural Verbs

In contrast to subjects, adding an *s* to a present tense *verb* (except the *be* verb) makes it singular in nature, not plural. Look at these *singular* verbs:

The student learn*s*.

The teacher enjoy*s*.

The box glitter*s*.

The class respond*s*.

If these verbs were made to agree with a plural noun, there would be no *s* on them:

The students learn.

The teachers enjoy.

The boxes glitter.

The classes respond.

The fact that singular verbs end in *s* holds true even for three "difficult verbs" that do not form the present tense in a regular manner: *go/goes, do/does, have/has*. Look at these *singular* verbs:

The student goes.

The teacher does.

The box has.

If these verbs were made to agree with a plural noun, there would be no *s* on them:

The students go.

The teachers do.

The boxes have.

In the present tense, all third-person singular verbs end in *s*.

In the past tense (with the exception of the *be* verb), the same verb is used for both the singular and plural subjects:

Singular	Plural
The boy walked.	The boys walked.

The only exception to this rule is the *be* verb. In the past tense, the third-person verb changes form:

	Singular	Plural
Third person	he wa*s*	they *were*
	she wa*s*	
	it wa*s*	

Three-Step Test for Determining Whether the Subject Is Singular or Plural

Most students can easily distinguish between singular and plural forms of subjects and verbs. Yet, errors in subject/verb agreement are common in student writing. To eliminate these errors, we suggest the following three-step test:

1. Identify the word that is the subject of the sentence. Because students sometimes neglect to analyze the structure of a sentence, they fail to identify the correct subject. Failing to identify the correct subject is the main cause of student errors in subject/verb agreement.

2. Determine whether the subject is singular or plural.

3. If the subject is singular, substitute *he* or *it* and read the sentence aloud. If the subject is plural, substitute *they* and read the sentence aloud. By doing this, sometimes your ear can "hear" the correct verb.

For example, you would use the test as follows:

Her reasons for the new schedule (seem, seems) logical.

1. *Reasons* is the subject.
2. *Reasons* is plural.
3. *They seem* sounds better than *They seems* (for those of you who can "hear" the correct verb).

© NTC/CONTEMPORARY PUBLISHING COMPANY

His reason to reject the new schedule (seem, seems) logical.

1. *Reason* is the subject.
2. *Reason* is singular.
3. *It seems* sounds better than *It seem* (for those of you who can "hear" the correct verb).

You should recognize that there are very few times when a student's ear can hear whether grammar is correct. This is one of those times, however. If your ear can help you make the judgment, then do so. But *if you find it does not work for you*, then learn the "*s*-rules" for making subject and verb agree.

FIVE COMMON CAUSES OF SUBJECT/VERB AGREEMENT ERRORS

If you mastered the material in Chapter 1, you will have little trouble finding the subject of a sentence. You may choose to review that chapter, however. Beware of the five common causes of incorrect subject identification. Because failure to identify the correct subject is the main cause of student errors in subject/verb agreement, knowing the five most common traps students fall into will help you avoid them.

First Trap: Phrase Between Subject and Verb

Failure to identify the correct subject of a sentence usually occurs when there is a group of words between the subject and the verb. This group of words is often either a prepositional or parenthetical phrase. You want to *ignore these phrases.*

PREPOSITIONAL PHRASES BETWEEN SUBJECT AND VERB. The number of the subject is not usually changed by a prepositional phrase that intervenes between the subject and the verb. Do not mistake the object of a preposition for the subject of the sentence:

This backpack for my books and papers is handy.

The runners in the last race of the day are Hae and Monica.

In the first sentence, the singular subject *backpack* is followed by a prepositional phrase that has plural objects: *books* and *papers*. In the second sentence, the plural subject *runners* is followed by two prepositional phrases that have singular objects: *race* and *day*.

TRY-IT

EXERCISE

In the following sentences, first underline the subject of each. Then underline the correct verb.

1. The houses (have, has) been built this year.
2. The houses in this block (have, has) been built this year.

In the first sentence, the subject is *houses* and it is plural. You would say *They have* rather than *They has* and probably would have no problem choosing the correct verb. In the second sentence, the subject is also *houses,* but a careless student will try to make the verb agree with the word closest to it—in this case the word *block,* which is the object of the preposition *in.* Unless you invest the time to analyze the parts of each sentence, you will try to make the verb agree with the object of the preposition, rather than with the actual subject of the sentence. Beware of this common error. Remember that the subject of a sentence is never in a prepositional phrase.

PARENTHETICAL PHRASES BETWEEN SUBJECT AND VERB. The number of the subject is not changed by a parenthetical phrase that intervenes between the subject and the verb. Do not get confused by a parenthetical phrase that is tucked between a subject and a verb. Some common introductions to parenthetical phrases are *along with, as well as, accompanied by, in addition to, together with,* and *including.* Consider the following sentences:

The team members, along with the coach, are excited.

Austin Brown, as well as his coaches, is excited.

In the first sentence, the plural subject *members* is followed by the parenthetical phrase *along with the coach.* In the second sentence, the singular subject *Austin Brown* is followed by the parenthetical phrase *as well as his coaches.*

TRY-IT
EXERCISE

In the following sentences, first underline the subject. Then underline the correct verb.

1. Mr. Lee (have, has) gone fishing.
2. Mr. Lee, together with his sons, (have, has) gone fishing.

In the first sentence, the subject is *Mr. Lee* and is singular. You would say *He has* rather than *He have.* In the second sentence, the correct verb is again *has.* The parenthetical phrase *together with his sons* does not change the fact that *Mr. Lee* is the subject of the sentence. Beware of making verbs agree with the last word of a parenthetical phrase.

PRACTICE EXERCISE 5-1

SUBJECT-VERB AGREEMENT– PHRASES BETWEEN SUBJECT AND VERB

Underline the subject of each sentence. Then underline the verb that would be preferred in standard formal writing.

EXAMPLE: That <u>tree</u> with the tiny leaves on its delicate branches (look, <u>looks</u>) fragile.

1. Those houses in the woods by the stream (become, becomes) more valuable each year.

2. That house among all those trees (become, becomes) more valuable each year.

3. The captain, as well as the coaches, (know, knows) that the team must win the next game.

4. The coaches, as well as the captain, (know, knows) that the team must win the next game.

5. The opinion of a teenager's friends (determine, determines) his or her behavior.

6. The opinions of a teenager's mother (determine, determines) his or her behavior.

7. A teen's best friend, in addition to his or her parents, (serve, serves) as a role model.

8. The peers of a teenager (serve, serves) as his or her role models.

9. The sound of the traffic on the two interstates (get, gets) annoying.

10. The cars on the interstate highways near our home (cause, causes) noise and air pollution.

NAME _____ DATE _____

INSTRUCTOR _____ CLASS TIME _____

PRACTICE	# USING SUBJECT-VERB
EXERCISE 5-2	# AGREEMENT—PHRASES

USING SUBJECT-VERB AGREEMENT—PHRASES BETWEEN SUBJECT AND VERB

Rewrite each of the following sentences by making three changes. (1) If the subject is singular, make it plural, and if it is plural, make it singular. (2) Insert a prepositional or parenthetical phrase between the subject and the verb. (3) Make the verb agree with the subject.

EXAMPLE: The flowers feel like artificial ones.

The flower on the desk feels like an artificial one.

1. Both daughters agree with the new rule.

    _____

2. Students seldom see the advantages of required courses.

    _____

3. A professor prefers teaching an elective course.

    _____

4. The badminton nets need to be repaired.

    _____

5. My kitten continues to shred the upholstered furniture.

    _____

6. My brothers save all sorts of unneeded items.

    _____

7. The artist attracts the attention of onlookers.

    _____

8. The workers eagerly wait for break to arrive.

    _____

9. A song influences people's moods.

    _____

10. The light flickers on and off.

    _____

NAME _____ DATE _____

INSTRUCTOR _____ CLASS TIME _____

Second Trap: Subject After the Verb

Failure to identify the correct subject of a sentence can occur when there is a word or phrase at the beginning of a sentence, followed by the main verb and the subject. This construction puts the subject after the verb. Both introductory words and introductory phrases create this common trap:

> Here are the books.
>
> Under the desk are the books.

Though the most common word order in the English language is subject first and verb second, there are other acceptable sentence constructions. You need to be aware that the verb can come before the subject, as in the previous sample sentences. In both of these sentences, the verb is *are* and the subject is *books*. In the first sentence, the word *here* is an introductory word; it is not the subject. In the second sentence, the prepositional phrase *under the desk* has as the object of the preposition the singular word *desk*. Only with care will a student ignore the word *here* in the first sentence and the word *desk* in the second. The best way to avoid falling into this common trap is to use the three-step test given on page 181.

INTRODUCTORY WORDS: THERE, HERE, AND WHERE. When the subject comes after the verb, do not mistake some introductory word for the subject of the sentence. In sentences beginning with *there, here,* or *where,* the subject of the sentence will follow the verb. The words *there, here,* and *where* are never the subject of a sentence. The most common errors with these introductory words occur in daily conversation when we make contractions of these words, saying *there's, here's,* and *where's.* Each of these is a contraction for the verb *is.* Thus, each must be paired with a singular subject:

> There is the test.
>
> There are the tests.
>
> Here is the test.
>
> Here are the tests.
>
> Where is the test?
>
> Where are the tests?

In the first sentence of each pair, the singular verb is *is;* in the second sentence of each pair, the plural verb is *are.* In the above sentences, the introductory words *there, here,* and *where* are not the subject. The subject appears after the verb.

TRY-IT
EXERCISE

Identify the subject of each of the following sentences. If the verb agrees with the subject, write *C* in the blank. If it does not agree, write *I*.

_____ 1. There is too many mistakes in this essay.
_____ 2. There's too many mistakes in this essay.
_____ 3. There are too many mistakes in this essay.

This construction demands that you analyze the sentence to find the correct subject. The subject of each of these sentences is *mistakes*. It is a plural subject and takes a plural verb—in this case the verb *are*. The first two sentences are incorrect because each has the singular verb *is*.

TRY-IT
EXERCISE

Identify the subject of each of the following sentences. If the verb agrees with the subject, write *C* in the blank. If it does not agree, write *I*.

_____ 1. Here is the diskettes that you wanted.
_____ 2. Here's the diskettes that you wanted.
_____ 3. Here are the diskettes that you wanted.

The subject of each of these sentences is *diskettes* and takes a plural verb. The first two sentences are incorrect because each has the singular verb *is*.

TRY-IT
EXERCISE

Identify the subject of each of the following sentences. If the verb agrees with it, write *C* in the blank. If it does not agree, write *I*.

_____ 1. Where is Heather and Angela?
_____ 2. Where's Heather and Angela?
_____ 3. Where are Heather and Angela?

Each of these sentences has the compound subject *Heather* and *Angela* and takes a plural verb. Therefore, the first two sentences are incorrect because each has the singular verb *is*.

INTRODUCTORY PREPOSITIONAL PHRASES. When the subject comes after the verb, do not mistake some introductory phrase for the subject of the sentence. Do not confuse the object of a preposition with the subject in sentences with introductory prepositional phrases:

Among the students in the classes was Shamika.

On the table near the window are our children's pictures.

In the first sentence, the singular verb *was* takes the singular subject *Shamika.* The introductory prepositional phrases are *among the students* and *in the classes.* In the second sentence, the plural verb *are* takes the plural subject *pictures.* The introductory prepositional phrases are *on the table* and *near the window.* Students are sometimes tempted to call these objects of prepositions the subject of the sentence. Remember, however, that an object of a preposition is never the subject of a sentence. If you were to place parentheses around the introductory prepositional phrases to eliminate them as choices, the only words remaining as possible subjects would be after the verb.

<table>
<tr><td>**TRY-IT**
EXERCISE</td></tr>
</table>

Identify the subject of each of the following sentences and underline the correct verb.

1. Behind the ornate gate (stand, stands) a house and a garden.
2. On their farm (grow, grows) fields of soybeans.

Each of these sentences begins with a prepositional phrase. In the first sentence, the compound subject *house* and *garden* comes after the verb and would take the plural verb *stand.* A careless student might make the verb agree with *gate* because it precedes the verb. The word *gate,* however, is the object of a preposition, not the subject of the sentence. In the second sentence, the subject *fields* comes after the verb and would take the plural verb *grow*. In each case, you must be careful to find the correct subject of the sentence; otherwise, you might try to make the verb agree with the object of the preposition.

© NTC/CONTEMPORARY PUBLISHING COMPANY

| PRACTICE | # SUBJECT-VERB AGREEMENT– |
| EXERCISE 5-3 | # SUBJECT AFTER THE VERB |

Underline the subject of each sentence. Then underline the verb that would be preferred in standard formal writing.

EXAMPLE: There (<u>were</u>, was) twenty <u>runners</u> in the marathon.

1.   (There's, There are) three routes I can take to the college.

2.   In the picture on the wall (were, was) a man and his dog.

3.   Here (is, are) the reasons I can't go with you.

4.   Here (is, are) the reason I can't go with you.

5.   Underneath the desk (were, was) a chemistry book and a laboratory manual.

6.   Behind the house (grow, grows) hundreds of wild flowers.

7.   (Where's, Where are) the shopping lists?

8.   On the edge of the driveway (bloom, blooms) many pink rose bushes.

9.   (Where's, Where are) the notes you took in chemistry?

10.   Among this mess of papers and books (is, are) my class schedule for next quarter.

NAME _____   DATE _____

INSTRUCTOR _____   CLASS TIME _____

PRACTICE
EXERCISE 5-4 # USING SUBJECT-VERB AGREEMENT—SUBJECT AFTER THE VERB

Rewrite the following sentences to make the subject follow the verb.

EXAMPLE: Many students are currently graduating from community colleges.

Currently graduating from community colleges are many students.

1. Several students were in the library during exam week.

   _____

2. Three exchange students are in my history course.

   _____

3. A cardinal and a bluejay were at the birdfeeder by the magnolia tree.

   _____

4. Lots of ads are in the mail every day.

   _____

5. An old tractor and plow were in the barn deep in the woods.

   _____

6. Your test grade is posted on the office door.

   _____

7. Students from various colleges were on the dance floor.

   _____

8. Manuel and his father were at the initiation ceremony each year.

   _____

9. Numerous exercises on verbs are in our English workbook.

   _____

10. Ten songs in a row are played on several FM radio stations.

    _____

NAME _____ DATE _____

INSTRUCTOR _____ CLASS TIME _____

© NTC/CONTEMPORARY PUBLISHING COMPANY

Third Trap: Singular Indefinite Pronoun As Subject

When standing alone or followed by phrases, singular indefinite pronouns take singular verbs. The most common singular pronouns are *each, either, neither, one, everyone, everybody, everything, anyone, anybody, anything, someone, somebody, something, no one, nobody, nothing.* These words are called indefinite pronouns because they refer in a general sense to an indefinite person or thing. Notice that many of these sixteen pronouns are compound. Also notice that the last half of the compound is obviously *singular,* while the first half sounds plural. To avoid making mistakes, look only at the last half of these compound pronouns. Even after learning that these pronouns are singular, you may get confused when a singular pronoun is followed by a prepositional phrase with a plural noun as an object.

Look at the following sentences:

Each is taking the test.
Each of the students is taking the test.

Either (Neither) is taking the test.
Either (Neither) of the students is taking the test.

One has taken the test.
One of the students has taken the test.

The subject of each sentence above is an indefinite pronoun (*Each, Either, One*), is singular, and takes a singular verb. In the second sentence of each pair, the singular pronoun is followed by a prepositional phrase with a plural object. Be careful not to make the verb plural to agree with the object of the preposition rather than with the subject. Concentrate on these sixteen indefinite pronouns that always are singular. Most errors in pronoun usage involve these sixteen words.

There is also a small group of indefinite pronouns that always is plural: *few, many, several, others, both.* To help you remember this plural list, memorize a sentence using a plural subject to remind you that these words are always plural in number: "Few men sob." With this sentence, the word *few,* is already one of the five, the word *men* begins with the same letter as *many,* and *sob* contains the first letter of each of the last three words: *several, others,* and *both.* Of course, if you prefer, you should create whatever memory devices work for you. We are simply suggesting some that have helped us and might help you.

The best way to avoid confusion, then, is to recognize that the indefinite pronouns *each, either, neither, one, everyone, everybody, everything, anyone, anybody, anything, someone, somebody, something, no one, nobody, nothing* (when standing alone or followed by a prepositional phrase) are always singular. In addition, know that the indefinite pronouns *few, many, several, others, both* (when standing alone or followed by a prepositional phrase) are always plural.

TRY-IT

EXERCISE

Identify the subject of each of the following sentences and underline the correct verb.

1. Everyone in this school (want/wants) less homework.
2. Anybody in the school relays (need/needs) endurance.
3. Someone in the first three rows of bleachers (cheer/cheers) too loudly.
4. Each of the competitors (practice/practices) daily.
5. Either of the runners in the relays (deserve/deserves) the trophy.
6. Few of the students in this school (want/wants) more homework.
7. Many of those runners in the relays (need/needs) endurance.
8. Several of the fans at the game (cheer/cheers) loudly.
9. Others in the stadium (listen/listens) to their radios.
10. Both of these types of fans (enjoy/enjoys) the relays.

In the first sentence, the subject *everyone* is singular and takes the singular verb *wants*. In the second sentence, the subject *anybody* is singular and takes the singular verb *needs*. In the third sentence, the subject *someone* is singular and takes the verb *cheers*. In the fourth sentence, the subject *each* is singular and takes the singular verb *practices*. In the fifth sentence, the subject *either* is singular and takes the singular verb *deserves*. In the sixth sentence, the subject *few* is plural and takes the plural verb *want*. In the seventh sentence, the subject *many* is plural and takes the plural verb *need*. In the eighth sentence, the subject *several* is plural and takes the plural verb *cheer*. In the ninth sentence, the subject *others* is plural and takes the plural verb *listen*. In the tenth sentence, the subject *both* is plural and takes the plural verb *enjoy*.

To help you learn these indefinite pronouns, review Table 5.1 and Table 5.2.

© NTC/CONTEMPORARY PUBLISHING COMPANY

TABLE 5.1	*Singular Indefinite Pronouns*		
either	somebody	no one	everything
anybody	neither	someone	nothing
everybody	anyone	each	something
nobody	everyone	anything	one

TABLE 5.2	*Plural Indefinite Pronouns*	
few	many	several
others	both	

PRACTICE	# SUBJECT-VERB AGREEMENT–
EXERCISE 5-5	# SINGULAR PRONOUNS

Underline the subject of each of the following sentences. Put parentheses around each prepositional phrase (if any) that comes between the subject and the verb. Underline the verb that would be preferred in standard formal writing.

EXAMPLE: Each (of you) (face, faces) a difficult decision.

1. Everyone in the dorms (seem, seems) to be going to the play.

2. Anybody in the tournaments (get, gets) Friday off.

3. Neither (require, requires) technical knowledge.

4. Neither of the jobs (require, requires) technical knowledge.

5. Either (enjoy, enjoys) a good income.

6. Either of the lawyers (enjoy, enjoys) a good income.

7. Each of the players (goes, go) to the tourney.

8. Everybody in the tourney (compete, competes) for the trophy.

9. One of the teachers (give, gives) more tests than the other.

10. Anyone in economics classes (need, needs) help sometimes.

NAME _____ DATE _____

INSTRUCTOR _____ CLASS TIME _____

PRACTICE	# USING SUBJECT-VERB AGREEMENT—SINGULAR PRONOUNS
EXERCISE 5-6	

Rewrite the following sentences by inserting a prepositional phrase between the subject and the verb. Do not use the same prepositional phrase more than once in these exercises.

EXAMPLE: Nobody asks enough questions.

Nobody in the class asks enough questions.

1.   Somebody suggests writing questions in the text whle studying.

   _____

2.   Everybody applauds the idea.

   _____

3.   Sometimes one has difficulty in remembering questions from a day ago.

   _____

4.   Neither finds time to allow for questions during class.

   _____

5.   Anyone allows students time to request information.

   _____

6.   Either agrees with the ideas of Melissa.

   _____

7.   Everyone suggests solutions to the present problems.

   _____

8.   Each is a potential remedy.

   _____

9.   Someone tells of the format in math class.

   _____

10.   Anybody finds answers before the test.

   _____

NAME _____   DATE _____

INSTRUCTOR _____   CLASS TIME _____

© NTC/CONTEMPORARY PUBLISHING COMPANY

Fourth Trap: Compound Subject

Compound subjects can be either singular or plural. As you learned in Chapter 1, a compound subject consists of two or more words joined by *and, or,* or *nor.* Three basic rules will help you determine the number of a compound subject.

COMPOUND SUBJECTS JOINED BY AND RULE.   Most compound subjects joined by *and* are plural and take a plural verb. Consider the following sentences:

> Jesse and Yolanda *go* to the island each weekend.
>
> Winnie and Pearl *prepare* the evening meal.
>
> The introduction and the conclusion of your essay *need* revision.

COMPOUND SUBJECTS JOINED BY OR OR NOR RULE.   Most compound subjects joined by *or* or *nor* are singular and take a singular verb. If one subject is singular and one is plural, make the verb agree with the nearer subject:

> Jesse or Yolanda *goes* to the island each weekend.
>
> Winnie or Pearl *prepares* the evening meal.
>
> The introduction or the conclusion of your essay *needs* revision.
>
> Nora or her parents *pay* her tuition.

COMPOUND SUBJECTS JOINED BY EITHER...OR OR NEITHER...NOR RULE.   When two compound subjects are joined by *either-or* or *neither-nor,* the verb agrees with the nearer subject:

> Either the judges or the lawyer *is* wrong.
>
> Either the lawyer or the judges *are* wrong.
>
> Neither the students nor the teacher *seems* bored.
>
> Neither the teacher nor the students *seem* bored.

In each of the above sentences, the verb agrees with the half of the compound subject that is nearer to it. In the first and third sentence, the words *lawyer* and *teacher* are singular and take a singular verb. In the second and fourth sentences, the words *judges* and *students* are plural and take a plural verb. Because these are awkward constructions, most writers agree that it is best to avoid using them whenever possible. Nevertheless, at those times when they are used, they should be used correctly.

TRY-IT
EXERCISE

Identify the subject of each of the following sentences and underline the correct verb.

1. Keisha and Heather (like/likes) chocolate pie.
2. Keisha or Heather (like/likes) chocolate pie.
3. Neither Keisha nor Heather (like/likes) chocolate pie.
4. Either Keisha or her brothers (like/likes) chocolate pie.
5. Neither her parents nor Heather (like/likes) chocolate pie.

In the first sentence, the compound subject *Keisha* and *Heather* is joined by *and;* the correct answer is the plural verb *like.* In the second sentence, the compound subject is joined by *or* and takes the singular verb *likes.* In the third sentence, the half of the compound subject nearest the verb is *Heather* and takes the singular verb *likes.* In the fourth sentence, the half of the compound subject nearest the verb is *brothers* and takes the plural verb *like.* In the fifth sentence, the half of the compound subject nearest the verb is *Heather* and takes the singular verb *likes.*

| PRACTICE | # SUBJECT-VERB AGREEMENT– |
| EXERCISE 5-7 | # COMPOUND SUBJECT |

Underline the word (or words) in the subject that determines the verb you will use. Then underline the verb that would be preferred in standard formal writing.

EXAMPLE: Mother or <u>Dad</u> (buy, <u>buys</u>) groceries each Friday.

EXAMPLE: <u>Mother</u> and my <u>sister</u> (<u>like</u>, likes) to shop.

1.   Shayna and Jamal (know, knows) who gave the gift.

2.   Shayna nor Jamal (know, knows) who gave the gift.

3.   Shayna or Jamal (know, knows) who gave the gift.

4.   Neither Jan nor her brothers (have, has) left yet.

5.   Jan's brothers and her younger sister (have, has) already left.

6.   Neither Jan's older brother nor her younger sister (have, has) left.

7.   Choon says that either those cookies or this apple pie (taste, tastes) great.

8.   Choon told me that either this apple pie or those cookies (taste, tastes) great.

9.   *The Enquirer* or *The Post* (contain, contains) reliable news.

10. *The Enquirer* and *The Post* (contain, contains) reliable news.

NAME _____   DATE _____

INSTRUCTOR _____   CLASS TIME _____

PRACTICE	# SUBJECT-VERB AGREEMENT
EXERCISE 5-8	

For the first five sentences, change the subjects connected by *and* to subjects connected by *or* or *nor* and make the verb agree.

EXAMPLE: The boys and the girls are on the team.

The boys or the girls are on the team.

1. Bill and his dad own a business.

   Bill or his dad own a business

2. Bill and his parents own a business.

   Bill or his parents own business

3. Susan and Raoul want an accounting degree.

   Susan nor Raoul want an acting degree

4. A leaky radiator hose and loose fan belts cause problems with a car.

   a leaky radiator hose nor loose fan belt causes problem w/ a car

5. Loose fan belts and a leaky radiator hose cause problems with a car.

   loose fan belts or a leaky radiator hose cause problem w/ a car

For the last five sentences, change the subjects connected by *or, nor, either-or,* or *neither-nor* to subjects connected by *and* and make the verb agree.

6. Neither July nor August is a good time for school.

7. The teachers or the students have an investment in education.

8. Either the professor or the student has an investment in education.

9. Neither the seller nor the buyer agrees with the contract.

10. The seller or the buyers agree with the contract.

NAME _____ DATE _____

INSTRUCTOR _____ CLASS TIME _____

© NTC/CONTEMPORARY PUBLISHING COMPANY

Fifth Trap: Verb Followed By Predicate Nominative

As you learned in Chapter 1, a predicate nominative is a complement that follows a linking verb and renames the subject: Mother is my best friend. In this example, the subject *Mother* and the predicate nominative *friend* are each singular. It is possible, however, for the subject and the predicate nominative to be different in number: *Mother* is my best *friend* and *critic*. When a subject and a predicate nominative are different in number, the verb agrees with the subject—not the predicate nominative. Although this is an unusual construction, when it occurs it needs to be handled correctly. Consider the following sentences:

The best part of the meal is the coffee and cookies.

The coffee and cookies are the best part of the meal.

A cause of inflation is rising wages and prices.

Rising wages and prices are a cause of inflation.

In the first sentence, the subject is *part;* in the third sentence the subject is *cause.* Each is singular and takes a singular verb. In the second and fourth sentences, the compound subject is plural and takes a plural verb. In the second sentence, it is *coffee* and *cookies;* in the fourth sentence, it is *wages* and *prices.* Beware of making the verb agree with the predicate nominative rather than with the subject.

TRY-IT

EXERCISE

Identify the subject of each of the following sentences and underline the correct verb.

1. Rising prices (are/is) the red flag of inflation.
2. The red flag of inflation (are/is) rising prices.
3. Low test grades (are/is) Dorita's major concern.
4. Dorita's major concern (are/is) low test grades.

In the first sentence, the subject is *prices;* in the third sentence, the subject is *grades.* Each of these is plural and takes the plural verb *are.* In the second sentence, the subject is *flag;* in the fourth sentence, the subject is *concern.* Each of these is singular and takes the singular verb *is.*

PRACTICE	**SUBJECT-VERB AGREEMENT—**
EXERCISE 5-9	**VERB FOLLOWED BY PREDICATE**

SUBJECT-VERB AGREEMENT— VERB FOLLOWED BY PREDICATE NOMINATIVE

Underline the correct verb in the following sentences.

EXAMPLE: The best thing about this class (<u>is</u>, are) the interesting students.

1. The discussions (is, are) the best part of class.

2. The best part of class (is, are) the discussions.

3. The thing that impressed me (was, were) the discussions.

4. The discussions (was, were) the thing that impressed me.

5. Material possessions (is, are) his goal in life.

6. His goal in life (is, are) material possessions.

7. Paying rent and buying food (is, are) a necessity of life.

8. A necessity of life (is, are) paying rent and buying food.

9. Listening and forgiving (is, are) an important ingredient of love.

10. An important ingredient of love (is, are) listening and forgiving.

NAME _____ DATE _____

INSTRUCTOR _____ CLASS TIME _____

PRACTICE EXERCISE 5-10	# USING SUBECT-VERB AGREEMENT—VERB FOLLOWED BY PREDICATE NOMINATIVE

Change the following sentences by switching the subject and the predicate nominative. Then make the verb agree with the subject.

EXAMPLE: The surprise was a new car and a trip to Disneyland.

A new car and a trip to Disneyland were the surprise.

1. The assignment is an oral report and a paper.

   _____

2. The evidence convicting him was his fingerprints and a lock of his hair.

   _____

3. The main problem is the expenses.

   _____

4. The audience is doctors and nurses.

   _____

5. Eggs, bacon, and pancakes were my breakfast.

   _____

6. The panel is the dean, the assistant dean, and the department chairs.

   _____

7. Cassette players are the company's only product.

   _____

8. More money and longer vacations are the issue.

   _____

9. Buying gifts, planning parties, and sharing secrets are the best part of Christmas.

   _____

10. The mountains were the most impressive sight on the trip.

   _____

NAME _____ DATE _____

INSTRUCTOR _____ CLASS TIME _____

REVIEW
EXERCISE 5-1

SUBJECT-VERB AGREEMENT

DIRECTIONS: First, underline the subject(s) of each sentence. Then, underline the verb that would be preferred in standard formal writing.

1. Aromas from every restaurant (beg, begs) us to eat.

2. Within one block on Montgomery Road (is, are) a McDonald's and a Wendy's.

3. (There are, There's) a Baskin-Robbins and a Graeter's in Kenwood.

4. Pete and Jim, along with their sister, (does, do) the yard work.

5. Pete or Jim (does, do) the yard work.

6. Everyone (take, takes) the final test on the same day.

7. Everyone in the classes (know, knows) the date of the final test.

8. The manager or the owner of the team (plan, plans) a change in rules.

9. The manager and the owner (care, cares) about the change.

10. Neither the players nor the coach (know, knows) about the change.

11. Neither the coach nor the players (know, knows) about the change.

12. Neither of the teams (want, wants) the change.

13. Either of the players (seem, seems) qualified to mediate.

14. Each of the players on the four teams (appear, appears) prepared.

15. My classes in history (were, was) the best part of college.

16. The best part of college (were, was) my classes in history.

17. Across the hall (were, was) Dr. Douglas's history class and Dr. Thomas's psychology class.

18. The students in Dr. Douglas's class (learn, learns) history.

19. In Dr. Thomas's psychology class (were, was) thirty students.

20. The students, as well as every teacher, (need, needs) a vacation.

NAME _____ DATE _____

INSTRUCTOR _____ CLASS TIME _____

REVIEW
EXERCISE 5-2

SUBJECT-VERB AGREEMENT

DIRECTIONS: First, underline the subject(s) of each sentence. Then underline the verb that would be preferred in standard formal writing.

1. A sophomore and a junior (collect, collects) the tickets.

2. A sophomore or a junior (collect, collects) the tickets.

3. Neither of those women (look, looks) tired.

4. Either the chocolate cake or the butterscotch pie (call, calls) for brown sugar.

5. Neither teachers nor students (enjoy, enjoys) evaluation.

6. Either of those teachers (require, requires) five essays each quarter.

7. Reading the text and taking notes in class (is, are) an important part of school.

8. An important part of school (is, are) reading the text and taking notes in class.

9. Each of the students in his classes (say, says) good things about him.

10. (Where are, Where's) the exercises for today?

11. (There are, There's) an exercise that I didn't understand.

12. In the reception room of the admission office (was, were) a father and his son.

13. Everybody on our debate teams (work, works) very hard.

14. The students, along with the coach, (travel, travels) miles each year.

15. (Do, Does) either of these classes fit into your present schedule?

16. Everyone in the English classes (know, knows) the date of the exit exam.

17. Neither the boy in the back row nor the girls beside him (participate, participates) in class discussion.

NAME _____ DATE _____

INSTRUCTOR _____ CLASS TIME _____

18. Neither of those boys (participate, participates) in class discussion.

19. Studying during the day and working during the evening (require, requires) self-discipline.

20. English, including literature and composition, (demand, demands) effort.

REVIEW EXERCISE 5-3

SUBJECT-VERB AGREEMENT

DIRECTIONS: Determine whether the correct verb is used in each sentence. If it is correct, write *C* in the blank provided. If it is not, write the correct verb.

_____ 1.   Neither the teacher nor the students know the answer.

_____ 2.   Neither of you students knows the answer.

_____ 3.   Hard rain, late frost, and strong wind hurts delicate spring flowers.

_____ 4.   In Caroline's bedroom are a stereo, a TV, and a videocassette recorder.

_____ 5.   One of the reasons for the rules concern the safety of the students.

_____ 6.   Organization, self-discipline, and a good memory helps a student.

_____ 7.   Tamela, accompanied by her preschool children, goes to the grocery store.

_____ 8.   On the desk by the window was a computer and a telephone.

_____ 9.   There's things in this chapter that are important.

_____ 10. Everybody in both classes compete for the teacher's approval.

_____ 11. The howl of those cats reverberates through the neighborhood every evening.

_____ 12. Each of the men finishes work around 3 P.M.

_____ 13. Finishing work, getting groceries, and driving home takes nearly an hour.

_____ 14. The sentences on the final page of the last test illustrate various problems that students are having.

_____ 15. To the teacher falls the responsibilities of making lesson plans and grading essays.

NAME _____   DATE _____

INSTRUCTOR _____   CLASS TIME _____

_____ 16. Are either Sue or Dave Williams here?

_____ 17. Are Sue and Dave Williams here?

_____ 18. A salad and hot soup makes a good meal.

_____ 19. A salad or hot soup makes a good meal.

_____ 20. Either a salad or one of a variety of hot soups make a good meal.

CHAPTER
QUIZ 5-1

SUBJECT-VERB AGREEMENT

DIRECTIONS: Determine whether the correct verb is used in each sentence. If it is correct, write *C* in the blank provided. If it is not, write the correct verb.

_____ 1. The flowers in the large garden turns many shades of pink in June.

_____ 2. Over in the east yard grows lilacs, daffodils, and tulips.

_____ 3. The first robin, as well as some winter chickadees, sing at my window.

_____ 4. The nicest part of spring is the smell of the rain and the feel of the air.

_____ 5. Neither my younger sisters nor my older brother enjoys weeding the garden.

_____ 6. Either of my parents plant the vegetable garden in early May.

_____ 7. Neither of my younger sisters work in the garden many hours a day.

_____ 8. Either the squirrels or my pet rabbit eat the vegetables before we do.

_____ 9. The garden, in addition to the house and yard, requires a lot of Mother's time.

_____ 10. Here's some lilacs and tulips from our flower garden.

_____ 11. Each of the owners of the houses plants bulbs in the fall.

_____ 12. Waiting quietly and watching carefully takes patience.

_____ 13. The goldfinches, daffodils, and forsythia makes golden beauty in our yard each spring.

_____ 14. The feathers of the goldfinch turns bright yellow in April.

_____ 15. The daffodils are the first bright spot of yellow in the yard.

NAME _____   DATE _____

INSTRUCTOR _____   CLASS TIME _____

_____ 16. Across the creek behind our house blooms a pink dogwood and a purple magnolia.

_____ 17. Planting the garden, together with canning and freezing, demands hours of time.

_____ 18. The biggest problem in gardening are the insects.

_____ 19. Everybody in the homes near us mow grass every Saturday morning.

_____ 20. Are either the dogwood or the magnolia blooming?

CHAPTER
QUIZ 5-2

SUBJECT-VERB AGREEMENT

DIRECTIONS: Determine whether the correct verb is used in each sentence. If it is correct, write *C* in the blank provided. If it is not, write the correct verb.

_____ 1.   The vitamins and minerals in a person's diet affects energy and health.

_____ 2.   Within every bite of broccoli is vitamin A and vitamin C.

_____ 3.   Many foods, including oranges, spinach, and cantaloupe, contains vitamin C.

_____ 4.   An essential of nutritious diets is carbohydrates, protein, and fat.

_____ 5.   Either a fast-food hamburger or milkshake has too much sodium and fat for good health.

_____ 6.   Either of those foods sound nutritious, but neither of them is.

_____ 7.   Foods with an abundant content of sodium causes heart disease.

_____ 8.   Milk, in addition to apples, broccoli, potatoes, and whole wheat bread, are very nutritious.

_____ 9.   Milk and liver contain nearly all the essentials for good health.

_____ 10. Winter squash or carrots give us vitamin A.

_____ 11. There's vitamins and minerals in many foods.

_____ 12. Preparing fish for the evening meal and eating yogurt for lunch has become popular.

_____ 13. Everybody in the lines at the grocery stores were carrying cartons of yogurt and packages of fish.

_____ 14. There's many good reasons for buying fish and yogurt.

_____ 15. Fish, potatoes, and a vegetable makes a nutritious meal.

_____ 16. The calcium and protein in yogurt causes bones to break less easily.

NAME _____   DATE _____

INSTRUCTOR _____   CLASS TIME _____

_____ 17. Eating yogurt, together with milk, cheese, and ice cream, give the body needed calcium.

_____ 18. The biggest hurdle in eating well is fast-food restaurants.

_____ 19. Each of you go to a fast-food restaurant when time is short.

_____ 20. Many prepared dinners in the frozen food section of the grocery store contain little nutrition.

6 VERBS

Learning to correctly use verbs will help you communicate clearly what action is occurring and when it occurred. Verbs give you the power to write precise and specific sentences. You have already discovered how to identify a verb in Chapter 1 and how to create subject/verb agreement in Chapter 5. Now you are going to learn how to choose the right principal part of a verb.

Verbs indicate the time of an action by their form. The form tells whether the action is in the past, the present, or the future. These verb forms are called *tenses*, from the Latin word meaning time. The English language has six tenses to indicate past, present, or future time; however, we will study only the four principal parts these tense forms are based on. The six tenses can be learned later in your writing development. All these tenses are based on the four principal parts of a verb: the present, the past, the past participle, and the present participle.

By using these four principal parts, the writer indicates the time of an action. The **present** form may, or may not, have a helping verb. The **past** form, in contrast, will not have a helping verb before it. The **past participle** is always preceded by a form of the helping verb *have* (*have, has, had*). The **present participle** is always preceded by some form of the helping verb *be* (*am, are, is, was, were, be, been*).

Present	Past	Past Participle	Present Participle
walk	walked	(have) walked	(is) walking

Look at these sentences:

Each day I *walk* to school. (present)

Last year I seldom *walked* to school. (past)

I *have walked* to school all year. (past participle)

I *am walking* to school. (present participle)

English rules are a reflection of the way the educated public uses the language. Since this usage changes over time, the rules of English also change. A particular change that has made our language easier concerns verbs. In past centuries, verbs were much more confusing than they are today because they had many different principal parts. Over time these various forms evolved into a simplified pattern. The verbs that fit into this easily remembered and regular pattern are called *regular verbs*.

REGULAR VERBS

Most English verbs are regular: to form both the past and the past participle of a regular verb, you merely add *-ed* to the present form. If the verb in present form already ends in an *e,* form the past tenses by adding only the *-d.* The four principal parts of two regular verbs (*to sigh* and *to dance*) are given in the chart below.

Present	Past	Past Participle	Present Participle
sigh	sighed	(have) sighed	(is) sighing
dance	danced	(have) danced	(is) dancing

In the list above, note that the first two principal parts contain only one word—past or present. The last two principal parts include the additional word *participle* in their names. Since the word *participle* is an additional word, think of the verb you create as also having an additional word—a helping verb. The helping verbs for the past participle will be either *have, has,* or *had.* The helping verbs for the present participle will be either *am, are, is was, were, be,* or *been.* Consider these sentences:

We *sigh* when we remember our last test. (present)

We *sighed* when we saw our grades. (past)

That boy *has sighed* all class period. (past participle)

That boy *is sighing.* (present participle)

They *dance* well together. (present)

They *danced* at King's Island last summer. (past)

They *had danced* for many years. (past participle)

They *are dancing* in the show this summer. (present participle)

© NTC/CONTEMPORARY PUBLISHING COMPANY

An easy way to select the correct *present* time (or tense as it is called) is to say to yourself "Today I _____" and then fill in the blank with the verb. To choose the correct *past* tense, say "Yesterday I _____" and again fill in the blank with the verb. Likewise, to create the correct *past participle,* say "I have _____" and fill in the verb form. The past participle is preceded by some form of the *have* verb: *have, has, had.* To distinguish the correct *present participle,* say "I am _____" and fill in the verb form. The *-ing* form of the verb is preceded by some form of the *be* verb: *am, are, is, was, were, be, been.*

Look at these sentences:

Today I sigh. (present)

Yesterday I sighed. (past)

I have sighed. (past participle)

I am sighing. (present participle)

Today I dance. (present)

Yesterday I danced. (past)

I have danced. (past participle)

I am dancing. (present participle)

TRY-IT
EXERCISE

Fill in the correct past, past participle, and present participle form of the verb used.

1. Today I like carrots.
   Yesterday I _____ carrots.
   I have _____ carrots for years.
   I am _____ carrots.

2. Today I start the diet.
   Yesterday I _____ the diet.
   I have _____ the diet.
   I am _____ the diet.

The answers to the first group are *liked, liked,* and *liking.* The answers to the second group are *started, started,* and *starting.*

A regular verb that frequently confuses students is *ask*. The past and past participle should end in *-ed*, but often this ending is incorrectly dropped. For example, many students will write the past or past participle as they hear it pronounced: "After class I ask the teacher for my assignment." This sentence is incorrect because the rule for forming the past tense has been ignored. The verb should be changed to *asked*.

IRREGULAR VERBS

Though most verbs in our language adapted to the regular way of indicating past time, some refused this convenient change. These are irregular verbs. Unlike regular verbs, they do not form the past and past participle simply by adding *-ed*. Though the number of these verbs is not large compared to regular verbs, these are the verbs that give us the most trouble.

The key to success with these verbs is to discover which ones you do not know. To help you determine that, refer to the following list of thirty of the most commonly misused irregular verbs in their present tense. Write what you believe to be the past and the past participle of each of these thirty verbs. Do not look ahead to see whether you are correct. Complete this exercise and check your answers, then list the verbs you did not know. Now you can concentrate on learning these and cease to worry about the verbs you got right. By narrowing your personal list to only the few verbs that challenge you, your studying will be more effective.

TRY-IT

EXERCISE

For each of the following verbs, write what you believe to be the past, past participle, and present participle. An example of what you will do has been done for you. Remember to say "Yesterday I (verb)" to determine the past tense, "I have (verb)" to determine the past participle, and "I am (verb)" to determine the present participle forms.

Present	Past	Past Participle	Present Participle
bite	bit	bitten	biting

1. begin _____
2. blow _____
3. break _____
4. choose _____

© NTC/CONTEMPORARY PUBLISHING COMPANY

5. do _____
6. drink _____
7. drive _____
8. eat _____
9. fly _____
10. freeze _____
11. give _____
12. go _____
13. hide _____
14. know _____
15. lead _____
16. meet _____
17. ride _____
18. ring _____
19. run _____
20. see _____
21. sing _____
22. speak _____
23. spring _____
24. steal _____
25. swim _____
26. take _____
27. tear _____
28. throw _____
29. wear _____
30. write _____

Whenever you are writing and do not know the past or past participle of a verb, you will find the information in your dictionary. If the verb is irregular, the dictionary will list the principal parts for you. If there are no principal parts given, form the past and past participle using the regular method. Below are the principal parts for the irregular verbs. Now check your list against this one and learn the verbs you do not know.

Present	Past	Past Participle	Present Participle
begin	began	begun	beginning
blow	blew	blown	blowing
break	broke	broken	breaking
choose	chose	chosen	choosing
do	did	done	doing
drink	drank	drunk	drinking

Present	Past	Past Participle	Present Participle
drive	drove	driven	driving
eat	ate	eaten	eating
fly	flew	flown	flying
freeze	froze	frozen	freezing
give	gave	given	giving
go	went	gone	going
hide	hid	hidden	hiding
know	knew	known	knowing
lead	led	led	leading
meet	met	met	meeting
ride	rode	ridden	riding
ring	rang	rung	ringing
run	ran	run	running
see	saw	seen	seeing
sing	sang	sung	singing
speak	spoke	spoken	speaking
spring	sprang	sprung	springing
steal	stole	stolen	stealing
swim	swam	swum	swimming
take	took	taken	taking
tear	tore	torn	tearing
throw	threw	thrown	throwing
wear	wore	worn	wearing
write	wrote	written	writing

PRACTICE	# PRINCIPAL PARTS OF
EXERCISE 6-1	# IRREGULAR VERBS

For the following exercises remember that the principal parts or tenses of a verb indicate time. To use the correct present verb say, "Today I _____" and fill in the blank. The difference between past and past participle is that the past participle will have a helping verb with it. To select the correct past tense verb say, "Yesterday I _____" and fill in the blank. For the correct past participle say, "I have _____" and fill in the blank.

Underline the correct verb.

EXAMPLE: I should have (spoke, <u>spoken</u>) to him yesterday.

1. By the time I get my car paid for, it will have (wore, worn) out.

2. We have just (began, begun) the unit on verbs.

3. Have you and Trevor (chose, chosen) your new jobs yet?

4. The rain must have really (blew, blown) hard last night.

5. Tracy has already (ate, eaten) breakfast.

6. Last fall, Conrad (lead, led) the United Fund campaign.

7. She has (drank, drunk) three cups of coffee.

8. Yoko just recently (saw, seen) her ring.

9. Have you kids (wrote, written) those thank-you notes?

10. Have any of you (hid, hidden) the Sunday paper?

NAME _____ DATE _____

INSTRUCTOR _____ CLASS TIME _____

| PRACTICE EXERCISE 6-2 | # USING PRINCIPAL PARTS OF IRREGULAR VERBS |

For each of the following verbs, create four sentences, the first in present tense, the second in past, the third in past participle, and the fourth in present participle.

EXAMPLE: break

present: *The waitress breaks a lot of dishes.*

past: *I broke one of Mother's pieces of china.*

past participle: *Kevin has broken his leg.*

present participle: *I am breaking some bad habits.*

1. do

_____

_____

_____

2. give

_____

_____

_____

3. fly

_____

_____

_____

_____

NAME _____ DATE _____

INSTRUCTOR _____ CLASS TIME _____

4. drive

_____

_____

_____

_____

5. freeze

_____

_____

_____

_____

6. go

_____

_____

_____

_____

7. run

_____

_____

_____

_____

8. know

_____

_____

_____

_____

9. meet

_____

_____

_____

_____

10. speak

_____

_____

_____

_____

TRANSITIVE AND INTRANSITIVE VERBS: THE SIX MOST DIFFICULT

Though we attempt to keep terminology to a minimum, certain terms are necessary to improve your understanding. Such is the case with the terms *transitive* and *intransitive*. If it were not for six particular verbs, you would not even need these terms. But because these verbs are often used (and, more often than not, misused), you need to learn to use each correctly.

A verb is transitive when there is a transfer of action from the subject to the object. In Chapter 1 you learned that the receiver of an action verb is called the direct object. So a transitive verb always has a direct object. Note that both *transitive* and *transfer* begin with the same prefix. *Trans* means to move across, so if you can remember the logic of a transitive verb transferring action across to an object, you will easily remember that transitive and direct object always go together.

A verb is intransitive when there is no direct object and no transfer of action. Note the logic of this term. The prefix *in-* has the meaning of *not*. For example, people who are *not* sincere are *in*sincere. Likewise, people are either active or inactive, competent or incompetent, direct or indirect, and so on. Therefore, an intransitive verb is *not* transitive and does not have an object.

In the following sentences, the transitive verbs have their direct objects italicized. The sentences with no italicizing have no direct objects and, therefore, contain intransitive verbs:

1. Pedro's nervousness increased his *restlessness.*
2. Pedro's nervousness increased with each passing minute.
3. Letitia grew all her own *food.*
4. Letitia grew tired of waiting.
5. Earl read the *textbook.*
6. Earl read each evening after supper.
7. Mother felt the baby's *diaper.*
8. Mother felt exhausted.
9. Natasha got a bonus *check.*
10. Natasha got excited.

© NTC/CONTEMPORARY PUBLISHING COMPANY

TRY-IT
EXERCISE

Many verbs can be either transitive or intransitive, depending on how they are used in a sentence. In the following sentences, identify each verb as transitive (T) or intransitive (I).

_____ 1. Darnell feels fine.
_____ 2. Darnell feels his foot.
_____ 3. Joe called at three o'clock.
_____ 4. Joe called Barbara.

The second and fourth sentences each have a direct object, so the verbs are transitive. The first and third sentences do not have direct objects, and the verbs are, therefore, intransitive.

It would not matter so much that you learn the meanings of *transitive* and *intransitive* except that it will aid your understanding of three pairs of difficult verbs. Below are the pairs and their principal parts.

Present	Past	Past Participle	Present Participle
raise	raised	raised	raising
rise	rose	risen	rising
lay	laid	laid	laying
lie	lay	lain	lying
set	set	set	setting
sit	sat	sat	sitting

The first verb of each pair is transitive and will therefore have a direct object, whether in the present form, in one of the past forms, or in the *-ing* form. The second verb of each pair is intransitive; no direct object will be present. One way to help you remember which verb is intransitive is to look at the present tense spellings. *Rise, lie,* and *sit* each contain the letter *i*. Make that letter *i* stand for intransitive. Also the verbs *raise* and *lay*, which are transitive, form their past tenses by ending in a *d*. Make that *d* stand for direct object so you can easily remember they are the transitive ones. Make the memorization of these verbs logical to save yourself time and confusion.

Below are sample sentences for these six verbs in the *present* tense. The first three sentences are the transitive ones of the pairs and have italicized direct objects. The last three sentences are the intransitive verbs and have no direct object:

1. Please raise the *window*.
2. Lay your *books* under your desk.
3. Set the *date* for the test.
4. Rise when a judge enters the courtroom.
5. Lie down and take a nap.
6. Sit down and rest.

In order to know which verb from this list of six is correct, you must know whether the verb is transitive or intransitive and the principal parts for each of the six. Once you learn these basics, you will no longer be confused about which form to use.

PRACTICE EXERCISE 6-3

PRINCIPAL PARTS—THE SIX MOST DIFFICULT VERBS

Without looking at the previous chart, write in the blanks the past ("Yesterday I _____"), past participle ("I have _____"), and the present participle (*-ing* ending) of each of the following verbs.

Present	Past	Past Participle	Present Participle
raise			
rise			
lay			
lie			
set			
sit			

NAME _____ DATE _____

INSTRUCTOR _____ CLASS TIME _____

| PRACTICE EXERCISE 6-4 | # USING THE SIX MOST DIFFICULT VERBS |

Before each sentence are two trios of present tense verbs. If there is no direct object in the sentence given, choose the correct verb from the intransitive trio; if the sentence has a direct object, underline that word and choose the correct verb from the transitive trio. Write the correct principal part of the verb in the blank.

EXAMPLE: *lie/lay/lain* or *lay/laid/laid*

The poker player has __*laid*__ his <u>cards</u> on the table.

1. *sit/sat/sat* or *set/set/set*

   Yesterday Dwight _____ at his desk for twelve hours.

2. *sit/sat/sat* or *set/set/set*

   Today he _____ a new rule about working long hours.

3. *rise/rose/risen* or *raise/raised/raised*

   Whatever the circumstances, Gladys has always _____ to the occasion.

4. *rise/rose/risen* or *raise/raised/raised*

   Whenever they are nearby, they _____ people's spirits.

5. *lie/lay/lain* or *lay/laid/laid*

   Today I will _____ in the backyard and get a tan.

6. *lie/lay/lain* or *lay/laid/laid*

   I have _____ several medicines on my desk.

7. *sit/sat/sat* or *set/set/set*

   Some people _____ their values based on introspection.

8. *sit/sat/sat* or *set/set/set*

   Others _____ idly by and accept the values of the past without thinking.

9. *lie/lay/lain* or *lay/laid/laid*

   Yesterday Howard _____ carpet for the last time.

10. *lie/lay/lain* or *lay/laid/laid*

    He has _____ in traction for weeks since hurting his back.

NAME _____ DATE _____

INSTRUCTOR _____ CLASS TIME _____

© NTC/CONTEMPORARY PUBLISHING COMPANY

PRACTICE
EXERCISE 6-5
CHOOSING THE CORRECT VERB FROM THE SIX MOST DIFFICULT

Underline the correct verb. If there is a direct object, underline it also.

EXAMPLE: The teacher had (<u>laid</u>, lain) our graded <u>tests</u> on his desk.

1. My father has been (sitting, setting) tulip bulbs in the garden.

2. I had (laid, lain) my ring on the sink.

3. The colorful hot-air balloons (raise, rise) to the sky.

4. The doctor walked into the bedroom and (set, sat) on the bed.

5. Then she (set, sat) her bag on the bed to open it.

6. I was (lying, laying) on a lawn chair in sunny Florida.

7. The people in the stadium silently stood as the flag (raised, rose) to the top of the pole.

8. The cost of renting an apartment has (raised, risen) alarmingly.

9. Who has (laid, lain) these textbooks on my desk?

10. Taxes have been (raising, rising) every year since I began paying them.

NAME _____ DATE _____

INSTRUCTOR _____ CLASS TIME _____

PRACTICE EXERCISE 6-6	# CHOOSING THE CORRECT VERB FROM THE SIX MOST DIFFICULT

Underline the correct verb. If there is a direct object, underline it also.

EXAMPLE: Which one of you has (<u>laid</u>, lain) her <u>coat</u> on the chair?

1. Inflation has recently (risen, rose) beyond 5 percent a year.

2. It has been steadily (rising, raising) for over a year.

3. High inflation will (raise, rise) interest rates.

4. I have (lain, laid) my book under the desk.

5. I have (lain, laid) in the sun all afternoon.

6. (Lay, Lie) your books on the table.

7. The baby is (lying, laying) on the bed.

8. Yesterday I (lay, laid) the baby on the bed.

9. Yesterday I (lay, laid) in bed.

10. I have (set, sat) here for over an hour.

NAME _____ DATE _____

INSTRUCTOR _____ CLASS TIME _____

REVIEW EXERCISE 6-1 | IRREGULAR VERBS

DIRECTIONS: Underline any incorrect verb form; write the accepted form in the blank provided. Mark all correct sentences with a *C.*

_____ 1.   If he had drunk anymore, he'd be sick.

_____ 2.   Has he ever went to a class reunion?

_____ 3.   Has the whistle blew yet?

_____ 4.   After an hour, his stomach begun to feel better.

_____ 5.   Why didn't you say you had threw it away?

_____ 6.   Had you broke the news more gently, it would have been better.

_____ 7.   I might have swam yesterday, but it was too cold.

_____ 8.   They have ridden those motorcycles all day.

_____ 9.   Last winter the ice froze early.

_____ 10.   Has the bell rung for class yet?

_____ 11.   Last weekend I ask everyone to come to the party.

_____ 12.   He has chose his committee.

_____ 13.   Someone had tore the draperies.

_____ 14.   How far have we drove today?

_____ 15.   I done that job yesterday.

_____ 16.   If I had only wrote her earlier, she could have come.

_____ 17.   They have just recently stole those ideas.

_____ 18.   We have ran all over this park.

_____ 19.   At the game yesterday, we lead the parade.

_____ 20.   I have saw all these verbs before.

NAME _____ DATE _____

INSTRUCTOR _____ CLASS TIME _____

| REVIEW | # TRANSITIVE AND INTRANSITIVE |
| EXERCISE 6-2 | # VERBS: THE SIX MOST DIFFICULT |

DIRECTIONS: Underline the correct verb. If the verb is transitive, underline its direct object.

1. You've been (laying, lying) in the sun too long.

2. You should be (laying, lying) a towel over your sunburned face.

3. I have (set, sat) at the desk for three hours.

4. I had them (set, sit) my desk in front of the window.

5. Will you (raise, rise) when the speaker enters?

6. Will the speech (raise, rise) controversy?

7. Why don't you (lay, lie) down and take a nap?

8. Why don't you (lay, lie) the knapsack down and take a break?

9. I have been (setting, sitting) in this doctor's office for over an hour.

10. They have been (setting, sitting) the date for their wedding.

11. The smoke has (raised, risen) in the sky.

12. The pollution has (raised, risen) some questions by the public.

13. She has (laid, lain) her highest cards on the table.

14. The child has (laid, lain) in bed with a very high fever.

15. He (sets, sits) his dog in the passenger seat of his car.

16. When the owner goes into a store, his dog (sets, sits) in the driver's seat behind the steering wheel.

17. Fat yeast rolls were (raising, rising) in the oven.

18. The good smell of food was (raising, rising) hopes that dinner would soon be served.

19. Yesterday she (set, sat) and cried about her lack of a promising future.

20. Today she (set, sat) some goals and is entering college to earn a nursing degree.

NAME _____ DATE _____

INSTRUCTOR _____ CLASS TIME _____

REVIEW
EXERCISE 6-3

IRREGULAR VERBS, INCLUDING THE SIX MOST DIFFICULT

DIRECTIONS: Underline any incorrect verb; write the corrected form in the blank provided. Mark all correct sentences with a *C*.

_____ 1. If we set here much longer, we'll be late to our next class.

_____ 2. Has she ever wore that dress she bought?

_____ 3. All our dishes have been broke by the movers.

_____ 4. Since the election, stocks have been raising steadily.

_____ 5. I think that I have wrote seven pages of lecture notes today.

_____ 6. Have you spoke to the teacher about this?

_____ 7. I forgot that I had lain the flashlight on the roof of the car.

_____ 8. Had you ever flew before?

_____ 9. Set the baby on the chair where I was sitting.

_____ 10. Had you given him a chance, he would have ask to come.

_____ 11. I will lie down and rest until the alarm rings.

_____ 12. She can lay on the beach all afternoon.

_____ 13. Beyond this point the road raises rapidly.

_____ 14. Had you ever sang that song before tonight?

_____ 15. Piles of tests and papers were laying on the teacher's desk.

_____ 16. That dog has lain in the sun all afternoon.

_____ 17. Call the doctor if the child's temperature raises.

_____ 18. He forgot that the dog was lying under the porch.

_____ 19. Yesterday he chose his classes for next quarter.

_____ 20. We hardly set down at all during the final quarter of the game.

NAME _____ DATE _____

INSTRUCTOR _____ CLASS TIME _____

CHAPTER	**THE SIX MOST DIFFICULT**
QUIZ 6-1	**VERBS**

DIRECTIONS: Underline any verbs that are incorrect for standard formal writing. Then write the correct verb beside the sentence. Mark correct sentences with a *C.*

_____ 1. It has set there undisturbed all day.

_____ 2. I've been laying in bed watching TV and eating all day long.

_____ 3. Set next to me and you can see better.

_____ 4. Please sit the baby in the bassinet.

_____ 5. Let the baby set in his playpen.

_____ 6. If you will lay the baby on the floor, she will lie there peacefully.

_____ 7. We were setting beside the fireplace.

_____ 8. The book is lying exactly where you left it.

_____ 9. His adrenaline level was rising so quickly that his face lost color.

_____ 10. The waves had raised to great height.

_____ 11. She has sat there in that chair ever since you left.

_____ 12. Rover, lay down!

_____ 13. He hasn't lain the shingles on the right roof.

_____ 14. The roaring river has been rising higher during the night.

_____ 15. Have you laid in the sun all afternoon?

_____ 16. Please set this centerpiece on the table.

_____ 17. Have they been laying in the tanning booth too long?

_____ 18. The sweater had lain in the box for days.

NAME _____ DATE _____

INSTRUCTOR _____ CLASS TIME _____

_____ 19. I saw the nurse sit the medicine on the table.

_____ 20. Set down and talk to me.

CHAPTER	**PRINCIPAL PARTS OF ALL**
QUIZ 6-2	**VERBS**

DIRECTIONS: Underline any verb forms that would not be acceptable in formal written usage and write the correct form beside the sentence. Mark all correct sentences with a *C*.

_____ 1. "I wish I never had chose this dress!" she exclaimed.

_____ 2. He had spoke to every new person in the meeting and had given each a personal welcome.

_____ 3. If he had not sprang out of bed, he wouldn't have broken his ankle.

_____ 4. She assured her friends that she had absolutely never did the stunt before, for many people had begun to question her.

_____ 5. Had he flew his plane more carefully, he could have broken the records.

_____ 6. We enjoyed sitting by the lake, so we sat there all day.

_____ 7. Will you please sit this iced tea in the refrigerator?

_____ 8. She has lead the debate team to victory for four years.

_____ 9. She forgot where she had laid her purse and wondered if someone had hid it.

_____ 10. When I was younger, I wish I had drunk more milk and eaten more vegetables.

_____ 11. Last night for the first time since we met, I ask Yolanda for a date.

_____ 12. I'll raise this window before I lie down and rest.

_____ 13. Some of the students had not wrote an essay since junior high English.

NAME _____ DATE _____

INSTRUCTOR _____ CLASS TIME _____

© NTC/CONTEMPORARY PUBLISHING COMPANY

_____ 14. The kitten has laid under my bed the entire afternoon and will probably lie there until dinner time.

_____ 15. The box is setting on the top shelf of the cupboard.

_____ 16. Yesterday, I sat in my bedroom until my sister decided to lay down and take a nap.

_____ 17. Though we had never laid logs for a fire, we began following her instructions.

_____ 18. Haven't you ever went to a three-ring circus?

_____ 19. She had tore her skirt so badly that she wore her coat around her waist.

_____ 20. The hose has lain in the yard all winter and will probably be lying there when June arrives.

PRONOUNS

Assume you read the following paragraph in a book: "Ashley got up very early in the morning. After Ashley got out of bed and took Ashley's shower, Ashley dressed and drove to the gas station. After putting gasoline in Ashley's car, Ashley then drove quickly to work. When Ashley arrived, Ashley's boss asked to talk with Ashley."

Isn't this passage childlike, choppy, and boring? Through the use of pronouns, you can avoid needless repetition such as in the paragraph above. If you use pronouns correctly, you can write interesting, flowing paragraphs and avoid the bumpy and dull writing style you just read.

If you break the word *pronoun* into its two syllables, you can understand better what a pronoun does. *Pro* is a prefix meaning "for," and a *noun* names a person, place, object, event, substance, or idea. In other words, a pronoun is a replacement *for a noun*. That is, a pronoun functions as a noun does, though there are some differences.

While there are thousands and thousands of nouns, there are few pronouns. A noun is specific and clear in meaning, but a pronoun can be general and unclear. Hence, caution is necessary when using any pronoun. Also, pronouns have various forms, and a writer must use a given form in a given instance. Let's begin learning these forms by classifying the pronouns into their three cases: **nominative, objective**, and **possessive**. All three case forms show the relationship of that pronoun to other words in the sentence, and each takes its name from that relationship. Specifically, a pronoun that is the subject of a verb is in the nominative case; a pronoun that acts as the object of a verb or preposition is in the objective case; a pronoun that possesses something is in the possessive case. Consider the following sentences:

▼ **Pronoun as subject:**   *He* talked to the teacher.
▼ **Pronoun as object:**   The teacher understood *him.*
▲ **Possessive pronoun:**   *Their* discussion was helpful.

The pronoun *he* is the subject of the verb *talked;* the pronoun *him* is the direct object of the verb *understood;* the pronoun *their* shows whose discussion and is possessive.

NOMINATIVE CASE

The word *nominative* is from Latin, meaning "belonging to a name." In grammar, nominative case, sometimes called *subject case,* designates the subject of a verb, as well as words that refer back to that subject. As you learned in Chapter 1, predicate nominatives refer back to the subject and rename it. Therefore, any *subject* or *predicate nominative* is said to be in the nominative case. Look at the following sentences:

> *Gerald* is getting good grades.
>
> *He* is getting good grades.
>
> The student with the good grades is *Gerald.*
>
> The student with the good grades is *he.*

Each of these sentences is about a student named Gerald: Gerald = student = he. In each, the noun *student* or *Gerald* (or a pronoun standing for him) is the subject. In the first and third sentences, his name is used. In the second and fourth sentences, a pronoun "stands for" his name. In all four sentences, *Gerald*—or a pronoun standing for him—is either the subject of the sentence or a word referring back to the subject. All subjects, and words referring back to the subjects, are in the nominative case.

Students usually have little trouble with single subjects and predicate nominatives. Be careful, however, when a pronoun is half of a compound element. Pronouns in compound elements can be simplified by testing each element of the compound separately. For example, "She is getting good grades" causes no trouble. But when changed to "Gerald and (she/her) are getting good grades," we must handle each half of the compound by itself: "Gerald" and "(she/her)." Testing each separately, it is easier to see that the correct pronoun still is *she.*

As the name implies, a predicate nominative is in the nominative case. Be aware that in informal, colloquial English, however, it is acceptable to use objective case for predicate nominatives. In standard, formal written English, however, use nominative case for all predicate nominatives. Any subject or predicate nominative is said to be in the nominative case.

© NTC/CONTEMPORARY PUBLISHING COMPANY

TRY-IT
EXERCISE

In the following sentences, underline the subject and the predicate nominative (if any) in each sentence.

1. Sandra was asking the questions.
2. She was asking the questions.
3. The student asking the questions was Sandra.
4. The student asking the questions was she.

In the first sentence, the subject is *Sandra* and there is no predicate nominative. In the second sentence, *she* is the subject, and there is no predicate nominative. In the third sentence, the subject is *student,* and the predicate nominative is *Sandra.* In the fourth sentence, the subject is *student,* and the predicate nominative is *she.* Each of these sentences is about a student named Sandra: Sandra = student = she. In each, the noun *student* or *Sandra* is the subject. In the first and third sentences, her name is used. In the second and fourth sentences, a pronoun "stands for" her name. In all four sentences, *Sandra*—or a pronoun standing for her—is either the subject of the sentence or a word referring back to the subject. All subjects, and words referring back to subjects, are in the nominative case.

Remember that the nominative case is used for (1) the subject or (2) the predicate nominative. Table 7.1 is a chart of personal pronouns in the nominative case.

It might help you to remember the pronouns in the column labeled *Singular* by thinking of the number "1" as an I; after all, *I* is the first person in anyone's life. The word *you* (or some form of *you*) is always the second person. If you (second person) and I (first person) are talking about someone or something else, we would refer to this third person as *he, she,* or *it.* Once you know the *Singular* column, you create the *Plural* column by assuming there are more than one gathered. Several *I*s become *we*, several *you*s become *you* (the plural of *you* never has an *s* sound on the end, though), and several *he*s, *she*s, or *it*s become *they*.

TABLE 7.1 *Nominative Pronoun Chart*		
	Singular	**Plural**
First person	I	we
Second person	you	you
Third person	he, she, it	they

Once you memorize this first pronoun chart, the other two charts will be easy to remember because they derive from the nominative chart.

PRACTICE
EXERCISE 7-1
IDENTIFICATION OF THE NOMINATIVE CASE

Underline any words in the following sentences that are used in the nominative case. On the line below, identify these words as subjects (S) or predicate nominatives (PN).

EXAMPLE: <u>Joan</u> and <u>George</u> are pleasant <u>people</u>.

Joan—S   George—S   people—PN _____

1. Joan is a nurse.

    _____

2. José became a manager at State Farm Insurance.

    _____

3. They are parents of six children.

    _____

4. To their children, they were friends and advisors.

    _____

5. Joan and he have been parents for twenty-five years.

    _____

6. She was Joe's mother before she was Juanita's mother.

    _____

7. When someone asks for Joan on the phone, she says, "This is she."

    _____

8. George and she are gardeners on Sunday afternoons.

    _____

9. He and Joan have a lovely yard.

    _____

10. They are good neighbors.

    _____

NAME _____   DATE _____

INSTRUCTOR _____   CLASS TIME _____

PRACTICE	# USING THE NOMINATIVE CASE
EXERCISE 7-2	

Create a sentence using the listed pronoun as indicated. You may need to review the linking verbs listed in Chapter 1.

EXAMPLE: *She* as subject

She is working hard on these exercises.

1. *I* as subject

   _____

2. *You* as subject

   _____

3. *He* as subject

   _____

4. *It* as subject

   _____

5. *We* as subject

   _____

6. *They* as subject

   _____

7. *I* as predicate nominative

   _____

8. *He* as predicate nominative

   _____

9. *She* as predicate nominative

   _____

10. *They* as predicate nominative

    _____

NAME _____ DATE _____

INSTRUCTOR _____ CLASS TIME _____

OBJECTIVE CASE

The term *objective case* appropriately contains within it the word *object*. The reasoning is simple: any noun or pronoun used as an object is in the objective case. The objects we already know are direct objects, indirect objects, or objects of a preposition. Look at the following sentences:

My teacher told *me* about the study session.

I thanked *her* for the advice.

She gives *us* extra help in the evening.

She handed *them* the practice exercises.

They studied with *me*.

I gave my notes to *her*.

In the first sentence, the pronoun *me* is the direct object of the verb *told*. In the second sentence, the pronoun *her* is the direct object of the verb *thanked*. In the third sentence, the pronoun *us* is the indirect object of the verb *gives*. In the fourth sentence, the pronoun *them* is the indirect object of the verb *handed*. In the fifth sentence, the pronoun *me* is the object of the preposition *with*. In the sixth sentence, the pronoun *her* is the object of the preposition *to*.

Students usually have little trouble with single objects. Be careful, however, when a pronoun is half of a compound element. Pronouns in compound elements can be simplified by testing each element of the compound separately. For example, "This test is for *me*" causes no trouble. But when changed to "This test is for Jan and (I/me)," we must handle each half of the compound by itself: "for Jan" and "for (I/me)." Testing each separately, it is easier to see that the correct pronoun still is *me*.

TRY-IT
EXERCISE

In the following sentences, underline and identify the pronouns used as direct object (DO), indirect object (IO), or object of the preposition (OP) in each sentence.

_____ 1. Darnell told the other students and me about the study session.

_____ 2. Brandon called Austin and her that evening.

_____ 3. She gives Brandon and us advice.

_____ 4. Darnell offered Austin and them popcorn.

© NTC/CONTEMPORARY PUBLISHING COMPANY

_____ 5. They studied with Darnell and me.
_____ 6. Tests are hard for Brandon and him.

In the first sentence, the pronoun *me* is half the compound direct object of the verb *told.* In the second sentence, the pronoun *her* is half the compound direct object of the verb *called.* In the third sentence, the pronoun *us* is half the compound indirect object of the verb *gives,* and in the fourth sentence, the pronoun *them* is half the compound indirect object of the verb *offered.* In the fifth sentence, the pronoun *me* is half the compound object of the preposition *with.* In the sixth sentence, the pronoun *him* is half the compound object of the preposition *for.*

We said that once you learn the nominative personal pronoun chart, the other charts will be easy to remember. This simplicity is possible because you recall the nominative chart to create the objective. All you have to do is think of a simple sentence with an open slot for an object, maybe a direct object: "I like _____." Then look at the nominative chart, repeat the sentence, and fill in the pronoun slot. For example, to transfer the first person nominative singular pronoun to the objective case, you would not say "I like *I*," but, rather, "I like *me*." As you continue repeating and completing the simple sentence, you will create a chart as shown in Table 7.2.

TABLE 7.2 *Objective Pronoun Chart*		
	Singular	**Plural**
First person	me	us
Second person	you	you
Third person	him, her, it	them

Use the objective form if a pronoun is a direct object, indirect object, or object of a preposition.

PRACTICE	**IDENTIFICATION OF THE**
EXERCISE 7-3	**OBJECTIVE CASE**

Underline any words in the following sentences that are used in the objective case. These words will be both nouns and pronouns. On the line below, identify these words as direct object (DO), indirect object (IO), or object of a preposition (OP).

EXAMPLE: Hae and Tony met <u>us</u> at the <u>restaurant</u>.

Answer: us—DO   restaurant—OP

1. Choon and Peter had three children in school at one time.

_____

2. All of them now live in other cities.

_____

3. Choon cooks Peter great meals.

_____

4. Between you and me, she spoils him.

_____

5. We asked them to a party.

_____

6. Choon brought us cake for dessert.

_____

7. Joan invited her and me for lunch.

_____

8. Around him and her, I feel comfortable.

_____

9. For Peter and her, the children have been a pleasure.

_____

10. Like you and me, they want a good life for their children.

_____

NAME _____ DATE _____

INSTRUCTOR _____ CLASS TIME _____

PRACTICE	# USING THE OBJECTIVE CASE
EXERCISE 7-4	

Fill in the blanks for items 1 through 5 using the listed nominative pronoun in its *objective case*. Then indicate whether the pronoun is used as a direct object (DO), indirect object (IO), or object of a preposition (OP).

EXAMPLE: *I*   The girl with _____*me*_____ is my sister.   *OP*

1. *you*   I like _____ very much.

2. *he*   I gave _____ a picture of Sarah.

3. *it*   He listened to the idea and then made fun of _____.

4. *she*   The doctors asked questions about _____.

5. *they*   Their boss awarded _____ a plaque.

For items 6 through 10, change the listed nominative pronoun to its *objective case* and create a sentence using the objective pronoun as indicated.

6. *I* as direct object

    _____

7. *we* as object of a preposition

    _____

8. *I* as object of a preposition

    _____

9. *she* as indirect object

    _____

10. *they* as direct object

    _____

NAME _____   DATE _____

INSTRUCTOR _____   CLASS TIME _____

© NTC/CONTEMPORARY PUBLISHING COMPANY

POSSESSIVE CASE

The last case for a pronoun is possessive, which means that possession or ownership is evident. Again, the easiest way to create this chart, shown in Table 7.3, is by thinking of a brief sentence with a blank where the possessive pronoun will fit and then working your way through the nominative case chart, changing each pronoun to its possessive counterpart. You need to create two sentences here, however, because each block in the chart has two possible answers. Your sentences might be "This is _____ problem. This problem is _____."

Look at the following sentences:

Here is *my* last assignment.

Shayna gave me *her* class notes.

His opinion is very important to her.

Have you done *your* assignment for tomorrow?

Are these *their* tests?

The test on the desk is *mine.*

Each of the italicized words (*my, her, his, your, their,* and *mine*) shows possession or ownership. Each is in the possessive case.

TABLE 7.3 *Possessive Pronoun Chart*		
	Singular	**Plural**
First person	my/mine	our/ours
Second person	your/yours	your/yours
Third person	his, her/hers, its	their/theirs

TRY-IT
EXERCISE

In the following sentences, underline the pronouns used in the possessive case.

1. Luther and Melinda showed me their essays.
2. Melinda told me that she wrote her thesis statement a week ago.
3. Luther said that his essay will be four pages long.

4. He will receive a high grade on the essay; its introductory paragraph is great.
5. I hope his thesis statement is as good as hers.

In the first sentence, the possessive pronoun is *their*. (Notice that the possessive pronoun is *their,* not *there*). In the second sentence, the possessive pronoun is *her*. In the third sentence, the possessive pronoun is *his*. In the fourth sentence, the possessive pronoun is *its*. (As a possessive pronoun, *its* has no apostrophe). In the fifth sentence, the possessive pronouns are *his* and *hers*. (As a possessive pronoun, *hers* has no apostrophe).

There are some very important cautions concerning the spelling of these possessive pronouns. First of all, the third person plural is *their,* never *there*. Also, note that the pronouns ending in *-s* never need apostrophes. The form and spelling of the pronoun automatically indicate that it is from the possessive chart; therefore, there is no need to tack on an apostrophe. In addition, the spelling of the possessive pronoun *its* automatically announces to the reader that ownership is present. Again, there is no need for an apostrophe. In fact, an added apostrophe changes the idea of possession altogether and creates a contraction: *it's* always means *it is*. As a memory aid, think of the apostrophe in *it's* as the dot over an imaginary *i*, because that is always the meaning when the apostrophe is present in this pronoun.

Now you know the rules for nominative, objective, and possessive use of nouns and pronouns, as well as the three pronoun charts. As you practice choosing the correct pronoun from the respective chart, you will discover a pattern that will eventually help your selection of the correct pronoun become automatic.

© NTC/CONTEMPORARY PUBLISHING COMPANY

PRACTICE
EXERCISE 7-5

IDENTIFICATION OF POSSESSIVE CASE

Underline any pronouns in the following sentences that are used in the possessive case.

EXAMPLE: JoAn and Roger built <u>their</u> house in a woods near <u>ours</u>.

1. In <u>my</u> opinion, <u>their</u> home is beautiful.

2. <u>Their</u> yard has more trees than <u>mine</u>.

3. JoAn's house reflects <u>her</u> artistic nature.

4. She says, "<u>Your</u> tastes are similar to <u>mine</u>."

5. I reply, "I wish I had <u>your</u> view out <u>my</u> windows."

6. <u>Their</u> home grew from JoAn's dreams and Roger's blueprints.

7. Roger has <u>his</u> work areas, and JoAn has <u>hers</u>.

8. We always wanted a woods like <u>theirs</u>.

9. We told them, "<u>Our</u> yard is bare compared to <u>yours</u>."

10. The woods around <u>their</u> home with <u>its</u> multitude of birds is <u>our</u> delight.

NAME _____ DATE _____

INSTRUCTOR _____ CLASS TIME _____

PRACTICE EXERCISE 7-6

USING THE POSSESSIVE CASE

For items 1 through 7, change the listed nominative pronoun to its possessive case and create a sentence.

EXAMPLE: *I* _My mail has arrived._

1. *you* _____

2. *he* _____

3. *she* _____

4. *it* _____

5. *we* _____

6. *they* _____

7. *you* _____

For items 8 through 10, use the possessive pronoun correctly in a sentence.

8. *its* _____

9. *hers* _____

10. *theirs* _____

NAME _____ DATE _____

INSTRUCTOR _____ CLASS TIME _____

© NTC/CONTEMPORARY PUBLISHING COMPANY

PRACTICE
EXERCISE 7-7

NOMINATIVE, OBJECTIVE, AND POSSESSIVE CASE OF PERSONAL PRONOUNS

Underline the correct pronoun and indicate how the pronoun is used in the sentence: subject (S), predicate nominative (PN), direct object (DO), indirect object (IO), object of a preposition (OP), or possesion (P).

EXAMPLE: _____S_____ Jack and (I, me) make a good pair.

_____ 1. Have you met Yolanda and (he, him)?

_____ 2. The winners of the lottery were (they, them).

_____ 3. I wonder if this textbook is (yours, your's).

_____ 4. The auctioneer awarded (she, her) the famous picture.

_____ 5. (We, Us) and our supporters would not let the issue die.

_____ 6. That handsome man with my husband and (I, me) is a famous ball player.

_____ 7. I really do not believe that expensive car is (theirs, theirs').

_____ 8. Just between you and (I, me), I got the job.

_____ 9. The jeweler said my watch had a scratch on (its, it's) crystal.

_____ 10. (She, Her) and the radio station are sponsoring the benefit.

NAME _____ DATE _____

INSTRUCTOR _____ CLASS TIME _____

PRACTICE	# NOMINATIVE, OBJECTIVE, AND POSSESSIVE CASE OF PERSONAL PRONOUNS
EXERCISE 7-8	

Without looking at your answers to the previous exercise, underline the correct pronoun from the parentheses and indicate whether the word is in the nominative (N), objective (O), or possessive (P) case.

EXAMPLE: _____N_____ Jack and (I, me) make a good pair.

_____ 1. Have you met Yolanda and (he, him)?

_____ 2. The winners of the lottery were (they, them).

_____ 3. I wonder if this textbook is (yours, your's).

_____ 4. The auctioneer awarded (she, her) the famous picture.

_____ 5. (We, Us) and our supporters would not let the issue die.

_____ 6. That handsome man with my husband and (I, me) is a famous ball player.

_____ 7. I really do not believe that expensive car is (theirs, theirs').

_____ 8. Just between you and (I, me), I got the job.

_____ 9. The jeweler said my watch had a scratch on (its, it's) crystal.

_____ 10. (She, Her) and the radio station are sponsoring the benefit.

NAME _____ DATE _____

INSTRUCTOR _____ CLASS TIME _____

© NTC/CONTEMPORARY PUBLISHING COMPANY

AGREEMENT OF PRONOUN AND ANTECEDENT

You learned about subject-verb agreement in Chapter 5, and we discussed the definition for a pronoun at the beginning of this chapter. Now we will focus on the meaning of the word *antecedent*. The prefix *ante-* means *before*. So the noun that goes *before* or precedes the pronoun, and that the pronoun points back to, is called the pronoun's antecedent. The personal pronouns in Table 7.4 are often used in place of a noun.

When one of these personal pronouns is written within a paragraph or a sentence, it points back to another noun (that noun for which it is a stand-in). Pronouns are used to avoid repeating the same noun over and over in a monotonous fashion. For example, consider the following sentence: *Melissa took Melissa's purse and placed the purse on Melissa's car seat.*

This sentence is conspicuously repetitious and loses effectiveness as a result. By replacing the nouns with pronouns, however, the sentence improves. *Melissa took her purse and placed it on her car seat.* Notice the pronoun *her* is the stand-in for the antecedent *Melissa,* and the pronoun *it* is the replacement for the antecedent *purse.* Such pronoun usage makes sentences less repetitious and helps them to flow more smoothly.

Pronouns and Antecedents Agree in Number

The basic rule is that if the antecedent is singular, the associated pronoun must be singular. If the antecedent is plural, the pronoun must be plural. In other words, the pronoun and its antecedent must agree in number. Look at the following sentences:

The boy asked his father for some money.

The boys asked their father for some money.

In the first sentence, the pronoun *his* is singular because it points back to the antecedent *boy,* which also is singular. In the second sentence, the pronoun *their* is plural because it must match the plural antecedent *boys.*

TABLE 7.4 *Personal Pronouns*

	Singular	Plural
First person	I, me, my, mine	we, us, our, ours
Second person	you, your, yours	you, your, yours
Third person	he, him, his, she, her, hers, it, its	they, them, their, theirs

COMPOUND ANTECEDENTS.   Similar to the rules you have already learned for subject-verb agreement, two antecedents joined by *and* are plural and, therefore, the pronoun should be plural. Likewise, when two antecedents are joined by *or* or *nor,* the pronoun agrees with the number of the nearest one. Look at the following examples:

> The Cadillac and the Lincoln give pleasure to their owners.
>
> Either the Cadillac or the Lincoln gives its owner driving pleasure.

The first sentence has the two antecedents, *Cadillac* and *Lincoln,* connected by *and,* creating a plural. The pronoun *their* is plural to agree in number. The second sentence connects these same two antecedents with an *or,* and the antecedent nearest the pronoun is singular. Therefore, the singular pronoun *its* is used.

TRY-IT
EXERCISE

In each of the following sentences, underline the correct pronoun.

1. Lucille and Hyeon had finished (her/their) assignments.
2. Lucille or Hyeon had not finished (her/their) assignments.
3. When Joel and Itamar get here, tell (him/them) to eat.
4. If Joel or Itamar gets here, tell (him/them) to eat.
5. Neither Jesse nor Jasper was home for (his/their) dinner.
6. Jesse and Jasper will be home tonight for (his/their) dinner.
7. When Stella or Ariel comes for supper, give (her/them) a piece of Grandma's banana pie.
8. Stella and Ariel are coming for supper to get (her/their) piece of banana pie.
9. After Lu Ann or Leona does those dishes, ask (her/them) to come over for some pie.
10. When Lu Ann and Leona finish the dishes, ask (her/them) to come over for some pie.

In sentence one, the correct pronoun is *their* because the antecedent is joined by *and.* In sentence two, the correct pronoun is *her* because the antecedent is joined by *or*. In sentence three, the correct pronoun is *them* because the antecedent is joined by *and*. In sentence four, the correct pronoun is *him* because the antecedent is joined by *or*. In sentence five, the correct pronoun is *his* because the antecedent is joined by *nor*. In sentence six, the correct pronoun is *their* because the antecedent is joined by *and*. In sentence seven, the correct pronoun is *her* because the antecedent is joined by *or*. In sentence eight, the correct pronoun is *their* because the antecedent is joined by *and*. In sentence nine, the correct pronoun is *her* because the antecedent is joined by *or*. In sentence ten, the correct pronoun is *them* because the antecedent is joined by *and*.

SINGULAR INDEFINITE PRONOUNS. You learned some of the indefinite pronouns in Chapter 5 while discussing subject-verb agreement. These pronouns are called indefinite because the words themselves are nonspecific or indefinite. The easiest way to remember these pronouns is to arrange them logically into singular and plural groups and to memorize each group. The indefinite pronouns that are *singular* are in Table 7.5.

TABLE 7.5 *Singular Indefinite Pronouns*			
either	neither	each	one
anybody	anyone	anything	
everybody	everyone	everything	
nobody	no one	nothing	
somebody	someone	something	

In the chapter on subject-verb agreement, you learned that when used as the subject, these words are singular. When used as an antecedent, these words still are singular. After you learn the first row of *either, neither, each, one*, memorize the remainder of the indefinite pronouns: *anybody, anyone, anything, everybody, everyone, everything, nobody, no one, nothing, somebody, someone, something*. Your job will be simplified if you learn the four base words and the three endings that are added to each base, as indicated in Table 7.6.

TABLE 7.6 *Compound Singular Indefinite Pronouns*	
Base	**Endings**
any-	-body
every-	-one
no-	-thing
some-	

Each base word uses all three endings to create three separate words. For example, the base word *any* becomes *anybody, anyone,* and *anything,* and so on with each base. An important point here is that pronouns beginning with *every*- appear to be plural, but are singular. The way to remember this is that any-time you see *every* in front of a word, think of *each and every one.* This wording will emphasize the singularity of *every.* Consider the following sentences:

Everyone in the girls' dorms paid *her* fees before the September deadline.

Each of the men took *his* car to have the oil changed.

Neither of the women liked *her* high tuition at the private college.

Everybody in the sorority cleaned *her* room each week.

Somebody left *his* wallet in the men's rest room.

In each of the above sentences, the italicized pronoun is singular to agree with the singular indefinite pronoun that is its antecedent. Be careful, however, not to call the object of the preposition the antecedent of the pronoun.

TRY-IT
EXERCISE

In the following sentences, underline the pronoun that would be correct in standard, formal usage.

1. Each of the girls had done (her/their) share of the cooking.
2. Either of those men accepted (his/their) share of the cooking.
3. One of those women misplaced (her/their) car in the parking lot.
4. Someone left (her/their) purse in the ladies' rest room.
5. Everyone on the men's basketball team thinks that (he/they) will be the best player.
6. Neither of the men wanted (his/their) wife to work the night shift.
7. Everybody on the women's soccer team took (her/their) turn as goalie.
8. Anyone in the men's campus dorms might get (his/their) fees raised for next year.
9. Somebody left (his/their) watch in the men's rest room on the third floor.

10. Nobody in the men's fraternity could allow (his/their) GPA to go below 3.0.

In the first sentence, the pronoun *her* agrees with the antecedent *each*. In the second sentence, the pronoun *his* agrees with the antecedent *either*. In the third sentence, the pronoun *her* agrees with the antecedent *one*. In the fourth sentence, the pronoun *her* agrees with the antecedent *someone*. In the fifth sentence, the pronoun *he* agrees with the antecedent *everyone*. In the sixth sentence, the pronoun *his* agrees with the antecedent *neither*. In the seventh sentence, the pronoun *her* agrees with the antecedent *everybody*. In the eighth sentence, the pronoun *his* agrees with the antecedent *anyone*. In the ninth sentence, the pronoun *his* agrees with the antecedent *somebody*. In the tenth sentence, the pronoun *his* agrees with the antecedent *nobody*.

PLURAL INDEFINITE PRONOUNS. As mentioned in Chapter Five, to help you remember the plural list, create a sentence using a plural subject to remind you that these words are always plural in number: "Few men sob." With this sentence, the first word, *few*, is already one of the five, the second word, *men*, begins with the same letter as *many*, and *sob* contains the first letter of each of the last three words: *several, others, both* (see Table 7.7).

Notice the agreement between the italicized words in each of the following sentences:

Few of the students in the class thought that *they* would fail the test.

Many of the people in our class were excited about *their* essay grade.

Several of the teachers were ready for *their* vacation.

Others at the school would teach *their* students during summer school.

Both of the girls believed that *they* should attend summer school.

TABLE 7.7 *Plural Indefinite Pronouns*

few
many
several
others
both

TRY-IT
EXERCISE

For each of the following, underline the antecedent and the correct pronoun. These sentences have both singular and plural indefinite pronouns as antecedents.

1. Everybody on the girls' basketball teams wanted (their/her) coach to praise (them/her).
2. Several of the men on the football team wanted (their/his) coach to praise (them/him).
3. If anyone in that Catholic girls' school wants good grades, (they/she) must study.
4. Many of the men in English must study (their/his) lessons daily.
5. Either of those men sitting by the windows will earn (their/his) high grades.

In the first sentence, the antecedent is *everybody,* and the correct pronouns are *her* and *her.* In the second sentence, the antecedent is *several,* and the correct pronoun is *their* and *them.* In the third sentence, the antecedent is *anyone,* and the correct pronoun is *she.* In the fourth sentence, the antecedent is *many,* and the correct pronoun is *their.* In the fifth sentence, the antecedent is *either,* and the correct pronoun is *his.*

Pronouns and Antecedents Agree in Gender

A pronoun agrees with its antecedent in gender, as well as number. In the past, whenever the sex of a singular antecedent was unclear, common practice was to use the masculine pronouns. However, today that practice is questioned by those who believe it to be unfair to women. Hence, many teachers suggest the use of phrases such as *him or her,* which treat the sexes equally. Others suggest that using either *him* or *her* is correct for singular. Therefore, you must consider your audience before choosing singular gender. Although each of the following is acceptable in standard, formal English, not everyone agrees which usage is best. Your job as a writer is to know your audience. Consider the following sentences:

Everyone will review his or her lesson tonight.

Everyone will review his/her lesson tonight.

© NTC/CONTEMPORARY PUBLISHING COMPANY

Everyone will review his lesson tonight.

Everyone will review her lesson tonight.

Of course, if the indefinite pronoun is followed by a prepositional phrase that clearly tells the gender, use it. For example, in the sentence, "Each of the girls wanted her test grade," the prepositional phrase makes the indefinite pronoun feminine gender. Often, however, the indefinite pronouns mean both genders: "Each of the students wanted his/her test grade." At times this practice of using "his or her" is awkward. Avoid it by using a plural antecedent rather than a singular one. For example, look at the following sentences:

My neighbor's dog cannot walk past a person without growling at him or her (him/her).

My neighbor's dog cannot walk past people without growling at them.

The first sentence is awkward. The change to a plural antecedent in the second sentence did not change the meaning of the first sentence, but improved readability. Whenever you can make an antecedent plural without changing the intended meaning of a sentence, you will want to do so in order to avoid awkwardness. Whenever you cannot make the antecedent plural, ask your instructors how they prefer you handle the choice of singular gender and then be consistent.

Pronouns and Antecedents Agree in Person

As shown in the Nominative Pronoun Chart (Table 7.1), pronouns are classified into groups called persons: first person, second person, and third person. Just as pronouns and antecedents must agree in number and gender, they also must agree in person. One of the most common pronoun mistakes made by beginning writers is a shift into the second personal pronoun *you* when the antecedent requires third person be used. Consider the following sentences:

▼ INCORRECT: If someone wants to leave practice early, you should tell the coach. (The sentence shifts from third person *someone* to second person *you*.)

▲ CORRECT: If someone wants to leave practice early, he/she should tell the coach. (The sentence is consistently third person.)

▼ INCORRECT: If students have problems with an exercise, you can ask for help. (The sentence shifts from third person *students* to second person *you*.)

▲ CORRECT: If students have problems with an exercise, they can ask for help. (The sentence is consistently third person.)

TRY-IT

EXERCISE

For each of the following, indicate whether the pronoun and antecedent agree by marking in the blank provided A for agreement or N for no agreement.

_____ 1. If a student wants to gain confidence in writing, you must first learn the fundamentals of English.

_____ 2. If students want to gain confidence in writing, they must first learn the fundamentals of English.

_____ 3. If you want to gain confidence in writing, you must first learn the fundamentals of English.

_____ 4. A student may find a course difficult, but you can usually get help from the instructor.

_____ 5. Students may find some classes challenging, but they can usually get help from the instructor.

_____ 6. You may find some classes difficult, but you can usually get help from the instructor.

The first sentence is incorrect because the pronoun and antecedent do not agree: the pronoun *you* has as its antecedent *student,* which requires the third person pronoun. The second sentence is correctly written with the third person plural pronoun. Also, the third sentence is correct because *you* is consistently used throughout. The fourth sentence is incorrect because the pronoun *you* has its antecedent *student,* which requires the third person pronoun. The fifth sentence is correctly written with the third person used throughout. Also, the sixth sentence is correct because second person is used throughout.

You should avoid shifting to the person *you* not only within exercise sentences but also within paragraphs and essays. If you check your antecedents whenever you write a pronoun, you will learn to use correct pronoun/antecedent agreement in number, gender, and person.

Reflexive/Intensive Pronouns

Personal pronouns combined with *-self* may be used to *refer* to another word in the sentence (called reflexive) or to *emphasize* another word in the sentence (called intensive). Look at these sentences.

Reflexive (To refer to another word in the sentence)

Elaine is not herself.

Elaine gave herself a present.

Elaine's grandchild bathed himself.

Elaine promised to buy tickets for herself and me.

Intensive (To emphasize another word in the sentence)

Elaine herself went to the meeting.

Elaine's husband himself made the phone call.

Elaine will go herself.

Elaine and Pat themselves went to the meeting.

These -*self* pronouns are given in Table 7.8.

It is important that you avoid the common mistakes concerning these pronouns with the suffix -*self*. First of all, some of the -*self* words come from the objective pronoun chart (see page 250), while others are formed from the possessive pronoun chart (see page 253). You may put the suffix

TABLE 7.8	*The -self Pronoun Chart*	
	Singular	**Plural**
First person	myself	ourselves
Second person	yourself	yourselves
Third person	herself/himself/itself	themselves

-*self only* on the third person objective pronouns and *only* on the first and second person possessive pronouns. If you will refer to your objective pronoun chart, you will create the words *herself, himself, itself,* and *themselves* (not *themself,* because *them* is plural and -*self* must be changed to the plural -*selves* to agree).

No other third person -*self* words are correct. Some people incorrectly create the third person -*self* pronouns from the possessive chart. But there is no such word as *hisself, theirself,* or *theirselves.* When you want to make the first and second person into -*self* words, you must go to the possessive chart: *myself, ourselves* (not *ourself,* because *our* is plural), and *yourself* or *yourselves* (depending on whether the antecedent is singular or plural). These -*self* words must be used along with another noun or pronoun. They are never used by themselves in a sentence.

▼ CORRECT: Jerome bought tickets for himself. (Reflexive)
Jerome himself bought the tickets. (Intensive)

▼ INCORRECT: Jerome and myself are going to the show.
▲ CORRECT: Jerome and I are going to the show.

▼ **INCORRECT:** Jerome bought tickets for myself.

▲ **CORRECT:** Jerome bought tickets for me. (In the incorrect sentences, *myself* does not refer back to an antecedent.)

TRY-IT
EXERCISE

For each of the following, identify whether the personal pronoun is correctly or incorrectly used by placing a *C* or an *I* in the blank provided.

_____ 1. Naomi gave herself a present.
_____ 2. Naomi and myself went to the mall.
_____ 3. Jake himself will go to the mall.
_____ 4. The purchases were made by themselves.
_____ 5. They themselves chose to spend too much money.
_____ 6. The bus took themselves to the mall.
_____ 7. Isaac chose Bernice's present by himself.
_____ 8. The wise shoppers were Frieda and myself.
_____ 9. Ebony herself told Clifford about our shopping trip.
_____ 10. Jillian saw Edwin, LaToya, and myself at the mall.

The first, third, fifth, seventh, and ninth sentences are correct. In the first sentence, the pronoun *herself* refers to *Naomi;* in the third, the pronoun *himself* emphasizes *Jake;* in the fifth, the pronoun *themselves* emphasizes *they;* in the seventh, the pronoun *himself* refers to *Isaac;* in the ninth, the pronoun *herself* emphasizes *Ebony.* The second, fourth, sixth, eighth, and tenth sentences are incorrect. In the second sentence, the pronoun *myself* does not refer to a noun. Since it fills the subject slot in the sentence, it should be nominative case *I.* In the fourth sentence, the pronoun *themselves* does not refer to a noun. Since it is the object of the preposition *by,* it should be the objective case *them.* In the sixth sentence, the pronoun *themselves* does not refer to the noun. Since it is the direct object of the verb *took,* it should be the objective case *them.* In the eighth sentence, the pronoun *myself* does not refer to the noun. Since it is a predicate nominative, it should be the nominative case *I.* In the tenth sentence, the pronoun *myself* does not refer to the noun. Since it is the direct object of *saw,* it should be the objective case *me.*

PRACTICE	# PRONOUN/ANTECEDENT
EXERCISE 7-9	# AGREEMENT

For each of the following, underline the incorrect pronoun and write the corrected form.

EXAMPLE: ____*his*____ Either Tom or Pete can drive <u>their</u> parents' RV.

_____ 1. Every town in the United States has their own laws.

_____ 2. Some students like to study their lessons by themself.

_____ 3. Everyone on the boys' baseball team must have their registration in before leaving for vacation.

_____ 4. Both Beth and Kim achieved her goals.

_____ 5. Neither of the women realized their danger.

_____ 6. Many senior citizens prefer to live alone and take care of theirselves.

_____ 7. Each of the girls requested to see their test.

_____ 8. Neither Tom nor Jim knows where they parked the car.

_____ 9. We shouldn't let ourself lose control of our lives.

_____ 10. Many men have designed their own homes in great detail long before he can afford to hire a builder.

NAME _____ DATE _____

INSTRUCTOR _____ CLASS TIME _____

PRACTICE EXERCISE 7-10 | USING PRONOUNS

Create a grammatically correct sentence using the listed indefinite pronoun as the antecedent for another pronoun in the sentence.

EXAMPLE: *many*

Many people take their vacation in December.

1. *either*

   _____

2. *several*

   _____

3. *everybody*

   _____

4. *neither*

   _____

5. *few*

   _____

6. *each*

   _____

7. *something*

   _____

8. *both*

   _____

9. *another*

   _____

10. *somebody*

    _____

NAME _____ DATE _____

INSTRUCTOR _____ CLASS TIME _____

REVIEW EXERCISE 7-1

SHIFT IN PRONOUN <u>YOU</u>, -<u>SELF</u> WORDS, AND POSSESSIVE CASE

DIRECTIONS: Correct any shifts in pronouns by underlining the incorrect pronoun (do not change the antecedent) and writing the accepted pronoun form in the blank provided. Mark all correct sentences with a *C.*

_____ 1. People are spendthrifts to go in debt for a house you cannot afford.

_____ 2. Persons traveling abroad should check which side of the road you're supposed to drive on.

_____ 3. If you have ever watched the movie *Gandhi*, you'll never forget the man.

_____ 4. Interviewing for several jobs gives future employees a good idea of what working conditions you can expect.

_____ 5. Many of my friends are in business for themselves and ask me for advice, which makes you worried about saying the wrong thing.

_____ 6. Her job as a professional speaker is nerve-racking because you must constantly entertain people.

_____ 7. Drivers often dread the little bit of snow this city gets each winter because you have to maneuver the icy hills.

_____ 8. Several students have formed car pools in which you save a lot of wear and tear on the family car.

_____ 9. Students returning to school after several years find extra difficulties since you are often responsible for both school and family.

_____ 10. English students should realize that a shift in person is one of the most frequent mistakes you make.

NAME _____ DATE _____

INSTRUCTOR _____ CLASS TIME _____

DIRECTIONS: For each of the following, correct any incorrect pronouns by writing the accepted form in the blank provided. Mark all correct sentences with a *C*.

_____ 11. I have asked if these feelings are also hers'.

_____ 12. I completely understand the reasons for there joy.

_____ 13. If we know that we have a quick temper, we should learn to control ourself.

_____ 14. I suggest that you and Pat set up a study schedule for yourself.

_____ 15. We did not ask ourselves the right questions when we studied.

_____ 16. People need to be willing to think about the reasons for their actions, so they can better understand theirselves.

_____ 17. The children should be ashamed of theirself for acting that way in front of company.

_____ 18. My goals are the same as your's.

_____ 19. Sometimes a computer seems to have it's own mind.

_____ 20. The students want to finish there research papers by themselves.

REVIEW EXERCISE 7-2 | NOMINATIVE AND OBJECTIVE PRONOUNS

DIRECTIONS: For each of the following sentences, decide how the pronoun is used: subject (S), predicate nominative (PN), direct object (DO), indirect object (IO), object of the preposition (OP). Underline the correct pronoun and, in the blank provided, write the abbreviation for how it is used in the sentence.

_____ 1. Sandra and (I, me) have signed up for the next meeting of Weight Watchers.

_____ 2. Miguel and Juan are very supportive of Sandra and (I, me).

_____ 3. Miguel and Juan shared with Sandra and (I, me) secrets of weight loss.

_____ 4. Among the students on the Dean's List were Jamal and (I, me).

_____ 5. Neither her husband nor (her, she) had ever been through a disaster before.

_____ 6. After the tornado, members of the Red Cross took Mr. Kim and (her, she) to the shelter.

_____ 7. The problem only concerns Dave and (he, him).

_____ 8. Although (she, her) and I are majoring in different areas, we study together.

_____ 9. It must have been (he, him) on the phone when we were disconnected.

_____ 10. Please share this information with Tiffany and (I, me).

_____ 11. The children and (he, him) are having a great time this week at King's Island.

_____ 12. King's Island notified the children and (he, him) about free season passes to the park.

_____ 13. Among the people at the park were Jason and (I, me).

NAME _____ DATE _____

INSTRUCTOR _____ CLASS TIME _____

_____ 14. Jason and (I, me) go to King's Island each summer.

_____ 15. The correct response when a woman answers the phone is, "This is (she, her)."

_____ 16. This secret is just between you and (I, me).

_____ 17. I gave Maurizio and (she, her) tickets to Riverbend.

_____ 18. We asked Cathy and (he, him) to the concert at Riverbend.

_____ 19. The tickets to the concert were bought by Cathy and (I, me).

_____ 20. At the concert on Saturday night were Cathy and (I, me).

REVIEW EXERCISE 7-3 AGREEMENT OF PRONOUN AND ANTECEDENT

DIRECTIONS: For each of the following, correct any errors in pronoun/antecedent agreement by underlining the incorrect pronoun (do not change the antecedent) and writing the accepted form in the blank provided. Mark all correct sentences with a *C*.

_____ 1. At the restaurant, the student and the professor paid her own way.

_____ 2. Neither the foreman nor the workers could offer his assistance during working hours.

_____ 3. When you see Melissa and Michelle, tell her the date of the next test.

_____ 4. Each of the men in the cast decided to perform the scene their own way.

_____ 5. Both of the performers realized his mistake when the scene did not go smoothly.

_____ 6. Either Lia or Meechi wanted their test.

_____ 7. A woman is admired if actions coincide with their words.

_____ 8. Videocassette equipment has the special features of immediate recording and editing, which increase their cost.

_____ 9. Neither of those two men believed that they could win the nomination.

_____ 10. Few of the men in the class thought that he would get a low grade.

_____ 11. Every teacher should offer their students individual help.

_____ 12. Everybody in the sorority seemed to feel awkward when it was their turn to speak.

NAME _____ DATE _____

INSTRUCTOR _____ CLASS TIME _____

_____ 13. After graduation was over, many of our classmates moved to different states and went his separate ways.

_____ 14. Somebody left their purse in the women's rest room.

_____ 15. The child's red wagon had lost it's rear wheels.

_____ 16. If anyone wants more information on pronouns, they should consult a good English handbook.

_____ 17. Both studied hard and were eager to please his or her teacher.

_____ 18. Several of the women donated her time to the charity.

_____ 19. Lack of knowledge or lack of preparation leaves their negative mark on the world.

_____ 20. Every pronoun in our essays has their own separate use.

CHAPTER
QUIZ 7-1

CORRECT USE OF PRONOUNS

DIRECTIONS: For each of the following, correct any pronoun errors by underlining the incorrect pronoun (do not change the antecedent) and writing the accepted form in the blank provided. Mark all correct sentences with a *C.*

_____ 1. Either Paula or Kristy can give you their notes.

_____ 2. Both of the cars had its tires replaced.

_____ 3. It was him at the movie with Lia.

_____ 4. Does each of the men know where their car keys are?

_____ 5. Anyone should carefully proofread their test before handing it in.

_____ 6. Each woman at school is responsible for taking their child to the day care center before class.

_____ 7. Many of the mothers in our class earned good grades for themself.

_____ 8. Neither Sue nor Allyson wanted to leave their daughter alone for two hours in the afternoon.

_____ 9. I really enjoy spring break because you get to go to Florida and party with thousands of other students.

_____ 10. Neither Ms. Williams nor Ms. Sanchez would make their decision when to schedule our tests.

_____ 11. You probably have your checkbook and driver's license in your other pants if you would just go hunt for it.

_____ 12. Dogs are faithful animals and will endure much abuse from their owners' children.

_____ 13. The English professors have requested that each student bring their own notebooks to class for essay tests.

_____ 14. Few would argue against the petition if he had read it carefully.

NAME _____ DATE _____

INSTRUCTOR _____ CLASS TIME _____

_____ 15. The final signatures on the petition were by Mark and me.

_____ 16. Among those who signed the petition were Mark and me.

_____ 17. As Mark gave me the petition, he said, "Keep this just between you and I."

_____ 18. When they were around Mark and I, Hae and Mario did not discuss their opinions of the petition.

_____ 19. Darnell and she need more time for this decision.

_____ 20. Jason is going with Jamal and I to the Bahamas.

© NTC/CONTEMPORARY PUBLISHING COMPANY

CHAPTER
QUIZ 7-2

CORRECT USE OF PRONOUNS

DIRECTIONS: For each of the following, correct any pronoun errors by underlining the incorrect pronoun (do not change the antecedent) and writing the accepted form in the blank provided. Mark all correct sentences with a *C.*

_____ 1. Carol, Maria, Angela, and I wanted to get our college education.

_____ 2. Carol and Maria shared good advice about college with Angela and I.

_____ 3. Neither her neighbor nor her had gone to college after finishing high school.

_____ 4. Carol and Maria studied the lessons and reviewed all of her notes after supper.

_____ 5. When Carol's husband answers the phone and someone asks for him, he responds, "This is he."

_____ 6. Each of the husbands supported the new lifestyle of their former stay-at-home wife.

_____ 7. The teachers taught Carol, Angela, and I skills in English and math.

_____ 8. Both of the women sitting in the front row did well in classes and realized her potential was great.

_____ 9. The price of knowledge was paid by Angela and I as we studied hours each night.

_____ 10. Either Maurizio or Mike asked Carol if she would share her notes with him.

_____ 11. Maria's husband asked Angela and her to dinner on Friday night.

_____ 12. If there children needed them during class, the babysitter could call the college phone number.

NAME _____ DATE _____

INSTRUCTOR _____ CLASS TIME _____

_____ 13. Neither of those women had ever thought that they would get a college degree.

_____ 14. Few of the women in that class believed that she would earn such high grades.

_____ 15. Neither Maria nor her daughter could make up their mind where to go for vacation.

_____ 16. When Maria got home from her class, the family was being entertained by the cat looking at it's own face in the mirror.

_____ 17. Maria said to her husband, "Let's keep my return to college just between you and I for one quarter."

_____ 18. After they finished the test, the women were pleased with themselfs and felt reassured about their ability.

_____ 19. Among those sitting at their desks were Angela and I.

_____ 20. Does each of the students know when their tests will be graded and returned?

© NTC/CONTEMPORARY PUBLISHING COMPANY

PART

4

MECHANICS

© NTC/CONTEMPORARY PUBLISHING COMPANY

CHAPTER 8

APOSTROPHES, CAPITALIZATION, QUOTATION MARKS, AND UNDERLINING

Though numerous rules exist for apostrophes, capitalization, quotation marks, and underlining, we are going to present only those rules that are the most frequently used. These "rules" are simply a reflection of what the majority of educated people use in standard, written English. Knowing them will simplify your writing tasks and increase your confidence.

RELATIONSHIP OF PLURAL, SINGULAR, AND APOSTROPHE

Because all three major rules for using the apostrophe are based on whether a word is singular or plural, you must first be able to identify singular and plural nouns before learning placement of the apostrophe. In order to eliminate any problems with using the apostrophe, be absolutely sure you can correctly identify a plural noun.

Basic Rule for Forming Plurals

The word *singular* means that there is only a single one of something. The word *plural* means there is more than one. Below are the regular rules for making a word plural. Knowing these rules will make it easier to identify plural nouns and, as a result, easier to use the apostrophe correctly.

MOST NOUNS. The most common regular way to form a plural of a noun is to add an *s*.

Singular	Plural
student	students
teacher	teachers

NOUNS ENDING IN S, SH, CH, Z, AND X. The plural of words ending in *s, sh, ch, z,* and *x* is not formed by adding only *s;* it is formed by adding *es.* This ending allows for the extra syllable that is created in order for the word to be pronounced:

dress	dresses
box	boxes

NOUNS ENDING IN Y OR O. Words ending in *y* and *o* have some special rules that are based on whether their last letter is preceded by a *vowel* or a *consonant.* There are five vowels in the language: *a, e, i, o,* and *u.* The remaining letters of the alphabet are consonants.

Nouns Ending in *y* and *o*—Preceded by a Vowel. The plural of most nouns ending in a *y* preceded by a *vowel* is formed in the regular way by adding *s:*

monkey	monkeys
valley	valleys

The plural of most nouns ending in an *o* preceded by a *vowel* is formed in the regular way by adding *s:*

rodeo	rodeos
radio	radios

Nouns Ending in *y* and *o*—Preceded by a Consonant. The plural of most nouns ending in a *y* preceded by a consonant is formed by changing the *y* to *i* and then adding *es:*

fly	flies
lady	ladies

The plural of most nouns ending in an *o* preceded by a consonant is formed by adding *es:*

embargo	embargoes
tomato	tomatoes

© NTC/CONTEMPORARY PUBLISHING COMPANY

Nouns That Are Musical Terms. There is a deviant rule for nouns ending in *o*. The plural of all *musical terms* ending in *o* is formed by adding *s*, regardless of whether the *o* is preceded by a vowel or a consonant:

solo   solos

piano   pianos

USING THE APOSTROPHE TO FORM POSSESSIVES: THREE MAJOR RULES

Now that you understand the concept of singular and plural, you can apply the apostrophe rules. The most frequent use of the apostrophe is to show ownership (*Erin's bike*) or to indicate a close relationship between two words (*a day's wages*). The problem you might have is wanting to stick an apostrophe on every word that ends in an *s*. The fact is that many words that end in *s* do not need an apostrophe. One way for you to recognize a possible possessive case is that you will have two nouns together: *man's hat, girl's purse, friend's car.* But be aware that sometimes the second noun may be modified by adjectives: *man's brown hat, girl's leather purse, friend's new car.* Also, recognize that when you have the possessive case, the apostrophe will be placed on the first noun—never on the second one.

RULE ONE: SINGULAR NOUNS FORM THE POSSESSIVE BY ADDING AN APOSTROPHE AND AN S.
Note that if you recognize you have the possessive, your first job is not to drop an apostrophe in somewhere, but to check the first noun to see if it is singular, that is, if there is only one. If it is singular, then in order to make it possessive, you add *'s:*

Maurice's business is selling thousands of eggs each week.

A person's diet should have some eggs in it.

A meal's nutritional value is improved with eggs.

The nouns *Maurice, person,* and *meal* are all singular. In the first sentence, it is the business of *Maurice.* In the second sentence, it is the diet of a *person.* In the third sentence, it is the value of a *meal.* If the noun is singular, simply add an *'s* to show possession. *Never* put apostrophes on words that are plural but do not show possession or ownership, such as *thousands* in the first sentence.

TRY-IT
EXERCISE

For each of the following, decide whether the possessive noun is singular or plural and write S or P in the blank provided. Then correctly place the apostrophe in each.

———————— 1. Cole Porters songs
———————— 2. the ladys gloves
———————— 3. a workers wages
———————— 4. the wifes ring
———————— 5. a clients bill

Each of these possessive nouns is singular. Each has two nouns together and shows ownership; therefore, the first noun will need an apostrophe. In the first example, there is only one singer. Your job is to create his name in the singular form: Cole Porter. Then place an *'s* on the singular word *Porter* to read *Cole Porter's songs.* In the second example, the first noun is singular as indicated by the singular spelling of *lady.* Add the necessary *'s* to read *the lady's gloves.* In the third example, the *a* before the word *workers* indicates that it is singular. Add the necessary *'s* to read *a worker's wages.* In the fouth example, the first noun is singular as indicated by the singular spelling of *wife.* Add the necessary *'s* to read *the wife's ring.* In the fifth example, the *a* before the word *clients* indicates it is singular. Add the necessary *'s* to read *a client's bill.*

Some people prefer to use only an apostrophe (without the additional *s*) if the word already ends in *s*. We would like to encourage you to always add an *'s* until you know the rule very well. It is much easier to learn the rule through consistency, rather than be confused by unusual and rare exceptions. The only exception we make is for a two-or-more-syllable proper name ending in *s*, where it is almost impossible to pronounce the extra *s* created by the possessive. This exception can be seen in singular possessions such as *Sophocles' plays, Oedipus' mother,* or *Edwin Moses' gold medal.*

© NTC/CONTEMPORARY PUBLISHING COMPANY

PRACTICE	# FORMING THE SINGULAR
EXERCISE 8-1	# POSSESSIVE

For each of the following, rewrite the *of* phrases to create the possessive and then correctly place the apostrophe in each.

EXAMPLE: *the boy's bicycle* bicycle of the boy

_____ 1. garden of Mr. Lopez

_____ 2. laughter of a baby

_____ 3. responsibility of a man

_____ 4. books of a student

_____ 5. lines of an actress

_____ 6. money of Sue

_____ 7. charm of a lady

_____ 8. smile of a child

_____ 9. wages of a waitress

_____ 10. dog of Hae Kim

NAME _____   DATE _____

INSTRUCTOR _____   CLASS TIME _____

| PRACTICE EXERCISE 8-2 | # FORMING THE SINGULAR POSSESSIVE |

For each of the following, rewrite the sentences so that the *of* phrase is possessive. Correctly place the apostrophe in each sentence.

EXAMPLE: The seriousness of the doctor worried me.
The doctor's seriousness worried me.

1. The property of Mr. Ross has become very valuable.

   _____

2. The concerns of the wife were eliminated.

   _____

3. The suggestion of the attorney was to make a simple will.

   _____

4. The wish of the hostess is for everyone to have a good time.

   _____

5. The tail of the monkey got stuck in the door.

   _____

6. The skin of the potato became moldy.

   _____

7. The commands of the chief resulted in quick action.

   _____

8. The sad eyes of the child caused tears in my own.

   _____

9. The sound of the cello can be quite soothing.

   _____

10. The goal of his life is to earn a college degree.

    _____

NAME _____ DATE _____

INSTRUCTOR _____ CLASS TIME _____

© NTC/CONTEMPORARY PUBLISHING COMPANY

RULE TWO: PLURAL NOUNS ENDING IN s FORM THE POSSESSIVE BY ADDING AN APOSTROPHE ONLY.

Remember that the first item of business is to check the first noun to see whether it is plural in meaning—that is, if there is more than one. Then, if it is plural and possessive, does the word needing the apostrophe end in an *s*? If it does, all you have to do to show possession is to add an apostrophe:

The enemies' tactics were quickly observed.

We respect those teachers' opinion on grades.

Many students' winter coats were hung across the back of the classroom.

The words *enemies, teachers,* and *students* are all plural. In the first sentence, it is the tactics of *the enemies*. The spelling of *enemies* tells us it is plural. In the second sentence, it is the opinion of *those teachers*. The word *those* preceding the noun tells us it is plural. In the third sentence, it is the coats of *many students*. The word *many* preceding the noun tells us it is plural. If the noun is plural and ends in *s*, add only an apostrophe to show possession. *Never* put apostrophes on words that are plural but do not show possession or ownership, such as *coats* in the third sentence.

TRY-IT
EXERCISE

Correctly place the apostrophe in each of the following.

1. the Jameses house
2. ladies gloves
3. several waitresses wages

The first example is possessive because there are two nouns together and the first shows ownership. Names tend to be difficult for students because they want every name to have an apostrophe. You must check when you see a name to discover whether it is only plural (no apostrophe needed) or plural *and* possessive.

Though we see in this instance that the name happens to be possessive, our *first* job is to decide whether it is singular or plural. Otherwise, there is no way we can know where to place the apostrophe. Two clues tell us this name is plural. One is the spelling: A proper noun that ends in *s* forms its plural by adding *es*. The singular spelling is *James;* the plural is *Jameses.* The other clue is that the word *the* is in front of the last name. Ordinarily, when a last name is preceded by *the,* the name is understood to include all family members and is therefore considered plural. Since Rule 2 is about a plural possessive ending in *s,* we place the apostrophe at the end: *the Jameses' house.*

The second example is possessive. We know it is plural because of the spelling. If it were singular, the spelling would be *lady.* Once the *y* is changed to an *i* and *es* is added, we know we are dealing with the plural spelling; therefore, we place an apostrophe after the *s.* The plural possessive correctly written is *ladies' gloves.*

The third example is possessive. As with the first example, two clues tell us that the possessive noun is plural. One is the *es* ending. The plural of a singular noun ending in *s* is formed by adding an *es.* Secondly, the modifier *several* shows it to be plural. The plural ends in *s,* so we add an apostrophe only: *several waitresses' wages.*

PRACTICE	# FORMING THE POSSESSIVE OF
EXERCISE 8-3	# PLURALS THAT END IN <u>S</u>

For each of the following, rewrite the *of* phrases to create the possessive and then correctly place the apostrophe in each.

EXAMPLE: *the boys' bicycle* bicycle of the boys

_____ 1. garden of the Millers

_____ 2. laughter of the babies

_____ 3. lyrics of both songs

_____ 4. books of many students

_____ 5. lines of the actresses

_____ 6. game of the golfers

_____ 7. charm of the ladies

_____ 8. smiles of the two winners

_____ 9. wages of the waitresses

_____ 10. dog of the Joneses

© NTC/CONTEMPORARY PUBLISHING COMPANY

NAME _____ DATE _____

INSTRUCTOR _____ CLASS TIME _____

PRACTICE EXERCISE 8-4 — FORMING THE POSSESSIVE OF PLURALS THAT END IN S

For each of the following, rewrite the *of* phrases to create the plural possessive and then correctly place the apostrophe in each.

EXAMPLE: project of the kids *the kids' project*

1. flaws of the policies _____

2. jewels of the princesses _____

3. decision of those judges _____

4. donations of the Strausses _____

5. scars of the tattoos _____

6. worth of several dollars _____

7. traits of our heroes _____

8. strings of the banjos _____

9. rules of the authorities _____

10. grades of many students _____

NAME _____ DATE _____

INSTRUCTOR _____ CLASS TIME _____

RULE THREE: PLURAL NOUNS NOT ENDING IN <u>S</u> FORM THE POSSESSIVE BY ADDING AN APOSTROPHE AND AN <u>S</u>. At first, you may be confused by this rule since it seems similar to Rule 1. However, it does not need to be confusing at all if you merely ask your questions in a specific order. Once you recognize that you have a possessive, your *first* question is whether that noun which will eventually show possession is singular or plural. Only after you have answered the first question do you move to the *second* question: Do I now use Rule 1, 2, or 3? Consider the following:

The men's soccer team plays on Tuesday evenings.

Members of the women's softball league practice on the same evening.

While the parents relax, their boys and girls are playing in the children's area.

In these sentences, the nouns *men, women,* and *children* are plural. Each of these plural forms does *not* end in an *s*. In the first sentence, it is the team of the *men*. In the second sentence, it is the league of the *women*. In the third sentence, it is the area of the *children*. When a noun is plural and does not end in an *s,* create the possessive by adding *'s* to the word. *Never* add an apostrophe to plural words that do not show possession or ownership, such as *parents, boys*, and *girls* in the third sentence.

TRY-IT
EXERCISE

Correctly place the apostrophe in each of the following.

1. the childrens games
2. the mens room
3. the womens jewelry
4. the policemens new contract
5. the peoples votes

All of these nouns are possessive and all follow Rule 3. In the first example, *children* is the plural of *child*. Because *children* does not end in *s,* add *'s* and create *the children's games.* In the second example, *men* is the plural of *man*. Because *men* does not end in *s,* add *'s* and create *the men's room.* In the third example, create *the women's jewelry;* in the fourth example, create *the policemen's new contract;* in the fifth example, create *the people's votes. Women, policemen,* and *people* are all plural nouns that do not end in *s.*

PRACTICE	# FORMING THE POSSESSIVE OF
EXERCISE 8-5	# PLURALS THAT DO NOT END IN <u>S</u>

For each of the following, rewrite the *of* phrases to create the possessive and then correctly place the apostrophe in each.

EXAMPLE: *the men's responsibility*   responsibility of the men

The children Book   1.   book of the children

the women's clothes   2.   clothes of the women

the firemen uniform   3.   uniform of the firemen

the mens cars   4.   cars of the men

people opinion   5.   opinion of the people

the stepchildren mother   6.   mother of the stepchildren

the feets pain   7.   pain of the feet

mices tails   8.   tails of the mice

the geeses feathers   9.   feathers of the geese

the oxens leather hide   10.   leather hides of the oxen

NAME _____   DATE _____

INSTRUCTOR _____   CLASS TIME _____

| PRACTICE EXERCISE 8-6 | # FORMING SINGULAR AND PLURAL POSSESSIVES |

For each of the following, write a sentence in which the words show ownership or possession.

EXAMPLE: her mother

Her mother's car was in the garage.

1. that professor

_____

2. those students

_____

3. several owners

_____

4. my oldest cousin

_____

5. the people

_____

6. their youngest daughter

_____

7. someone

_____

8. the Kellers

_____

9. Steve Keller

_____

10. his best friend

_____

NAME _____ DATE _____

INSTRUCTOR _____ CLASS TIME _____

Use of the Apostrophe with Indefinite Possessive Pronouns

Like nouns, indefinite personal pronouns need apostrophes to show possession or close relationship. These pronouns follow the same three rules as nouns. First, you must decide whether the indefinite pronoun is singular or plural. If it is singular, add *'s*. If it is plural and ends in an *s*, add an apostrophe. If it is plural and does not end in an *s*, add *'s*.

Indefinite pronouns form the possessive by following the regular rules:

Everybody's job is to find meaning in life. (Rule 1 for singular)

Changed attitudes can bring meaning into someone's life. (Rule 1 for singular)

Others' handicaps are hard to comprehend. (Rule 2 for plural ending in an *s*.)

With indefinite pronouns, as with nouns, your first job is to determine whether the pronoun is singular or plural. In these sentences, the pronouns *everybody* and *someone* are singular, and the pronoun *others* is plural. In the first sentence, it is the job of *everybody*. In the second sentence, it is the life of *someone*. In the third sentence, it is the handicaps of *others*. Because *everybody* and *someone* are singular, add *'s*. Because *others* is plural, add an apostrophe.

Use of the Apostrophe with Personal Pronouns

Personal pronouns from the possessive chart (*my, his, hers, its, ours, yours, theirs*) are already possessive in form and therefore need no apostrophes. Remember that using an apostrophe on *it's* makes a contraction and means *it is*. Although *it's* can mean *it has* when spoken, this contraction more frequently means *it is* when written. As a personal pronoun showing possession, *its* never takes an apostrophe:

We thought those books were yours.   (not *yours'*)

She thought the books were hers.   (not *her's*)

The books were actually theirs.   (not *their's*)

The red book had its cover torn off.   (not *it's*)

Use of the Apostrophe with Contractions

Sometimes two words in our language can be merged into one by eliminating a letter from the second word and replacing it with an apostrophe. The apostrophe is placed exactly where the omitted letter or letters would ordinarily be. This merging of words using the apostrophe forms a *contraction*. Look at the following examples:

Two Words	**Contraction**
there is	there's
here is	here's
it is	it's
is not	isn't
can not	can't
have not	haven't
I have	I've
I am	I'm
you are	you're
they are	they're

It is important that you recognize the difference between the possessive pronouns and contractions.

TRY-IT

EXERCISE

Correctly use the apostrophe in each of the following examples.

1. Theyre sure that the recovered items are theirs.
2. Its a shame that the bicycle lost its chain during the race.
3. Your insistence to be punctual means youre likely to make a good impression.
4. I can honestly say that yours is the best pecan pie Ive ever eaten.
5. Theres a lot of difference between my pie and hers.

These sentences mix personal pronouns and contractions. In the first sentence, *They're* needs an apostrophe because it is a contraction for *they are,* and the pronoun *theirs* does not need an apostrophe because *theirs* is already the possessive case. In the second sentence, the first *Its* needs an apostrophe to represent the contraction *It is,* and the *its* before the word *chain* needs no apostrophe because *its* is already the possessive case. In the third sentence, *your* needs no apostrophe because *your* is already the possessive case, and *you're* needs an apostrophe to represent the contraction for *you are.* In the fourth sentence, *yours* needs no apostrophe because *yours* is the possessive pronoun, and *I've* needs an apostrophe to represent the contraction for *I have.* In the fifth sentence, *There's* needs an apostrophe to indicate the contraction for *There is,* and *hers* needs no apostrophe because *hers* is the possessive pronoun.

USE OF CAPITALS: NINE RULES CONCERNING CAPITALIZATION

Names of Specific Persons, Places, and Things

Capitalize the names of specific persons, places, and things.

▼ **NAMES OF SPECIFIC PERSONS:** Carolyn Monce is Maurice McDaniel's able business associate.

▲ **NAMES OF SPECIFIC PLACES:** Canberra, Australia, and Tokyo, Japan, are capital cities.

▼ **NAMES OF SPECIFIC INSTITUTIONS:** Medgar Evers College is named after the respected civil rights leader who was killed in 1963.
The University of California has locations in eight California cities.

▲ **NAMES OF HOLIDAYS:** Maurice and Hattie went to John and Paula's house for Christmas dinner.
Seth and Irwin went to Pittsburgh, Pennsylvania, to celebrate Hanukkah.

▼ **NAMES OF MONTHS:** During April we think of rebirth, but during October those thoughts turn to our mortality.

▲ **NAMES OF DAYS OF THE WEEK:** On Monday people face the week with energy; on Friday that energy has lessened.

Titles of Persons When Used with Their Names

Capitalize titles that go before a person's name, but do not capitalize them if they follow the name.

▼ **TITLES PRECEDING A NAME:** Capitalization would be used when a title is before a person's name: Senator John Glenn, Rabbi Goldman, Dean Bardes

© NTC/CONTEMPORARY PUBLISHING COMPANY

▲ **TITLES FOLLOWING A NAME:** Capitalization should not be used when the title follows a person's name: John Glenn, senator; Samuel Goldman, rabbi; Barbara Bardes, dean.

Names to Show Family Relationship

Capitalize the family-relationship words *aunt* and *uncle* when used with a name. Capitalize *mother* and *father* unless preceded by any of the possessive pronouns.

▼ **AUNT AND UNCLE WORDS:** Uncle Rubin operated two restaurants after his retirement.
Aunt Goldie enjoys traveling to new places.
She asked her uncle to the party.
We look forward to visits with our aunt.
My Aunt Loretta writes interesting letters.
Their Uncle Rodrigo lives in northern South America.

▲ **MOTHER AND FATHER WORDS:** I called Mother.
Father called me.
I called my mother.
My father called me.

© NTC/CONTEMPORARY PUBLISHING COMPANY

PRACTICE	# CAPITALIZATION OF NAMES, TITLES, AND FAMILY-RELATIONSHIP WORDS
EXERCISE 8-7	

For each of the following, using correct capitalization, rewrite any words that should be capitalized. If a sentence is correct, write *C*.

EXAMPLE: The candidate spoke to the auto workers in lansing, michigan.

Lansing, Michigan

1. I'm going shopping with mother.

   _____

2. I want you to meet my mother.

   _____

3. That is dr. paul kollman.

   _____

4. Paul kollman, doctor of medicine, works out of christ hospital.

   _____

5. Her aunt lives in eaton, indiana.

   _____

6. I want to visit aunt rosa next week.

   _____

7. On memorial day we had a picnic at coney island.

   _____

8. The services on good friday were held at first lutheran church.

   _____

9. Our university does not offer classes on labor day.

   _____

10. The conference at the college was organized by bob stevens, professor.

    _____

NAME _____ DATE _____

INSTRUCTOR _____ CLASS TIME _____

PRACTICE
EXERCISE 8-8

USING CAPITALIZATION OF NAMES, TITLES, AND FAMILY-RELATIONSHIP WORDS

For each of the following, write a sentence that includes the item(s) indicated.

EXAMPLE: Two days of the week

Nurses often have to work Saturday and Sunday.

1. A specific holiday

    _____

2. The first and last names of two friends

    _____

3. The name of someone with a title following the name

    _____

4. The name of a city and state

    _____

5. The name of an uncle with *uncle* preceding the name

    _____

6. The name of a college

    _____

7. The names of two months

    _____

8. The name of someone with a title preceding the name

    _____

9. The word *mother* preceded by the pronoun *their*

    _____

10. The word *father* not preceded by any pronoun

    _____

NAME _____ DATE _____

INSTRUCTOR _____ CLASS TIME _____

Names of Companies and Products

Capitalize names of companies and business products.

▼ **NAMES OF COMPANIES:** General Electric, International Business Machines
▲ **PROPER NAMES OF BUSINESS PRODUCTS:** Coca Cola, Pepsi Cola

Titles of Written Works

Capitalize all main words in titles of books, magazines, articles, poems, plays, movies, and TV shows. Always capitalize the first and last word of the title, but not intervening words that are minor, such as the articles *a, an,* and *the* and prepositions.

▼ **TITLES OF BOOKS:** The novel *The Great Gatsby* is an American classic.
John Powell tells us in *The Pain of Being Human* that our attitude influences our joy.

▲ **TITLES OF MAGAZINES:** Many people read *Newsweek* to keep up with current events.
The magazine *American Health* has articles about both mental and physical health.

▼ **TITLES OF ARTICLES:** Did you read that interesting article "From Homespun to Harvard"?
"Improving Your Health" is currently in *Reader's Digest.*

▲ **TITLES OF POEMS:** Two poems often read are "The Road Less Traveled" and "Richard Cory."

▼ **TITLES OF PLAYS:** Musicals such as *Phantom of the Opera* and *The King and I* have been well received.

▲ **TITLES OF MOVIES:** A film that delighted people was *Waiting to Exhale.*
As both a play and a movie, *West Side Story* is enjoyable.

▲ **TITLES OF TV SHOWS:** At some time, many families have watched the television shows *I Love Lucy* and *The Brady Bunch.*

First Word of a Sentence and a Direct Quotation

Capitalize the first word of a sentence and of a direct quotation used as a sentence.

▼ **DIRECT QUOTATION:** *Hamlet* says, "To be or not to be; that is the question."
Bob asked, "Which way to the bookstore?"

Academic Subjects

Capitalize exact titles of courses, but not general fields of study, with the exception of the names of languages, which are always capitalized.

▼ **EXACT TITLES OF COURSES:** Sun Keng is enrolled in Business Law 2465 and College Algebra 1000.
Her sister is taking Accounting 103 and Algebra 201.

▲ **GENERAL FIELDS OF STUDY:** Wanting to major in business and math, Cassandra is taking accounting and algebra.
Leon is enrolled in biology and psychology this quarter.

▼ **NAMES OF LANGUAGES:** Many students in Texas can speak both English and Spanish.

Direction Words

Capitalize direction words only if used to represent a region.

▼ **DIRECTION WORDS AS REGIONS:** Living in the East is expensive.
People choose to live in the South to avoid cold weather.

▲ **DIRECTION WORDS AS DIRECTIONS:** Go north on Interstate 75
Go west on Sharon Road.

Seasons

Do not capitalize the names of seasons.

▼ **SEASONS:** Each spring people become energized and hopeful.
Each fall thousands of students return to the classroom.

PRACTICE
EXERCISE 8-9
CAPITALIZATION

For each of the following, correctly write any words that should be capitalized. If no capitals are needed, write *C* in the blank provided.

EXAMPLE: John works for prudential insurance.

Prudential Insurance

1. I bought potato chips and pretzels.

   _____

2. These wheat crackers are made by nabisco.

   _____

3. Have you read the book *love, medicine, and miracles?*

   _____

4. Mike is enrolled in accounting and spanish.

   _____

5. He's taking american history II this quarter.

   _____

6. Shayna's major is business, and her minor is economics.

   _____

7. While campaigning in the north, she spoke in milwaukee.

   _____

8. They drove south on adventure lane.

   _____

9. This fall our family is visiting points of interest in the south.

   _____

10. My nose can't tell the difference between kleenex and puffs.

    _____

NAME _____ DATE _____

INSTRUCTOR _____ CLASS TIME _____

PRACTICE	# Using Capitalization
EXERCISE 8-10	

For each of the following, write a sentence that includes the item indicated.

EXAMPLE: Names of two companies

Ford and Mazda are allies in creating cars.

1. Names of two products

    _____

2. Name of a book

    _____

3. Names of two magazines

    _____

4. Names of two movies

    _____

5. Titles of two courses—needing no capitals

    _____

6. Titles of two courses—needing capitals

    _____

7. Your major area of study

    _____

8. A friend's major area of study

    _____

9. Direction word—as a region

    _____

10. Direction word—as a direction

    _____

NAME _____ DATE _____

INSTRUCTOR _____ CLASS TIME _____

PRACTICE	**CAPITALIZATION**
EXERCISE 8-11	

For each of the following, using correct capitalization, rewrite any words that should be capitalized.

EXAMPLE: My mother and father are going to visit my aunt in houston, texas, next spring after passover.

Houston, Texas   Passover

1. In our sociology class professor johnson asked if we had read *the closing of the american mind* by allan bloom.

   _____

2. Joanne's uncle taught accounting in muncie, indiana, and received his degree from columbia university in new york city.

   _____

3. Doctor james flavin, professor of english at shawnee state university, is married to professor louise flavin of the university of cincinnati.

   _____

4. At a banquet on july 4, I sat between senator harris and jim andrews, mayor of centerville.

   _____

5. Their doctor has his office east of town near bethesda hospital on montgomery road.

   _____

NAME _____ DATE _____

INSTRUCTOR _____ CLASS TIME _____

PRACTICE	# CAPITALIZATION
EXERCISE 8-12	

For each of the following, using correct capitalization, rewrite any words that should be capitalized.

1. If you drive south on Interstate 71, you'll see the home offices of procter and gamble, birthplace of tide, pampers, and crisco.

   _____

2. On your left is the ohio river and the stadium that was home to one of the midwest's well-known baseball teams: the cincinnati reds.

   _____

3. She's taking accounting, economics, and french this quarter and plans to transfer to a university in illinois in the fall.

   _____

4. On veterans day, when sycamore high school is closed, shirley's mother is taking her to see doctor stewart.

   _____

5. Aunt Rosa and uncle Luis are planning a party for mom and dad's wedding anniversary next june.

   _____

NAME _____ DATE _____

INSTRUCTOR _____ CLASS TIME _____

USE OF QUOTATION MARKS AND UNDERLINING

Quotation marks are used to enclose a person's exact words and to identify parts within a published work. Underlining, or italics, is used to identify works that are published as separate units. The rules are easy to learn once you understand their logic.

Quotation Marks to Enclose a Person's Exact Words

Use quotation marks to enclose a person's exact words, but do not use quotation marks if the wording is not exact.

▼ **DIRECT QUOTATION OF EXACT WORDS:** Keith said, "I do not like poetry because I do not understand it."

▲ **INDIRECT QUOTATION, NOT EXACT:** Keith said that he does not like poetry because he doesn't understand it.

Quotation Marks with Commas and Periods

Commas and periods always go *inside* the ending quotation marks.

▼ **COMMAS:** "We will have a test tomorrow," she said.
I had labeled the package "Handle With Care," but the glasses were broken.

▲ **PERIODS:** She said, "We will have a test tomorrow."
The glasses were broken even though I had labeled the package "Handle With Care."

Quotation Marks with Colons and Semicolons

Colons and semicolons always go *outside* the ending quotation marks.

▼ **COLONS:** An important message exists in the article "Dying To Be Thin": anorexia and bulemia are diseases that require professional help.

▲ **SEMICOLONS:** The teacher said, "Everyone passed the test"; I was so relieved that I didn't hear another word she said.

Quotation Marks with a Question Mark and an Exclamation Mark

The question mark and the exclamation mark are placed inside the ending quotation marks when they apply only to the quotation, but outside the ending quotation marks when they apply to the whole sentence.

▼ QUESTION MARK AND EXCLAMATION MARK INSIDE:
(applies only to quotation)

My students' favorite question is, "Can we get out of class early?"

Cathy exclaimed in delight, "I got an A on the last test!"

▲ QUESTION MARK AND EXCLAMATION MARK OUTSIDE:
(applies to whole sentence)

Why do some students respond, "We think we should get our money's worth"?

Don't tell me your excuse for that low grade is "I was tired and couldn't study"!

Quotation Marks vs. Underlining for Titles

Underline titles of works that are published as separate units, but place quotation marks around titles of parts within a published work, such as chapters within a book, articles within magazines or newspapers, and short stories. In addition, place quotation marks around song titles. Underlining is a substitute for italicizing words. When using a computer, italics are preferred to underlining.

  1. Works published as separate units are italicized (or underlined).

▼ BOOKS: *Lake Wobegon Days, Simplified Sentence Skills*
▲ MAGAZINES: *Reader's Digest, Consumer Reports*
▼ NEWSPAPERS: *The San Francisco Chronicle, The New York Times*
▲ PLAYS: *A Doll's House, Romeo and Juliet*
▼ MOVIES: *The Wizard of Oz, The Lion King*
▲ TELEVISION SHOWS: *Bonanza, Chicago Hope*

  2. Titles published within another work (chapters, articles, poems, and short stories), as well as songs, take quotation marks.

▼ CHAPTER WITHIN A BOOK: "Winter" in *Lake Wobegon Days*
▲ MAGAZINE ARTICLE: "When You're Embarrassed" in *Reader's Digest*
▼ NEWSPAPER ARTICLE: "Life in the Medical Aftermath" in *The Cincinnati Enquirer*
▲ POEMS: "The Road Not Taken," "The Unknown Citizen"
▼ SHORT STORIES: "The Lottery," "The Catbird Seat"
▲ SONGS: "Love Me Tender," "Amazing Grace"

The major rules for capitalization, quotation marks, and underlining follow logical patterns. The more you use them correctly, the more automatic their use becomes.

PRACTICE EXERCISE 8-13 QUOTATION MARKS AND UNDERLINING

In each of the following sentences, rewrite the titles correctly using quotation marks and underlining.

EXAMPLE: Our class read Cather's short story Paul's Case.

"Paul's Case"

1. Mother reads The Wall Street Journal every night.

   _____

2. There is a symbolic door slam at the end of the play A Doll's House.

   _____

3. Time is a magazine that gives a conservative view of the news.

   _____

4. Our professor assigned the chapter Cell Growth for tomorrow's lesson.

   _____

5. One of the best-selling songs is White Christmas.

   _____

6. When Joe read the poem Bereft, he felt the loneliness of the speaker.

   _____

7. The television show Rosie O'Donnell has received praise for being positive and upbeat.

   _____

8. Our class just read Faulkner's short story Spotted Horses in Perrine's book Literature.

   _____

9. The article Thin Thighs was recently in Redbook magazine.

   _____

10. The movie Big Business starred two well-known actresses.

   _____

NAME _____ DATE _____

INSTRUCTOR _____ CLASS TIME _____

PRACTICE	# USING QUOTATION MARKS AND UNDERLINING
EXERCISE 8-14	

For each of the following, write a sentence that includes the indicated item.

EXAMPLE: Names of two poems

"Stopping by Woods" and "Barter" give contrasting insights into life.

1.   Name of a book

_____

2.   Name of a chapter in a book

_____

3.   Name of a magazine

_____

4.   Name of an article in a magazine

_____

5.   Name of a newspaper

_____

6.   Name of an article in a newspaper

_____

7.   Names of two movies

_____

8.   Names of two TV shows

_____

9.   Names of two short stories

_____

10.   Names of two songs

_____

NAME _____ DATE _____

INSTRUCTOR _____ CLASS TIME _____

© NTC/CONTEMPORARY PUBLISHING COMPANY

REVIEW EXERCISE 8-1   APOSTROPHE

DIRECTIONS: For each of the following, underline any word that needs an apostrophe and then place the apostrophe where needed. Some sentences have more than one word needing an apostrophe. If a sentence is correct, place a *C* beside the number.

_____ 1. Mikes daughter was at the beach with Bills brother.

_____ 2. A girls clothes tell a lot about her, but they also say something about her parents income and taste.

_____ 3. Those girls grades show they have been studying; in fact, Sun Lee and Lia had a quiz session in the Rosses family room.

_____ 4. The families garage sale on our block was held on the Lees driveway.

_____ 5. The childrens attitudes often reflect what they have learned at home.

_____ 6. Cars tend to make statements about the personalities of the owners.

_____ 7. My English teachers have their office hours in the afternoon.

_____ 8. It is anybodys guess which questions will be on the test.

_____ 9. Someones paper got a high grade; Ann thinks it was hers, but I know it is not mine.

_____ 10. Teds chewing gum lost its flavor quickly.

_____ 11. Tomorrows assignment will be hard; I am going to Marys house to work on it.

_____ 12. She is the Joneses babysitter; Jane and Joe Jones are the Lewises neighbors.

_____ 13. The girls mother took her to the picnic that the Lewises gave for their son.

_____ 14. The mans hat and the childrens toys were lost.

NAME _____ DATE _____

INSTRUCTOR _____ CLASS TIME _____

_____ 15. The Mendozas and the Bushes take many vacations together.

_____ 16. This is Trevors shirt; it was left in the boys locker room at school.

_____ 17. We are going to Jamals party; unfortunately, its on the same night as the Harrises party for Jennifer.

_____ 18. They are not coming to Jamals party; rather, they are going with the Joneses to the party for the Harrises.

_____ 19. Richards fortune is in his paternal grandfathers gift of inherited stocks.

_____ 20. Hostesses often have to work as servers during their free moments.

REVIEW	# CAPITALIZATION
EXERCISE 8-2	

DIRECTIONS: In the blank provided, rewrite the following using correct capitalization. If correct as is, write *C* in the answer blank.

1. easter   _____

2. our aunt   _____

3. phillips petroleum company   _____

4. ivory (the soap)   _____

5. "death of a hired man" (poem)   _____

6. data structures I   _____

7. The store is four miles north.   _____

8. tuesday   _____

9. professor carol sue robinson   _____

10. northern kentucky university   _____

11. august   _____

12. uncle pete   _____

13. solomon goldberg, rabbi   _____

14. diet-rite cola   _____

15. bill gradison, representative   _____

16. the united states   _____

17. My mother is fine.   _____

18. winter   _____

19. A popular movie was *ironweed.*   _____

20. frances, my aunt   _____

NAME _____   DATE _____

INSTRUCTOR _____   CLASS TIME _____

REVIEW EXERCISE 8-3 | QUOTATION MARKS AND UNDERLINING

DIRECTIONS: For each of the following, use quotation marks and underlining correctly as you rewrite the item in the blank provided. Information in parentheses gives additional explanation for a given item.

1. Plural and Apostrophe (chapter in a book) _____

2. Type A Behavior (book) _____

3. He often asks, Can I have my allowance early? _____

4. He often asks if he can have his allowance early. _____

5. He often states, I want my allowance early. _____

6. Hedda Gabler (play) _____

7. Faith (song) _____

8. I will be unable to attend class, she stated. _____

9. She said, I will be unable to attend class;
   I did not know how to reply. _____

10. A Jury of Her Peers (short story) _____

11. The Indianapolis Star (newspaper) _____

12. Murphy Brown (television show) _____

13. He said, I've been in a wreck. _____

14. Positive Emotions: Love, Gratitude, and
    Determination (chapter in a book) _____

15. Gandhi (movie) _____

16. To His Coy Mistress (poem) _____

17. Bugging (magazine article) _____

18. Popular Science (magazine) _____

19. Reds Going South with Set Lineup
    (newspaper article) _____

20. He said, Yes, you are; I then told him that I was not. _____

NAME _____ DATE _____

INSTRUCTOR _____ CLASS TIME _____

CHAPTER
QUIZ 8-1

APOSTROPHE

DIRECTIONS: For each of the following, underline any word that needs an apostrophe and then place the apostrophe where needed. Some sentences have more than one word needing an apostrophe. If a sentence is correct, write *C* in the blank provided.

_____ 1. The girls gymnasium in our school is too small, but its pleasant.

_____ 2. Daytons biggest department store is having a sale in the boys clothing department.

_____ 3. He is the peoples choice to win, but he is not this persons choice.

_____ 4. Mendozas and Claytons were at yesterdays meeting.

_____ 5. The Smiths cat and Mike Stones dog are great friends.

_____ 6. The Patels are going with the Dickersons to Donnas party.

_____ 7. Its time all waitresses tips were given to represent service received.

_____ 8. After a long vacation, she was tired of giving tips to the waitresses.

_____ 9. The babys dresses are all in the back of Tiffanys closet.

_____ 10. The Joneses car is parked in Peter Kims garage.

_____ 11. These newspapers give the three judges decision on Jasons requests for parole.

_____ 12. The food is good in the students lunchroom; however, its true that several students prefer to eat at nearby restaurants.

_____ 13. Grace works at her fathers store and gets her wages on Friday.

_____ 14. My fathers boat was not working, so we borrowed the Goldbergs boat for the day.

_____ 15. Those monkeys faces are so funny that I am taking their pictures.

_____ 16. The five girls grades were excellent, and they rushed home to tell their parents.

NAME _____ DATE _____

INSTRUCTOR _____ CLASS TIME _____

_____ 17. That persons attitude shows he is not interested in the nations welfare.

_____ 18. We had a gentlemens agreement, but the mans ethics ruined it.

_____ 19. My house will be decorated soon, but even when its finished, it will not be as pretty as Juanitas house.

_____ 20. Paulas cakes are great; mine are good, but they are not as good as hers.

| CHAPTER | CAPITALIZATION, QUOTATION |
| QUIZ 8-2 | MARKS, AND UNDERLINING |

DIRECTIONS: For each of the following, underline any words that should have been capitalized. If a sentence is correct, write a *C* in the blank provided.

_____ 1. I heard Uncle Irwin say that buying in the fall, maybe in august or september, was the best time because prices are lower then.

_____ 2. Only a couple of mechanics, one in the south and one in the west, were able to find that a spark plug wire had been disconnected.

_____ 3. Probably the worst time to have automobile trouble is during the christmas holidays or over the fourth of july weekend.

_____ 4. Mark Twain says, "the humorous story is american; the comic story is english; the witty story is french."

_____ 5. My doctor's son is a priest working in zaire, africa.

_____ 6. Cologne advertisers lure buyers through the use of suggestive names: interlude, my sin, and obsession.

_____ 7. If you are having problems in math, history, or english, you might want to sign up for a tutor.

_____ 8. When senator glenn spoke here, he stated, "one area we need to give more attention is our education system."

_____ 9. My aunt and uncle traveled throughout the southwest when uncle bud had his annual army reunion.

_____ 10. My mother wrote a letter to my sociology professor telling him how much she and my father appreciate this university.

NAME _____ DATE _____

INSTRUCTOR _____ CLASS TIME _____

DIRECTIONS: For each of the following, insert quotation marks or underlining where needed. If a sentence is correct, write a *C* in the blank provided.

_____ 11. I asked the salesman, Won't I get more for my car if I sell it on my own?

_____ 12. The customer turned and said, I want to return these shoes I bought two years ago; the open-mouthed clerk stood looking at her in shock.

_____ 13. One reference book I highly recommend to secretaries is The Gregg Reference Manual by William Sabin.

_____ 14. When I asked Mother what her favorite song was, she said that she liked the song Some Enchanted Evening.

_____ 15. The movie Good Morning, Vietnam starring Robin Williams earned over fifty million dollars during the first month of its release.

_____ 16. An article in the February 1988 issue of Family Circle entitled Dying To Be Thin is about the battle with bulimia.

_____ 17. Our professor at the university assigned one paper on Thoreau's book Walden and another on his essay Civil Disobedience.

_____ 18. An article called Bad Dreams in Parents Magazine helps parents deal with children's nightmares.

_____ 19. The best children's educational show is Sesame Street.

_____ 20. Interesting themes are found in Robert Frost's two poems entitled Out, Out, and Birches.

USAGE: COMMONLY CONFUSED WORDS

There are words in our language that differ in spelling and meaning but have the same pronunciation; other words have like spellings but different definitions. Some words, on the other hand, are recognized simply because they often are misspelled. This chapter discusses three areas that seem to confuse students frequently.

HOMOPHONES

The first syllable of this term, *hom,* means "alike," and the last syllable, *phone,* means "sound." Homophones are words that sound alike yet have different spellings and different meanings. Following is a list of those homophones that are frequently used and, all too frequently, misused.

▼ **HEAR:** A verb meaning "to listen."
▲ **HERE:** An adverb meaning "at this place."
    1. I *hear* what you are saying.
    2. Please come *here.*

▼ **IT'S:** A contraction meaning "it is."
▲ **ITS:** A possessive pronoun meaning "belonging to it."
    1. I believe *it's* time for another test.
    2. The bell lost *its* clapper and could not be rung.

▼ **LED:** A past tense verb meaning "guided." Present tense is *lead;* rhymes with *weed* when pronounced.

▲ **LEAD:** A noun meaning the "metallic element." If *lead* has the same pronunciation as *led,* it is the noun, usually the lead in a pencil.
1. The blindfolded boy was *led* down the hall.
2. The *lead* in my pencil broke.

▼ **NO:** An adverb meaning "nothing," "none," or "not so."
▲ **KNOW:** A verb meaning "to understand."
1. He has been *no* help to the new employees.
2. I *know* that sounds a little harsh.

▼ **PASSED:** A past tense verb meaning "gone by" or "through" or "having satisfied requirements."
▲ **PAST:** An adjective meaning "formerly" or "beyond in time."
1. She has *passed* this test.
2. It is *past* time for her arrival.

PRACTICE EXERCISE 9-1 | COMMONLY CONFUSED HOMOPHONES

In each of the following sentences, underline the correct word within the parentheses.

EXAMPLE: I wish you had been (hear/<u>here</u>).

1. Michelle could (hear/here) the applause of the audience as she (led/lead) the cast back on stage for a curtain call.

2. Even though my high grade is a surprise, (it's/its) pleasant to (no/know) I can do good work.

3. My research paper had (it's/its) grade on the last page.

4. He wasn't (hear/here) that day, so he didn't (hear/here) that the test was postponed.

5. Are you sure (it's/its) time to hand in this research paper?

6. Is (it's/its) thesis clearly stated in the first paragraph?

7. Last Saturday Juan (led/lead) the homecoming parade.

8. With (no/know) training, I do not (no/know) how they (no/know) so much about gardening.

9. I'm amazed that I (past/passed) algebra this (past/passed) quarter.

10. Even though I had trouble with the (past/passed) tense of verbs, I (past/passed) English.

NAME _____ DATE _____

INSTRUCTOR _____ CLASS TIME _____

PRACTICE	**USING COMMONLY CONFUSED**
EXERCISE 9-2	**HOMOPHONES**

Write a sentence correctly using the word indicated.

EXAMPLE: past   *Lou's library books are past due.* _____

1.   hear _____

2.   here _____

3.   it's _____

4.   its _____

5.   led _____

6.   lead _____

7.   no _____

8.   know _____

9.   passed _____

10.   past _____

NAME _____ DATE _____

INSTRUCTOR _____ CLASS TIME _____

MORE HOMOPHONES

▼ PATIENTS: A noun meaning "people under medical care."
▲ PATIENCE: A noun meaning "steadiness or perseverance in performing a task."
    1. The *patients* were pleased with their rapid recovery.
    2. She does not have much *patience,* especially when having to wait in line.

▼ PIECE: A noun meaning "a part or a fragment."
▲ PEACE: A noun meaning "harmony" or "freedom from war."
    1. I wanted a *piece* of that cherry pie.
    2. While heads of state speak of *peace,* their soldiers are fighting wars.

▼ PLAIN: An adjective meaning "clearly understood" or "simple."
▲ PLANE: A noun meaning "carpenter's tool" or an "airplane."
    1. The *plain* fact is that your engine needs a complete overhaul.
    2. The *plane*'s landing was delayed an hour.

▼ STATIONARY: An adjective meaning "fixed," "unchanging," or "in one place." Remember the *ary* ending coincides with the *a* in "unch*a*nging" and in "pl*a*ce."
▲ STATIONERY: A noun meaning "paper on which a person writes." Remember the *ery* ending coincides with the *e* in "writ*e*" and in "l*e*tter."
    1. The water level remained *stationary.*
    2. The *stationery* I received for my birthday is beautiful.

▼ THEIR: A possessive pronoun meaning "belonging to them."
▼ THEY'RE: A contraction meaning "they are."
▲ THERE: An adverb meaning "in a certain place."
    1. That is *their* house.
    2. *They're* rarely home to enjoy their luxuries.
    3. Put the books *there* on the desk.

▼ TO: A preposition meaning "in the direction of" and telling where.
▼ TOO: An adverb meaning "also" or "more than enough."
▲ TWO: An adjective meaning "more than one" or "a pair."
    1. They are going *to* the study session.
    2. Television has *too* much influence on a young, developing mind.
    3. Many families have *two* cars.

▼   **WHO'S:**   A contraction meaning "who is."

▲   **WHOSE:**   A possessive pronoun meaning "belonging to whom."

    1.   I wonder *who's* going tonight.

    2.   I wonder *whose* gloves these are.

▼   **YOU'RE:**   A contraction meaning "you are."

▲   **YOUR:**   A possessive pronoun meaning "belonging to you."

    1.   I think *you're* supposed to see a program adviser.

    2.   I think *your* adviser is in her office.

© NTC/CONTEMPORARY PUBLISHING COMPANY

PRACTICE	# COMMONLY CONFUSED
EXERCISE 9-3	# HOMOPHONES

In each of the following sentences, underline the correct word within the parentheses.

EXAMPLE: People seldom want to hear the (<u>plain</u>/plane) truth.

1. A nurse needs (patients/patience) when dealing with grumpy (patients/patience).

2. There will be no (peace/piece) until you give him a (peace/piece) of cake.

3. This letter is written on expensive (stationery/stationary).

4. (Their/They're/There) are piles of dishes for Jim and Murali to wash.

5. (Their/They're/There) always skipping (their/they're/there) turn.

6. That's (to/too/two) much (to/too/two) spend on a meal for (to/too/two) people.

7. (Who's/Whose) going to tell me (who's/whose) sweater this is?

8. Since he's a person (who's/whose) always on time, I wonder (who's/whose) clock is wrong.

9. (You're/Your) my best friend, but some of (you're/your) ideas are crazy.

10. If (you're/your) interested in going, you should ask (you're/your) parents for their permission.

NAME _____ DATE _____

INSTRUCTOR _____ CLASS TIME _____

PRACTICE	**USING COMMONLY CONFUSED**
EXERCISE 9-4	**HOMOPHONES**

Write a sentence correctly using the word indicated.

EXAMPLE: peace *Geraldine said, "I need some peace and quiet."*

1. patience _____

2. stationary _____

3. their _____

4. there _____

5. they're _____

6. too _____

7. who's _____

8. whose _____

9. you're _____

10. your _____

NAME _____ DATE _____

INSTRUCTOR _____ CLASS TIME _____

COMMONLY CONFUSED WORDS

The English language contains pairs of words that are spelled similarly yet have different meanings and slightly different pronunciations. Learning the differences in pronunciation will help you to remember the different spellings and meanings for these commonly confused words.

▼ ACCEPT: A verb meaning "to take," "to receive," or "to believe."
▲ EXCEPT: A preposition meaning "leaving out," "other than," or "but."
1. I *accept* responsibility for my actions.
2. I like all my classes *except* chemistry.

▼ ADVICE: A noun meaning "opinion given."
▲ ADVISE: A verb meaning "to give an opinion" or "to recommend."
1. I asked for their *advice* on the matter.
2. They will *advise* me concerning my investments.

▼ AFFECT: A verb meaning "to influence."
▲ EFFECT: A noun meaning "a result." This spelling can be a verb but seldom is. If the word is preceded by *a, an,* or *the,* use *effect.*
1. They were deeply *affected* by her actions.
2. The injection for pain had an immediate *effect.*

▼ CHOOSE: A verb in present tense meaning "to select." Its pronunciation rhymes with *cruise.*
▲ CHOSE: A verb in past tense meaning "selected." Its pronunciation rhymes with *rose.*
1. I *choose* to take today as a vacation day.
2. Yesterday I *chose* to work overtime.

▼ CONSCIENCE: A noun meaning "a sense of right and wrong."
▲ CONSCIOUS: An adjective meaning "aware" or "able to feel and think."
1. His *conscience* was clear—he had not taken the money.
2. He was *conscious* of how the people who lost their money would feel.

▼ DESERT: A noun meaning "a dry, barren, sandy region." A verb meaning "to abandon one's duty."
▲ DESSERT: A noun meaning "a sweet course after a meal." You can remember the double *s* for the food by thinking how tempting it is to have two helpings.
1. The *desert* has some very beautiful flowering plants.
2. Her willpower will *desert* her when she sees this strawberry shortcake.
3. Some people can have all the *dessert* they want and never gain a pound.

PRACTICE
EXERCISE 9-5

COMMONLY CONFUSED WORDS

For each of the following sentences, underline the correct word within the parentheses.

EXAMPLE: We're having apple pie for (<u>dessert</u>/desert).

1. Everyone who received an invitation plans to (accept/except) the offer.

2. I'll (accept/except) the responsibility for every day (accept/except) Friday.

3. I'll (advise/advice) you only if you want my (advise/advice).

4. They will (advise/advice) me, but I don't like their (advise/advice).

5. The (affect/effect) of the cold medication will (affect/effect) my ability to concentrate while driving.

6. Unemployment has a ripple (affect/effect); lack of work (affects/effects) employees, employers, and the economy.

7. Tomorrow I'll (choose/chose) my schedule for next quarter.

8. Yesterday I (choose/chose) my schedule for next quarter.

9. Unless she makes a (conscience/conscious) effort to study, she goofs off; then her (conscience/conscious) bothers her.

10. I hope his willpower doesn't (desert/dessert) him when he sees that chocolate (desert/dessert).

NAME _____ DATE _____

INSTRUCTOR _____ CLASS TIME _____

| PRACTICE EXERCISE 9-6 | # USING COMMONLY CONFUSED WORDS |

Write a sentence correctly using the word indicated.

EXAMPLE: conscious *Gideon was conscious of Abigail staring at him.*

1. accept _____

2. except _____

3. advise _____

4. advice _____

5. affect _____

6. effect _____

7. choose _____

8. chose _____

9. conscience _____

10. dessert _____

NAME _____ DATE _____

INSTRUCTOR _____ CLASS TIME _____

MORE COMMONLY CONFUSED WORDS

▼ **LOOSE:** An adjective meaning "not securely fastened." The pronunciation rhymes with *moose.*

▲ **LOSE:** A verb meaning "to part with" or "misplace." The pronunciation rhymes with *cruise.*
1. The *loose* bolt caused the tire to wobble.
2. I was afraid I'd *lose* my tire.

▼ **QUIET:** An adjective meaning "still, calm, motionless, peaceful."

▼ **QUITE:** An adverb meaning "completely, entirely, really, positively."

▲ **QUIT:** A verb meaning "to stop," "to discontinue," or "to resign."
1. The house was *quiet* until the children returned.
2. The picnic was *quite* enjoyable.
3. We regretted having to *quit* our jobs.

▼ **THAN:** A conjunction used to introduce the second element in a comparison.

▲ **THEN:** An adverb meaning "at that time," "soon afterward," or "therefore."
1. She ran faster *than* he did.
2. I will run errands and *then* take a nap.

▼ **THOROUGH:** An adjective meaning "complete, accurate."

▲ **THROUGH:** A preposition or an adjective meaning "from the beginning to the end," or "finished."
1. He did a very *thorough* job.
2. He went *through* the house checking for damage.
3. He was *through* with all his classes.

▼ **WHETHER:** A conjunction used to introduce an indirect question or to introduce alternatives.

▲ **WEATHER:** A noun meaning atmospheric conditions.
1. She asked *whether* she could go.
2. The *weather* may prevent our going.

| PRACTICE EXERCISE 9-7 | COMMONLY CONFUSED WORDS |

In each of the following sentences, underline the correct word within the parentheses.

EXAMPLE: It's time to give this room a (<u>thorough</u>/through) cleaning.

1. The clasp on your necklace is so (loose/lose) that I'm afraid you'll (loose/lose) it.

2. Since I've started to (loose/lose) weight, these slacks are too (loose/lose).

3. This job is (quiet/quite/quit) stressful.

4. If things don't improve, I'll (quiet/quite/quit) and find a (quiet/quite/quit) job.

5. (Than/Then) she said, "Your essay is better (than/then) mine."

6. Andrew cleaned the vegetables and (than/then) made us better salads (than/then) I make.

7. I'm (thorough/through) with washing diapers and burping babies.

8. Ron did a (thorough/through) job on this research, but he's glad he's (thorough/through) with the project.

9. I wonder (whether/weather) the (whether/weather) will be decent today.

10. I don't know (whether/weather) to wear a sweater or a coat in this unpredictable spring (whether/weather).

NAME _____ DATE _____

INSTRUCTOR _____ CLASS TIME _____

PRACTICE EXERCISE 9-8	USING COMMONLY CONFUSED WORDS

Write a sentence correctly using the word indicated.

EXAMPLE: through *Farah ran through the hallway.* _____

1. loose _____
2. lose _____
3. quiet _____
4. quite _____
5. quit _____
6. than _____
7. then _____
8. whether _____
9. weather _____
10. thorough _____

NAME _____ DATE _____

INSTRUCTOR _____ CLASS TIME _____

MISSPELLINGS OF ELEVEN COMMON WORDS

Because the purpose of this chapter is to help you avoid incorrect usage, we want to introduce you to eleven commonly misspelled words. These words (in italics) quickly label a writer as ineffective and uneducated. Do not use them in either formal or informal writing.

▼   A LOT: This is always two words, never *alot.*

▼   ALL RIGHT: This is always two words, never *alright.*

▼   RECEIVE: This is one of the most frequently misspelled words in our language because of the *e* and *i.* Remember that whenever an *ei* combination comes after the letter *c* and the *ei* has a long *e* sound, as in *beet,* the *e* always comes before the letter *i: conceive, receive, deceit, receipt.* This word is never spelled *recieve.*

▼   COMING: There is only one *m* in this word. *Comming* is not a word.

▼   TRULY: There is no *e* before the *ly* ending. *Truely* is not a word.

▼   DIE/DYING AND LIE/LYING: The *-ing* form of *die* and *lie* is formed by changing the *ie* to a *y* and adding *-ing. Dieing* and *lieing* are not words.

▼   TRY/TRIES/TRIED: Note the spelling with the *s* and the *ed* endings. The spelling is never *trys* or *tryed.*

▼   LAY/LAID AND PAY/PAID: The past tense spelling of these two verbs is never just an *ed* ending. *Layed* or *payed* are not words.

Remember that none of the following is a word: *alot, alright, recieve, comming, truely, dieing, lieing, trys, tryed, layed,* or *payed.* Avoid these misspellings.

HOMOPHONES AND COMMONLY CONFUSED WORDS

REVIEW
EXERCISE 9-1

DIRECTIONS: For each of the following, underline the correct word in the parentheses.

1. School is (alot, a lot) more difficult this year.

2. We (laid, layed) our books on the table in the library.

3. We (paid, payed) our tuition in August.

4. We're having cheesecake for (dessert, desert).

5. While vacationing in California last year, we visited the (dessert, desert).

6. Their family (trys, tries) to be together for the holidays.

7. He hasn't even (tried, tryed) to prepare for the next test.

8. She (led, lead) the team to victory.

9. If you (led, lead) me, I'll follow.

10. This tooth is (loose, lose).

11. I don't want to (loose, lose) the tooth.

12. The first runner (past, passed) the finish line five seconds before the one who placed second.

13. From (past, passed) experience I know to take careful notes in his class.

14. (It's, its) time for another quarter to begin.

15. She had a place for everything and kept everything in (it's, its) proper place.

16. She writes all her letters on lavender (stationery, stationary).

17. To avoid being caught snooping, I stood (stationery, stationary) behind the living room draperies.

NAME _____ DATE _____

INSTRUCTOR _____ CLASS TIME _____

18. If you will (choose, chose) a class from this schedule, we can register you today.

19. Yesterday I (choose, chose) milk and an apple for my afternoon snack.

20. He always signs letters, "Yours (truly, truely)."

REVIEW EXERCISE 9-2 HOMOPHONES AND COMMONLY CONFUSED WORDS

DIRECTIONS: For each of the following, underline the correct word in the parentheses.

1. (Their, There, They're) going to (loose, lose) this game.

2. (Too, To, Two) many people try to give me (advice, advise).

3. I (know, no) (whose, who's) getting a good grade in English.

4. It is (your, you're) turn to (receive, recieve) a bonus.

5. (Your, You're) going to have some (desert, dessert), aren't you?

6. How I (past, passed) English is (quite, quit, quiet) a mystery!

7. Because this car is newer (than, then) (there, their, they're) car, I'd buy it.

8. I (payed, paid) (alot, a lot) to get the car that I wanted.

9. (It's, Its) expensive extras give it the sporty (effect, affect) I want.

10. This (passed, past) year I (tryed, tried) to save more money (than, then) last.

11. When I (lose, loose) my temper, my (conscious, conscience) bothers me (alot, a lot).

12. We are ready for spring break, (accept, except) some of us wish it were longer (than, then) it is.

13. (Who's, Whose) job is it to check that the bills are (paid, payed)?

14. I will (advice, advise) you when to (accept, except) the offer.

15. (Desert, Dessert) wildflowers bloom in (loose, lose) sand.

16. (It's, Its) not as important (whether, weather) she likes the class as it is that she (trys, tries) to learn something from it.

17. I lay in the sun (alot, a lot) this (past, passed) summer.

NAME _____   DATE _____

INSTRUCTOR _____   CLASS TIME _____

18. I'll be happy once these projects have (received, recieved) evaluations and I'm (thorough, through) with the mess.

19. I know that a low grade will (affect, effect) my grade average and also have a rotten (affect, effect) on my attitude.

20. After a (thorough, through) examination of my (conscious, conscience), I can (truly, truely) say that (there, their, they're) is no excuse for that low grade.

REVIEW EXERCISE 9-3 | HOMOPHONES AND COMMONLY CONFUSED WORDS

DIRECTIONS: For each of the following sentences, determine whether any words are misused. Write the correct words in the blank provided. (A sentence may include more than one error.) If the sentence is correct, write *C*.

1. To many people want to give me unasked-for advice.

   _____

2. If your one of these people who gives alot of advice, stop advising and start listening.

   _____

3. Tim trys too often to make my decisions for me; I think we all like to choose things by ourselves.

   _____

4. I asked him weather he likes to recieve unwanted advise.

   _____

5. Its hard for some people to except a compliment that's payed to them.

   _____

6. Quite often people hear only what they choose to hear.

   _____

7. I believe that a lot of the praise your hearing is truely sincere.

   _____

8. My conscious gives me advise that effects my choices.

   _____

9. When she lead the choir, she tryed to know who's voice was off-key.

   _____

NAME _____ DATE _____

INSTRUCTOR _____ CLASS TIME _____

10. The choir does only vocal exercises when their rushed before a program and no the songs quiet well.

_____

11. Their afraid that she knows more then they do and are dieing to learn more of the details.

_____

12. He layed all his cards on the table and said, "It's your deal."

_____

13. My grades will be alot better now that I have past all my required courses accept English.

_____

14. I'm going to chose the foods with the fewest calories, so I can loose weight.

_____

15. That chocolate desert with it's whipped-cream topping lead me to eat too much yesterday.

_____

16. If I'm conscious of calories, I'll not accept a piece of that tempting fudge when the plate is passed.

_____

17. Because of the damaged box, this good stationary is on sale.

_____

18. It takes a little patients and alot of time to answer the questions of a three-year-old.

_____

19. Everyone is coming except Tiffany; she always waits until the last minute to accept invitations she receives.

_____

20. This past quarter has had a good effect on their attitudes; high grades often affect students positively.

_____

CHAPTER QUIZ 9-1	# HOMOPHONES AND COMMONLY CONFUSED WORDS

DIRECTIONS: For each of the following sentences, determine whether any words are misused. Write the correct words in the blank provided. (A sentence may include more than one error.) If the sentence is correct, write *C*.

1. My advise to you is to do what you truely believe is right.

   _____

2. The children are ready to go to the beach, but today is to hot for lieing in the sun.

   _____

3. Our dog ran in circles as it tryed to catch it's tail.

   _____

4. Michelle lead the parade through downtown, and then she passed the reviewing stand.

   _____

5. It takes all the patients you've got to live with someone whose always giving advice.

   _____

6. This letter is written on lovely stationary; I'll bet it cost alot of money.

   _____

7. Their all quite sure that I payed to much for these clothes.

   _____

8. My parents are dying to know whether I past that last chemistry test.

   _____

NAME _____ DATE _____

INSTRUCTOR _____ CLASS TIME _____

9. Look who's finished with his dessert.

_____

10. She trys hard to choose the best advice, but it's not easy to know who's right.

_____

11. The boys layed there wet towels on the deck to dry.

_____

12. Your going to be better after this medicine has an affect on you.

_____

13. They know more then there letting you believe they do.

_____

14. Everyone accept Itamar has finished the first two exercises.

_____

15. Too many teens blindly follow their peers' advice.

_____

16. Since choosing to skip desserts, I'm losing weight.

_____

17. I recieve alot of unwanted advise from my conscience.

_____

18. The teacher will choose the best essay; then she'll tell us whose essay she chose.

_____

19. People should accept others' advice concerning the weaknesses in themselves.

_____

20. These jeans are too loose now that I've chosen to lose weight, but that's all right with me.

_____

CHAPTER QUIZ 9-2 HOMOPHONES AND COMMONLY CONFUSED WORDS

DIRECTIONS: For each of the following sentences, determine whether any words are misused. Write the correct words in the blank provided. (A sentence may include more than one error.) If the sentence is correct, write *C*.

1. I'm truely tired of wearing loose sweat suits, so following my doctor's advice, I'm choosing to eat alot less food each day.

   _____

2. My doctor says that its alright to use this diet because it has been approved by the AMA.

   _____

3. Since I started to lose weight, my slacks are looser then they used to be.

   _____

4. Look whose losing weight after she tryed on some clothes at Lazarus!

   _____

5. People think your lieing when you say it costs to lose weight.

   _____

6. I payed alot each time I refused a piece of pie on the dessert cart in a restaurant.

   _____

7. Now I hear my conscious asking whether I want to eat the pie or feel thin.

   _____

8. Do I want to recieve compliments and feel alright about myself, or will I chose to lead a life of loose sweat suits?

   _____

NAME _____ DATE _____

INSTRUCTOR _____ CLASS TIME _____

9.   My weight loss is having quite an affect on my boyfriend's eating.

_____

10. He trys to quite eating snacks, but its hard to do.

_____

11. I bribed myself: "Lose fifteen pounds and you can buy that pink suit with it's slim skirt."

_____

12. Then I wrote a note to myself on my best stationery: "Lose weight."

_____

13. Using patients and determination, I shed all the weight accept five stubborn, stationary pounds that refused to move.

_____

14. My girlfriend has tryed to lose weight before, but her love for food has lead her to accept being overweight.

_____

15. Her doctor told her to lose alot of weight, but she'd rather chose strawberry pie then plain strawberries.

_____

16. When our friends give us their advice about diets, they are truly trying to help.

_____

17. There is no safe way to lose weight accept by eating less and exercising more.

_____

18. Some people advise crash diets; their misleading us if they advise losing more then two pounds a week.

_____

19. Now that I accept my new looks, I am conscious of people's stares of approval.

_____

20. I know whose happiest about your weight loss. Its you!

_____

ANSWER KEY

CHAPTER 1: VERBS, SUBJECTS, COMPLEMENTS, AND COMPOUNDS

PRACTICE EXERCISE 1-1:
IDENTIFYING ACTION VERBS (PAGE 7)

1. ride
2. plays
3. lectures
4. thinks
5. agrees
6. define
7. gain
8. praise
9. blushes
10. enjoys

PRACTICE EXERCISE 1-3:
IDENTIFYING LINKING VERBS (PAGE 13)

1. was
2. were
3. is
4. is
5. is
6. looks
7. seems
8. feels
9. taste
10. appears

PRACTICE EXERCISE 1-5:
IDENTIFYING HELPING VERBS (PAGE 19)

1. has (H); been (H); walking
2. have (H); relaxed
3. have (H); followed
4. may (H); have (H); cared
5. do (H); ask
6. can (H); talk
7. must (H); be
8. might (H); have (H); been
9. can (H); walk
10. are (H); wanting

PRACTICE EXERCISE 1-7:
IDENTIFYING SUBJECTS (PAGE 29)

1. Days
2. fun
3. I
4. days
5. you
6. (you)
7. people
8. teens
9. place
10. we

PRACTICE EXERCISE 1-9:
IDENTIFYING VERBAL PHRASES (PAGE 37)

1. Laughing at Jan's jokes
2. Studying early in the evening
3. balancing work and play
4. Earning good grades
5. laughing at themselves
6. To graduate from college
7. to get a job
8. to ask their history teacher
9. to answer their questions on the Civil War
10. To give clear answers to questions

PRACTICE EXERCISE 1-11:
IDENTIFYING VERBS AND SUBJECTS (PAGE 39)

1. are (L); Parents (S)
2. feels (L); child (S)
3. may (H); occur (A); Jealousy (S)
4. create (A); parents (S)
5. may (H); have (H); wished (A); Many (S)
6. think (A); you (S)
7. may (H); experience (A); parents (S)
8. may (H); have (H); been (H); given (A); Neither (S)
9. is (L); Loving (S)
10. can (H); grow (L); children (S)

PRACTICE EXERCISE 1-13:
IDENTIFYING DIRECT OBJECTS AND INDIRECT
OBJECTS (PAGE 45)

1. bicycle
2. golf
3. clubs [Dad]
4. thoughts
5. none
6. health
7. fitness
8. praise [brother]
9. none
10. praise

PRACTICE EXERCISE 1-15:
IDENTIFYING PREDICATE ADJECTIVES AND PREDICATE
NOMINATIVES (PAGE 51)

1. winner (PN)
2. best (PA)
3. chocolate (PA)
4. hungry (PA)
5. recipe (PN)
6. tired (PA)
7. proud (PA)
8. excited (PA)
9. great (PA)
10. pleased (PA)

PRACTICE EXERCISE 1-17:
VERBS AND SUBJECTS (PAGE 53)

1. seemed (L); exercises (S)
2. are (H); spotted (A); Problems (S)
3. pass (A); few (S)
4. find (A); students (S)
5. ask (A); you (S)
6. will (H); help (A); Teachers (S)
7. Do (H); feel (L); you (S)
8. may (H); create (A); shyness (S)
9. must (H); have (H); chosen (A); I (S)
10. will (H); give (A); teachers (S)

PRACTICE EXERCISE 1-19:
IDENTIFYING COMPOUND ELEMENTS (PAGE 57)

1. P   before/after
2. OP   thinking/planning
3. V   chose/took
4. IO   coach/assistant
5. PA   calm/collected
6. V   are/have been
7. S   ranting/raving
8. DO   coach/assistant
9. PN   win/spot
10. S   players/coaches/parents

REVIEW EXERCISE 1-1:
PREPOSITIONAL PHRASES, VERBS, AND SUBJECTS (PAGE 59)

	VERBS/VERB PHRASES	SUBJECTS	PREPOSITIONAL PHRASES
1.	study	Students	in the first-period class
2.	should review	Students	in this college
3.	are reviewing	Many	of the students/in English
4.	am	I	in English class
5.	have been studying	We	of verbs/in common English sentences
6.	would remember	students	without a review
7.	has known	girl	in the front row/of our class/for years
8.	could have been learned	Several	of these skills/in middle school
9.	study	I	in English
10.	seems	teacher	from my point/of view/during class
11.	Did work	you	on verbs/in our assignment
12.	must have finished	I	in our workbook/until midnight
13.	did start	Jim	on the exercises/until late/at night
14.	study	you	on the next assignment
15.	has been	Neither	of those classes/in math
16.	sounds	assignment	in history
17.	might be	class	across the hall/from us/in psychology
18.	look	Many	of the classes/on my schedule/for next quarter
19.	appear	students	in this class/about basic English
20.	has been talking	teacher	In the room/above us/for the entire hour

© NTC/CONTEMPORARY PUBLISHING COMPANY

REVIEW EXERCISE 1-2:
IDENTIFYING VERBS, SUBJECTS, AND COMPLEMENTS (PAGE 61)

VERBS/VERB PHRASES	SUBJECT	COMPLEMENTS
1. lists	*TV Guide*	shows (DO)
2. are	shows/shows	popular (PA)
3. has hurt	television	ratings (DO)
4. has given	addition	competition (DO)
5. are renting	people	movies (DO)
6. are shown	shows	none
7. grow	movies	better (PA)
8. must have found	people	methods (DO)
9. might have been	Books, movies, sports	part (PN)
10. Do watch	you	television (DO)
11. takes	Being a single parent	time/energy (DO)
12. feels	Darlene	overwhelmed (PA)
13. seems	Paying the bills	difficult (PA)
14. have been living	Darlene/baby	none
15. works/studies	she	none
16. needs	she	job (DO)
17. will be studying	She	lessons (DO)
18. grows	Darlene	tired/impatient (PA)
19. causes	Parenting	frustration/joy (DO)
20. is	To be a good mother	goal (PN)

REVIEW EXERCISE 1-3:
VERBS, SUBJECTS, COMPLEMENTS, AND COMPOUNDS (PAGE 63)

VERBS/VERB PHRASES	SUBJECTS	COMPLEMENTS
1. work	Many	none
2. review	students/teachers	homework (DO)
3. get	both	review (DO)
4. get	teacher/students	hungry (PA)
5. is	French	class (PN)
6. can bring	Learning	pleasure (DO)
7. grow	chapters	harder/longer (PA)
8. am	I	student/waitress (PN)
9. Do know	you	tuition/fees (DO)
10. are	books/chart	none
11. feel	Thousands	exhausted (PA)
12. are	eyes/bodies	characteristics (PN)
13. met/adjourned	class	none
14. will be	Bruce/sister	students (PN)
15. attended/graduated	Several	none
16. will need	I	self-discipline/determination (DO)
17. asked	teacher	questions (DO) Josh/me (IO)
18. looks	boy	tall/thin (PA)
19. may have been	He	player (PN)
20. lost	Melinda	notes/textbook (DO)

CHAPTER 2: SENTENCE ERRORS

PRACTICE EXERCISE 2-1:
DEPENDENT CLAUSES BEGINNING WITH A SUBORDINATE CONJUNCTION (PAGE 75)

1. Because TV often gives a false image of life
2. Before TV told viewers how to look, think, and act
3. If TV stars become role models
4. Once a person sees six killings a night
5. since death can be watched on TV over 24 times a week
6. Although TV violence distorts viewers' values
7. While girls watch the lean, beautiful women on TV
8. when they mistake TV's reflection of life for reality
9. until they are ill from anorexia
10. Unless viewers maintain open minds

PRACTICE EXERCISE 2-3:
IDENTIFICATION OF FUSED SENTENCES AND COMMA SPLICES (PAGE 81)

1. CS; you, an
2. FS; test extreme
3. C
4. CS; early, we
5. CS; difficult, I
6. C
7. C
8. CS; spring, I
9. C
10. FS; here I

PRACTICE EXERCISE 2-5:
IDENTIFICATION OF SENTENCE FRAGMENTS (PAGE 87)

1. To get the major I want
2. Mastering Spanish and English at the same time
3. Studying Spanish with Ms. Brod and English with Ms. Hellyer
4. C
5. C
6. When I took my test in English
7. After I finish these classes in Spanish and English
8. On the stock market in New York or at a company like General Electric
9. In many fields such as transportation, business, or teaching
10. Because they are begging for teachers who know both English and Spanish

PRACTICE EXERCISE 2-7:
IDENTIFICATION OF FAULTY PARALLELISM (PAGE 91)

1. he dates Rachel
2. to tease
3. it's fun
4. his bike rides
5. self-discipline
6. are very determined
7. school
8. he'll play some softball
9. it's free
10. who has many friends

PRACTICE EXERCISE 2-9:
IDENTIFICATION OF DANGLING MODIFIERS (PAGE 95)

1. Juan
2. brother
3. hamburgers
4. car
5. doctors
6. dad
7. dishes
8. grass
9. Itamar
10. windows

REVIEW EXERCISE 2-1:
IDENTIFICATION OF COMMA SPLICES, FUSED SENTENCES, AND SENTENCE FRAGMENTS (PAGE 97)

1. CS; class, he
2. C
3. FS; fragments, many
4. FRAG
5. C
6. CS; Road, then
7. FRAG
8. FRAG
9. CS; coming, classes
10. FRAG
11. FRAG
12. C
13. FRAG
14. C
15. CS; quickly, then
16. CS; weather, spring
17. FRAG
18. CS; spring, I
19. FRAG
20. C

© NTC/CONTEMPORARY PUBLISHING COMPANY

REVIEW EXERCISE 2-2:
IDENTIFICATION OF COMMA SPLICES, FAULTY PARALLELISM, AND DANGLING MODIFIERS (PAGE 99)

1. FP
2. DM
3. CS
4. C
5. FP
6. CS
7. C
8. C
9. DM
10. C
11. DM
12. FP
13. DM
14. FP
15. CS
16. C
17. CS
18. CS
19. FP
20. DM

REVIEW EXERCISE 2-3:
COMMA SPLICES, FUSED SENTENCES, SENTENCE FRAGMENTS, FAULTY PARALLELISM, AND DANGLING MODIFIERS (PAGE 101)

1. FP
2. DM
3. CS
4. C
5. C
6. FS
7. C
8. DM
9. FP
10. CS
11. CS
12. C
13. FRAG
14. FRAG
15. DM
16. C
17. FS
18. CS
19. DM
20. C

CHAPTER 3: PUNCTUATION JOINING INDEPENDENT CLAUSES

PRACTICE EXERCISE 3-1:
COORDINATING CONJUNCTIONS (PAGE 113)

1. shoes, but
2. background, so
3. C
4. shirt, and
5. C
6. month, or
7. C
8. payment, nor
9. mall, yet
10. time, for

PRACTICE EXERCISE 3-3:
JOINING INDEPENDENT CLAUSES WITH NO JOINING WORD (PAGE 117)

1. class; he
2. lousy; he
3. student; self-discipline
4. written; others
5. amazing; they
6. students; our
7. tension; today
8. grade; she
9. shock; I
10. difficult; others

PRACTICE EXERCISE 3-5:
CONJUNCTIVE ADVERBS AND SENTENCE MODIFIERS (PAGE 125)

1. money; furthermore,
2. beautiful; in fact,
3. car; however,
4. gas; in addition,
5. year; on the contrary,
6. , on the contrary,
7. , on the other hand,
8. years; consequently,
9. car; otherwise,
10. start; hence,

REVIEW EXERCISE 3-1:
COORDINATING CONJUNCTIONS (PAGE 131)

1. wrecked, and
2. morning, but
3. none
4. times, so
5. money, or
6. none
7. tonight, nor
8. none
9. cheese, and
10. none
11. atmosphere, and
12. hurriedly, but
13. none
14. none
15. yourself, or
16. none
17. water, and
18. none
19. sweetheart, and
20. none

REVIEW EXERCISE 3-2:
CONJUNCTIVE ADVERBS, SENTENCE MODIFIERS,
AND INTERRUPTERS (PAGE 133)

1. month; however,
2. not, however,
3. haircut; on the other hand,
4. short; her boyfriend, on the other hand,
5. figures; in fact,
6. figures; her firm, in fact,
7. thought, in addition,
8. planes; in addition,
9. week; however,
10. week; students may, however,
11. homework; for example,
12. night, for example,
13. chapter; then
14. night; as a result,
15. and, as a result,
16. twins; hence,
17. long; nevertheless,
18. long; she enjoyed, nevertheless,
19. wonderful; indeed,
20. summer; thus,

REVIEW EXERCISE 3-3:
PUNCTUATION OF COMPOUND SENTENCES (PAGE 135)

1. deep; he
2. deep, and
3. deep; therefore,
4. deep; he did, however,
5. hazardous; nevertheless,
6. school, for
7. none
8. none
9. started; then
10. wet; moreover,
11. wet; the temperature, moreover,
12. start; consequently,
13. start; furthermore,
14. start; in other words,
15. car; the battery, in other words,
16. heavy; it
17. heavy; thus,
18. heavy, so
19. heavy; many children, as a result,
20. none

CHAPTER 4: PUNCTUATION SEPARATING ELEMENTS IN A SENTENCE

PRACTICE EXERCISE 4-1:
INTRODUCTORY DEPENDENT CLAUSES (PAGE 145)

1. game, the
2. game, the
3. C
4. C
5. game, it
6. pouring, we
7. C
8. team, we
9. game, we
10. game, the

PRACTICE EXERCISE 4-3:
IDENTIFICATION OF PREPOSITIONAL PHRASES (PAGE 149)

1. On; in; of
2. In; after; for
3. At; of
4. Before; during; at
5. After; in
6. Under; in
7. Behind; across; from
8. About; between
9. With; in
10. Around; at; on

© NTC/CONTEMPORARY PUBLISHING COMPANY

PRACTICE EXERCISE 4-5:
IDENTIFYING VERB + -ING PHRASES (PAGE 153)

1. sitting
2. Sitting
3. Selecting
4. sorting
5. Selecting
6. Working
7. working
8. Working
9. getting
10. Getting

PRACTICE EXERCISE 4-7:
IDENTIFICATION OF TO + A VERB PHRASES (PAGE 157)

1. To graduate
2. To earn
3. to borrow
4. to earn
5. To be
6. To work
7. to get
8. To make
9. To lend
10. to stop

PRACTICE EXERCISE 4-9:
PUNCTUATION OF ITEMS IN A SERIES (PAGE 163)

1. Hatch, Ms. McQuire, and
2. lessons, invite the speakers, hold discussions, and
3. educational, enjoyable, and
4. short, overweight, cheerful
5. lectures, discuss the readings, and
6. listening, reading, and
7. quarter, around midterm, and
8. lectures, to write five critiques, and
9. fall, Child Development II in the winter, and
10. Jamal, Lia, Chris, and

REVIEW EXERCISE 4-1:
PUNCTION OF INTRODUCTORY ELEMENTS (PAGE 167)

1. weekend,
2. flight,
3. none
4. Friday,
5. trouble,
6. none
7. sandwiches,
8. none
9. airport,
10. none
11. Alabama,
12. none
13. educational,
14. house,
15. yard,
16. advance,
17. flights,
18. airport,
19. flights,
20. friends,

REVIEW EXERCISE 4-2:
PUNCTUATION OF INTRODUCTORY ELEMENTS AND ITEMS IN A SERIES (PAGE 169)

1. care,
2. children,
3. wanted,
4. town,
5. advisor, filling out enrollment forms, and finding her classrooms,
6. advisor, filling out enrollment forms,
7. accounting,
8. control,
9. material, she finished the test, proofread each question,
10. notes,
11. answers, many students picked up their books, handed in their tests,
12. room,
13. finished, she took a deep breath, reviewed her answers,
14. teacher,
15. class,
16. none
17. college, she was exhausted, determined,
18. cities, she needed new interests, challenges,
19. everyone,
20. grade,

REVIEW EXERCISE 4-3:
SUMMARY OF PUNCTUATION RULES (PAGE 171)

1. vitamins,
2. none
3. day, some teens substitute pizza and Pepsi for oranges and apples; therefore,
4. manners; she did not, however,
5. manners; however,
6. manners, I feel comfortable when I am in public; in fact,
7. is, as a matter of fact,
8. research; indeed, it is an excellent place to study, read,
9. paper, I check the library's reference room;
10. night; as a result, I went home, ate a sandwich,
11. assignments, I seldom have time to watch television; many students, I am certain,
12. early; nevertheless,
13. ability; they often, I regret to say,
14. ability; on the contrary,
15. qtime, stick to a schedule, and attend classes regularly,
16. time,
17. none
18. none
19. education,
20. college,

CHAPTER 5: SUBJECT AND VERB AGREEMENT

PRACTICE EXERCISE 5-1:
SUBJECT-VERB AGREEMENT—PHRASES BETWEEN SUBJECT AND VERB (PAGE 185)

1. houses become
2. house becomes
3. captain knows
4. coaches know
5. opinion determines
6. opinions determine
7. friend serves
8. peers serve
9. sound gets
10. cars cause

PRACTICE EXERCISE 5-3:
SUBJECT-VERB AGREEMENT—SUBJECT AFTER THE VERB (PAGE 191)

1. routes are
2. man/dog were
3. reasons are
4. reason is
5. book/manual were
6. hundreds grow
7. lists are
8. bushes bloom
9. notes are
10. schedule is

PRACTICE EXERCISE 5-5:
SUBJECT-VERB AGREEMENT—SINGULAR PRONOUNS (PAGE 197)

1. Everyone (in the dorms) seems (to the play)
2. Anybody (in the tournaments) gets
3. Neither requires
4. Neither (of the jobs) requires
5. Either enjoys
6. Either (of the lawyers) enjoys
7. Each (of the players) goes (to that tourney)
8. Everybody (in the tourney) competes (for the trophy)
9. One (of the teachers) gives
10. Anyone (in economics classes) needs

PRACTICE EXERCISE 5-7:
SUBJECT-VERB AGREEMENT—COMPOUND SUBJECT (PAGE 201)

1. Shayna/Jamal know
2. Jamal knows
3. Jamal knows
4. brothers have
5. brothers/sister have
6. sister has
7. pie tastes
8. cookies taste
9. *The Post* contains
10. *The Enquirer/The Post* contain

Answer Key ◆ 357

PRACTICE EXERCISE 5-9:
SUBJECT-VERB AGREEMENT—VERB FOLLOWED BY
PREDICATE NOMINATIVE (PAGE 205)

1. are
2. is
3. was
4. were
5. are
6. is
7. are
8. is
9. are
10. is

REVIEW EXERCISE 5-1:
SUBJECT-VERB AGREEMENT (PAGE 207)

1. Aromas beg
2. McDonald's/Wendy's are
3. Baskin-Robbins/Graeter's are
4. Pete/Jim do
5. Pete (or) Jim does
6. Everyone takes
7. Everyone knows
8. manager (or) owner plans
9. manager/owner care
10. players (nor) coach knows
11. coach (nor) players know
12. Neither wants
13. Either seems
14. Each appears
15. classes were
16. part was
17. class/class were
18. students learn
19. students were
20. students need

REVIEW EXERCISE 5-2:
SUBJECT-VERB AGREEMENT (PAGE 209)

1. sophomore/junior collect
2. sophomore (or) junior collects
3. Neither looks
4. cake (or) pie calls
5. teachers (nor) students enjoy
6. Either requires
7. Reading/taking are
8. part is
9. Each says
10. exercises are
11. exercise There's
12. father/son were
13. Everybody works
14. students travel
15. either Does
16. Everyone knows
17. boy (nor) girls participate
18. Neither participates
19. Studying/working require
20. English demands

REVIEW EXERCISE 5-3:
SUBJECT-VERB AGREEMENT (PAGE 211)

1. C
2. C
3. hurt
4. C
5. concerns
6. help
7. C
8. were
9. are
10. competes
11. C
12. C
13. take
14. C
15. fall
16. Is
17. C
18. make
19. C
20. makes

© NTC/CONTEMPORARY PUBLISHING COMPANY

CHAPTER 6: VERBS

PRACTICE EXERCISE 6-1:
PRINCIPAL PARTS OF IRREGULAR VERBS (PAGE 223)

1. worn
2. begun
3. chosen
4. blown
5. eaten
6. led
7. drunk
8. saw
9. written
10. hidden

PRACTICE EXERCISE 6-3:
PRINCIPAL PARTS—THE SIX MOST DIFFICULT VERBS (PAGE 231)

PRESENT	PAST	PAST PARTICIPLE	PRESENT PARTICIPLE
raise	raised	raised	raising
rise	rose	risen	rising
lay	laid	laid	laying
lie	lay	lain	lying
set	set	set	setting
sit	sat	sat	sitting

PRACTICE EXERCISE 6-5:
CHOOSING THE CORRECT VERB FROM THE SIX MOST DIFFICULT (PAGE 233)

1. setting; bulbs
2. laid; ring
3. rise
4. sat
5. set; bag
6. lying
7. rose
8. risen
9. laid; textbooks
10. rising

REVIEW EXERCISE 6-1:
IRREGULAR VERBS (PAGE 235)

1. C
2. gone
3. blown
4. began
5. thrown
6. broken
7. swum
8. C
9. C
10. C
11. asked
12. chosen
13. torn
14. driven
15. did
16. written
17. stolen
18. run
19. led
20. seen

REVIEW EXERCISE 6-2:
TRANSITIVE AND INTRANSITIVE VERBS: THE SIX MOST DIFFICULT (PAGE 236)

1. lying
2. laying <u>towel</u>
3. sat
4. set <u>desk</u>
5. rise
6. raise <u>controversy</u>
7. lie
8. lay <u>knapsack</u>
9. sitting
10. setting <u>date</u>
11. risen
12. raised <u>questions</u>
13. laid <u>cards</u>
14. lain
15. sets <u>dog</u>
16. sits
17. rising
18. raising <u>hopes</u>
19. sat
20. set <u>goals</u>

© NTC/CONTEMPORARY PUBLISHING COMPANY

REVIEW EXERCISE 6-3:
IRREGULAR VERBS, INCLUDING THE SIX MOST DIFFICULT (PAGE 237)

1. sit
2. worn
3. broken
4. rising
5. written
6. spoken
7. laid
8. flown
9. C
10. asked
11. C
12. lie
13. rises
14. sung
15. lying
16. C
17. rises
18. C
19. C
20. sat

CHAPTER 7: PRONOUNS
PRACTICE EXERCISE 7-1:
IDENTIFICATION OF THE NOMINATIVE CASE (PAGE 247)

1. Joan (S); nurse (PN)
2. José (S); manager (PN)
3. They (S); parents (PN)
4. they (S); friends/advisors (PN)
5. Joan/he (S); parents (PN)
6. She (S); mother (PN); she(S); mother (PN)
7. someone (S); This (S); she (PN)
8. George/she (S); gardeners (PN)
9. He/Joan (S)
10. They (S); neighbors (PN)

PRACTICE EXERCISE 7-3:
IDENTIFICATION OF THE OBJECTIVE CASE (PAGE 251)

1. children (DO); school (OP); time (OP)
2. them (OP); cities (OP)
3. meals (DO); Peter (IO)
4. you/me (OP); him (DO)
5. them (DO); party (OP)
6. cake (DO); us (IO); dessert (OP)
7. her/me (DO); lunch (OP)
8. him/her (OP)
9. Peter/her (OP)
10. you/me (OP); life (DO); children (OP)

PRACTICE EXERCISE 7-5:
IDENTIFICATION OF POSSESSIVE CASE (PAGE 255)

1. my; their
2. Their; mine
3. her
4. Your; mine
5. your; my
6. Their
7. his; hers
8. theirs
9. Our; yours
10. their; its; our

PRACTICE EXERCISE 7-7:
NOMINATIVE, OBJECTIVE, AND POSSESSIVE CASE OF PERSONAL PRONOUNS (PAGE 257)

1. him (DO)
2. they (PN)
3. yours (P)
4. her (IO)
5. We (S)
6. me (OP)
7. theirs (P)
8. me (OP)
9. its (P)
10. She (S)

PRACTICE EXERCISE 7-9:
PRONOUN/ANTECEDENT AGREEMENT (PAGE 269)

	INCORRECT:	CORRECT:
1.	their	its
2.	themself	themselves
3.	their	his
4.	her	their
5.	their	her
6.	theirselves	themselves
7.	their	her
8.	they	he
9.	ourself	ourselves
10.	he	they

REVIEW EXERCISE 7-1:
SHIFT IN PRONOUN <u>YOU</u>, <u>-SELF</u> WORDS, AND POSSESSIVE CASE (PAGE 271)

	INCORRECT:	CORRECT:
1.	you	they
2.	you're	they're
3.	C	
4.	you	they
5.	you	me
6.	you	she
7.	you	they
8.	you	they
9.	you	they
10.	you	they
11.	hers'	hers
12.	there	their
13.	ourself	ourselves
14.	yourself	yourselves
15.	C	
16.	theirselves	themselves
17.	theirself	themselves
18.	your's	yours
19.	it's	its
20.	there	their

REVIEW EXERCISE 7-2:
NOMINATIVE AND OBJECTIVE PRONOUNS (PAGE 273)

1. I (S)
2. me (OP)
3. me (OP)
4. I (S)
5. She (S)
6. her (DO)
7. him (DO)
8. she (S)
9. he (PN)
10. me (OP)
11. he (S)
12. him (DO)
13. I (S)
14. I (S)
15. she (PN)
16. me (OP)
17. her (IO)
18. him (DO)
19. me (OP)
20. I (S)

REVIEW EXERCISE 7-3:
AGREEMENT OF PRONOUN AND ANTECEDENT (PAGE 275)

	INCORRECT:	CORRECT:
1.	her	their
2.	his	their
3.	her	them
4.	their	his
5.	his	their
6.	their	her
7.	their	her
8.	their	its
9.	they	he
10.	he	they
11.	their	his or her
12.	their	her
13.	his	their
14.	their	her
15.	it's	its
16.	they	he or she
17.	his or her	their
18.	her	their
19.	their	its
20.	their	its

CHAPTER 8: APOSTROPHES, CAPITALIZATION, QUOTATION MARKS, AND UNDERLINING

PRACTICE EXERCISE 8-1:
FORMING THE SINGULAR POSSESSIVE (PAGE 287)

1. Mr. Lopez's garden
2. baby's laughter
3. man's responsibility
4. student's books
5. actress's lines
6. Sue's money
7. lady's charm
8. child's smile
9. waitress's wages
10. Hae Kim's dog

PRACTICE EXERCISE 8-3:
FORMING THE POSSESSIVE OF PLURALS THAT END IN S (PAGE 291)

1. Millers' garden
2. babies' laughter
3. songs' lyrics
4. students' books
5. actresses' lines
6. golfers' game
7. ladies' charm
8. winners' smiles
9. waitresses' wages
10. Joneses' dog

PRACTICE EXERCISE 8-5:
FORMING THE POSSESSIVE OF PLURALS THAT DO NOT END IN S (PAGE 295)

1. children's book
2. women's clothes
3. firemen's uniform
4. men's cars
5. people's opinion
6. stepchildren's mother
7. feet's pain
8. mice's tail
9. geese's feathers
10. oxen's leather hides

PRACTICE EXERCISE 8-7:
CAPITALIZATION OF NAMES, TITLES, AND FAMILY-RELATIONSHIP WORDS (PAGE 301)

1. Mother
2. C
3. Dr. Paul Kollman
4. Kollman; Christ Hospital
5. Eaton, Indiana
6. Aunt Rosa
7. Memorial Day; Coney Island
8. Good Friday; First Lutheran Church
9. Labor Day
10. Bob Stevens

PRACTICE EXERCISE 8-9:
CAPITALIZATION (PAGE 305)

1. C
2. Nabisco
3. *Love, Medicine, and Miracles*
4. Spanish
5. American History II
6. C
7. North; Milwaukee
8. Adventure Lane
9. South
10. Kleenex; Puffs

PRACTICE EXERCISE 8-11:
CAPITALIZATION (PAGE 307)

1. Professor Johnson; *The Closing of the American Mind;* Allan Bloom
2. Muncie, Indiana; Columbia University; New York City
3. James Flavin; English; Shawnee State University; Professor Lousie Flavin; University of Cincinnati
4. July 4; Senator Harris; Jim Andrews; Centerville
5. Bethesda Hospital; Montgomery Road

PRACTICE EXERCISE 8-13:
QUOTATION MARKS AND UNDERLINING (PAGE 313)

1. <u>The Wall Street Journal</u>
2. <u>A Doll's House</u>
3. <u>Time</u>
4. "Cell Growth"
5. "White Christmas"
6. "Bereft"
7. <u>Rosie O'Donnell</u>
8. "Spotted Horses"; <u>Literature</u>
9. "Thin Thighs"; <u>Redbook</u>
10. <u>Big Business</u>

REVIEW EXERCISE 8-1:
APOSTROPHE (PAGE 315)

1. Mike's; Bill's
2. girl's; parents'
3. girls'; Rosses'
4. families'/Lees'
5. children's
6. C
7. C
8. anybody's
9. Someone's
10. Ted's
11. Tomorrow's; Mary's
12. Joneses'; Lewises'
13. girl's
14. man's; children's
15. C
16. Trevor's; boys'
17. Jamal's; it's; Harrises'
18. Jamal's
19. Richard's; grandfather's
20. C

© NTC/CONTEMPORARY PUBLISHING COMPANY

REVIEW EXERCISE 8-2:
CAPITALIZATION (PAGE 317)

1. Easter
2. C
3. Phillips Petroleum Company
4. Ivory
5. "Death of a Hired Man"
6. Data Structures I
7. C
8. Tuesday
9. Professor Carol Sue Robinson
10. Northern Kentucky University
11. August
12. Uncle Pete
13. Solomon Goldberg
14. Diet-Rite Cola
15. Bill Gradison
16. United States
17. C
18. C
19. Ironweed
20. Frances

REVIEW EXERCISE 8-3:
QUOTATION MARKS AND UNDERLINING (PAGE 318)

1. "Plural and Apostrophe"
2. Type A Behavior
3. "Can I have my allowance early?"
4. C
5. "I want my allowance early."
6. Hedda Gabler
7. "Faith"
8. "I will be unable to attend class,"
9. "I will be unable to attend class";
10. "A Jury of Her Peers"
11. The Indianapolis Star
12. Murphy Brown
13. "I've been in a wreck."
14. "Positive Emotions: Love, Gratitude, and Determination"
15. Ghandi
16. "To His Coy Mistress"
17. "Bugging"
18. Popular Science
19. "Reds Going South with Set Lineup"
20. "Yes, you are";

CHAPTER 9: USAGE: COMMONLY CONFUSED WORDS

PRACTICE EXERCISE 9-1:
COMMONLY CONFUSED HOMOPHONES (PAGE 325)

1. hear; led
2. it's; know
3. its
4. here; hear
5. it's
6. its
7. led
8. no; know; know
9. passed; past
10. past; passed

PRACTICE EXERCISE 9-3:
COMMONLY CONFUSED HOMOPHONES (PAGE 329)

1. patience; patients
2. peace; piece
3. stationary
4. There
5. They're; their
6. too; to; two
7. Who's; whose
8. who's; whose
9. You're; your
10. you're; your

PRACTICE EXERCISE 9-5:
COMMONLY CONFUSED WORDS (PAGE 333)

1. accept
2. accept; except
3. advise; advice
4. advise; advice
5. effect; affect
6. effect; affects
7. choose
8. chose
9. conscious; conscience
10. desert; dessert

PRACTICE EXERCISE 9-7:
COMMONLY CONFUSED WORDS (PAGE 337)

1. loose; lose
2. lose; loose
3. quite
4. quit; quiet
5. Then; than
6. then; than
7. through
8. thorough; through
9. whether; weather
10. whether; weather

REVIEW EXERCISE 9-1:
HOMOPHONES AND COMMONLY CONFUSED WORDS
(PAGE 341)

1. a lot
2. laid
3. paid
4. dessert
5. desert
6. tries
7. tried
8. led
9. lead
10. loose
11. lose
12. passed
13. past
14. It's
15. its
16. stationery
17. stationary
18. choose
19. chose
20. truly

REVIEW EXERCISE 9-2:
HOMOPHONES AND COMMONLY CONFUSED WORDS
(PAGE 343)

1. They're; lose
2. Too; advice
3. know; who's
4. your; receive
5. You're; dessert
6. passed; quite
7. than; their
8. paid; a lot
9. Its; effect
10. past; tried/than
11. lose; conscience; a lot
12. except; than
13. Whose; paid
14. advise; accept
15. Desert; loose
16. It's; whether; tries
17. a lot; past
18. received; through
19. affect; effect
20. thorough; conscience; truly; there

REVIEW EXERCISE 9-3:
HOMOPHONES AND COMMONLY CONFUSED WORDS
(PAGE 345)

1. Too
2. you're; a lot
3. tries
4. whether; receive; advice
5. It's; accept; paid
6. C
7. you're; truly
8. conscience; advice; affects
9. led; tried; whose
10. they're; know; quite
11. They're; than; dying
12. laid
13. a lot; passed; except
14. choose; lose
15. dessert; its; led
16. C
17. stationery
18. patience; a lot
19. C
20. C

INDEX